SOCIOLOGY OF PILGRIMS

SOCIOLOGY OF PILGRIMS

Paras Kumar Choudhary

KALPAZ PUBLICATIONS
Delhi-110052

Sociology of Pilgrims
(Sociology, Religion)

Rs. 590

ISBN : 81-7835-243-5

Published in 2004 in India by
Kalpaz Publications,
C-30, Satyawati Nagar, Delhi-110052
E-mail : Kalpaz@hotmail.com

Laser Typesetting at : Shree Vaishnavi Creations, Delhi
Printed at : Chawla Offset Press, Delhi

Dedication

The Present volume is
Dedicated to the memory
of Late Prof. Makhan Jha,
Anthropology Department,
Ranchi University, Ranchi.

Contents

Acknowledgements

First of all I express my deep sense of gratitude and respect to MAA DURGA Goddess, for her spiritual blessings to come out with this volume.

I wish to express my gratefulness to all those, who have helped me in completing this volume. The list of such person is indeed a very comprehensive one, but a few persons need special mention.

I am happy to express my obligation to all contributor's, who have contributed valuable article for this volume.

I wish to express my respect and gratefulness to all the Faculty members and Staff of Postgraduate Deptt. of Sociology, Ranchi University, Particularly to Dr. Sharad Kumar Prof-in-Charge, whose efforts and encouragements for this work.

I want to thank Miss Sapna, Miss Sharmistha, Miss Sandhya student of P.G. Deptt. of Sociology and Research Scholar Mr. Amar Kumar, Mr. Rajeswar Nath Alok, Mr. Sunil Kumar and Mr. Manoj Kumar for her/his time and energy in processing this volume.

List of Contributors

1. Paras Kumar Choudhary	:	P.G. Department, of Sociology Ranchi University, Ranchi Jharkhand, India.
2. B.N. Sahay	:	P.G. Department of Anthropology Ranchi University, Ranchi Jharkhand, India
3. Monika Sahay	:	A Lady Anthropologist P.G. Department of Anthropology, Jharkhand, India
4. Sharad Kumar	:	Prof.-in-charge P.G. Department of Sociology Ranchi University, Ranchi Jharkhand, India.
5. Leslie Ellen Straub	:	O.P. Department of Sociology and Anthropology Providence College, Providence, Rhode Isalnd 02918-0001, U.S.A.
6. Glenn Bowman	:	Department of Anthropology Eliot College University of Kent at Canterburg Canterburg, Kent CT2 7NS. U.K.

7. Sabita Acharya	:	Reader, Department of Anthropology Utkal University, Bhubaneswar-751004, Orissa, India
8. J. McKim Malville	:	Department of Astrophysical and Planetary Sciences; University of Colorado; Boulder, Colorado, U.S.A.
9. Rana P.B. Singh	:	Department of Geography Banaras Hindu University, Varanasi, U.P. India
10. Shashi Tiwari	:	Department of Sanskrit, Maitreyi College, University of Delhi, India
11. K.G. Gurumurthy	:	Professor, Department of Anthropology Karnatak University, Dharwad-580003, India
12. Y. Nath Pandey	:	P.G. Department of Anthropology Ranchi University, Ranchi Jharkhand, India
13. Purabi Nandi	:	A lady Sociologist Currently School Sub-Inspector, Govt. of West Bengal India.

Introduction

Pilgrimages are the historical sacred complex structure, which people accept as a matter of fact. Religions have various rituals, which people operationalize at the place of historical sacred pilgrimage. For example, Roman church, Catholic church, Lutharian church, Ayodhya and Mecca etc., are the places where people visit in order to get salvation through either performing rituals over there and thereby purchase and deliver sacred objects, which in P.R. Bourdievian sense called as "cultural capital" or "social capital". After all, religion is a matter of historical faith and convention and, sometime, Hegel says that religion is incarnation of God on the earth. Mecca is a place, where Muslim devotees visit regularly and worship Mohamad Sahab as a "matter of symbolic surrender of man to God". Man is the creation of God. Man gets all kinds of emotional support by performing social capital, symbolized by salvating God at various places. Rome is a Catholic city, where the hard cord believers of Catholic Christian worship for peace and tranquillity. Ayodhya is a place where Ram was born. The Hindus consider Ayodhya as a sacred complex or what L.P. Vidyarthi calls sacred complex. When religious city established the priest of temple, church or mosque, where priest is supposed to have secret personality. Its geographical location, where temple is situated, is considered as a sacred geography. Various religions have sometimes common element and sometimes different discourses. For example, J.P.S. Uberoi in his book *Religion, and civil society and state* argues that Sikhism developed out of mixture of Hinduism and Islam in Amritsar where the Golden Temple is situated. People generally go over there and pray to God in symbolic and actual sense. Similarly, where the birth of Ṣita is traced. In Chiana there is a historical pilgrimage which even Marxist Govts have not demolished, primarily because of the fact that they consider religious places and pilgrimage as a cementing force. Religion, sometimes, works as a libidonal energy, which keeps people mobile and energetic and to be human. It is necessary to practise rituals at the time of birth, marriage and festival ceremonies, which are essential for the transformation of biological into social individual. The change in the religious status is known as Rite de passage. In Hinduism, first of all, man is born as biophysical being and when he performs ritual, be in the form of sacrifice or salvation, be becomes religious. In religion just as in the marriage sacred and profane are combined and differentiated at the same time. For example, in Hindu marriage, the presence of the barber and the priest are equally important. Marriage is supposed to be a sacred event, which is sanctioned by the priest. The Priest is relatively supposed to be pure and the barber is relative as impure. But the question arises as to why the barber is present over there? Answer has been given by L. Dumont in his book *Religion in Society* when he says that presence of profane as equally important than presence of sacred. Major function of priest is to sanction and legitimize marriage. Which, can not be broken by heart of two combined souls. Marriage is not system of relation between only two individual, but it is system of relation between two groups. Function of barber is to prevent the profane element which, might contaminates the ceremony of marriage. Although the barber is relatively impure, but his function is highly pure. Dumont sees the relationship between caste and community, principle of religious hierarchy, which is based on binary opposition between pure and impure; But J.P.S.Uberai and Veena Das argue that the relationship between the two castes, which are the expression of the religious hierarchy, are sometimes reciprocal and are based upon the principle of equivalence.

The relationship between the social structures can be analytically divided into two spheres: first is based upon structure, second is based on super structure. Dumont says that the basic structure consists of ideological symbolic, identical abstract and super structure consists of economic and political organizations. The religious objects express the chief value and obligation of super structure, then he says that the social structure can be seen in terms of four of the spheres: the first is the economic, the second is the political sphere, the third is the family/kinship and the fourth is the religion/ideological sphere. In economic structure, the material object happens to supersede. The religious object whereas in ideological sphere symbolic sphere supersedes the material object. This happens because the society is not considered as an aggregation of the individual; it is more than mere aggregation of the individual. The society is the moral community.

The individual is a moral agent, said Dumont, that there is noncontractual element in religion. However, there is process of development in religious sphere, for example, the development of cult, sect, refers to process of structural differentiation and functional specialization of the system. Following Durkheim and Weber, we see that the social structure of religion as to symbolic expression lies in the form of pilgrimage in the evolutionary comparative and historic manner. Weber says that religious organization is also hierarchical as it is a case with economic organization. Emergence of lit-commoners and priest symbolized this idea that there is symbolic foundation of religion over which economic super-structure is created. Sometimes, religion is used for political legitimacy and political obligation as in the case with Islam.

T. Parsons says that K. Marx is wrong when he says that religion is the heart of heartless people and soul of soulless people. In fact, Parsons says that it is through religion by which people internalize behavioural activities. Parsons says that the economic structure performs the function of adaptation; the political structure performs the function of law and order; the family structure manages the tension or religion; and the community performs the function of integration. Parsons says that religion is an apex of the system that controls the social system, personality system and biological system through symbolic socialization of the individual, which is known as a social being as well as a religious being.

Coming to India, we find that the social structure consists of the reciprocal relationship between sacred and profane. For example, L. Dumont says that there is binary opposition between caste and individual; M.N. Srinivas says that the sacred can be divided into two parts: good sacred and bad sacred. According to our interpretation, Dumont's pune to equal of bad sacred and Dumont's pune is equal to good sacred. Dumont, in fact, legitimized Brahminical order, which has been challenged by M.N. Srinivas,

J.P.S. Uberoi, T.N. Madan, Veena Das, Prof. Yogendra Singh, T.K. Oommen in their respective writings.

Prof. T.K. Oommen says that the social structure can be seen in terms of existence of the religious imperative that is equal of pueralism and peaceful co-existence. In India, there is also correlation between cults. We find various pilgrimages like Agra, Jaipur, Sitamarhi, Ayodha, Rameshwaram, Deoghar, Orissa and other places come together voluntarily and submit their obligations to God.

Religion constitutes the essence over which major parts of culture of any society develop and reinforce over a period of time. Culture is the same as religion in some society, for example, the tribal. But, in advanced society, the religion is differentiated from the culture, as to why to look at the reality, which prescribes what to be done and what is not to be done. Religion basically as system of believes in spiritual God, which may be a supernatural force or a social body. According to Tylor, religious basic essence lies in the belief of supernatural force as the same has been told by other Sociologists and Anthropologists. J.G. Frazer and Max Muller have developed the concept of culture through cosmic views, projected by the individual, but functional interpretation that worshipping society is equal to worshipping God. The functional view has been provided by Radcliffe- Brown, Herskovits, Kroeber, M. Marriate, Majumdar, L.P. Vidyarthi and others who argued that the basic function of religion is to integrate individual to society via religious institutions like church, temple, mosque etc. The structural interpretation has been given by Levi-Strauss, Leach and L. Dumont. According to structuralism, society is a "Ideo Structure" or cogntive model, which determined the individual behaviour. The whole concept of structuralism is based upon interpretation of ideology, myth, kinship and religion terms of binary opposition. By binary opposition, we mean that society is more than aggregation and submission of parts. Structuralists also happen to advocate for dialectics. By dialectics, we mean what Hegel called principle of identity and difference. Identity means one element may be similar to another element in terms of certain trait but may be different from other elements, such as, terms of certain attributes, for example, two individual may be brother, because they have the same origin, but they may be different from each other in terms of their respective attitudes, moral, physical quality such as height, length, weight, etc. Another example in society is of one particular JATI (Caste) may be identical to another JATI because both JATI express maintain and transmit the universe of human stratification through human mind. But one JATI may be different from the other JATI in terms of name, dress, God, Goddess, symbol, culture and language, that is why the fixation of the status of JATI depends upon the specific historical configuration. The same is true in case of culture and religion, for example, Hinduism may be identical to Christianity in one sense, because both the religions perform function of integration of society, but the manner in which integration is germinated may be different from one religion to the other.

Behavioural approach has been adopted by R.K. Merton, David Eston, Almon, Coalman, David After, Simon Hatiton, Amrtsen. According to these intellectuals, the function of the culture of religion is to regulate the behaviour and action of group, nation or individual, depending upon choosing the unit for analysis. Behaviour is that action which germinated from ideas and values of society. There are five types of action, which Merton talks about in his book *Social Structure and Social Theory*. The first is the conformist behaviour or action in which actor correlationship between institutionalized means and institutionalized goal. This is particularly found in the American middle class people. Merton says that most of the American middle-class people go to church for two things: first, to get success of life by offering praying to God via priest and second, to get salvation in life for the realization and actualization of human existence in which he is placed and works as mediator in resolving contradiction of human essence and existence. Herbert Marcuse, in his book *One Dimensional Man* and second book *Reason and Revolution* argues that when ideological existence is transferred into historical existence or through them man creates process of actualization of dialectics between man, culture and society. Marcuse says that religion is an antidote to make man more sensible and receptive; similarly, Eric From, a Marxist of humanism, says that the basic thrust of human life is to return into his "Species" character. This point has been taken from Feuerbach, who wrote a book on "Essence of Christianity". He says that man is basically a sensual, social and cultural being, which differs from the animal society. K. Marx in his book *Economic and Philosophical Manuscripts*, says that there are two processes, which operate at the same time; First, humanization of nature; second, naturalization of man. This can be achieved by ethics, religion, and culture of society, which man creates in order to get salvation and self-actualization. Swami Vivekananda says that basis source of salvation is knowledge and knowledge is all encompassing because man is a Karmayogi, spiritual realization depends upon human conformity to his established goal. Goal fixation is of two types: first the ideal goal may be satisfied by knowledge and the material goal can be satisfied by money. That is the reason, Weber in his book *science as a Vocation* argues that a man of science is at the same time a man of religion. The major function of religion and science is to come out from the cave of darkness of light. This point has made particularly by Plato who talks about the realization of ideal, God in society. Hegel takes a clue from Plato when he says that whatever is ideal is real, real is rational, therefore state is the most rational organization. Similarly, Hegel says that the history is the process of self-actualization of freedom; freedom is not equal to anarchy, because anarchy is the state of lawlessness but freedom is the only source of developing human potential and capacity to develop his personality with the realization of social goal at the same time. Durkheim says that man is basically a religious being; however, he says that man is depended upon society, society is suigenens. But at the same time he says that the individual freedom is not rejected. Basically, he tries to locate the forces and sources, which make a man more social, ethical and moral. It was the Rousseau who, for the first time, says that social contract does not mean that individual has to surrender all obligations be-personal or be-social, when he pursues his goal, state is the natural referee in the west ,when the church was separated by the state, then there was clearly a distinction between man as religious being in one sector of life and as a political being in the other. After all salvation is a religious phenomenon and it can be achieved by sacrifice of material goal. Material object attracts an individual when he is young. But when he becomes mature and old, he aspires to get salvation by performing religious obligation. The whole process of initiation of social category starts with praxis, which generally is called as a "philosophy of praxis". Religion is not a veil of childhood, which will disappear as some people argue, it is basically a system of relationship. Associational norm is the only source for getting salvation in the west. Only difference between society in the west and society in India is that in west salvation is achieved by what Merton says "success theme principle" whereas in India it is achieved by rejection of material world and acceptance of ideal, actual and adaptive norms, which can be seen through by Ashram Viyavastha, life cycle, principles of rebirth, Dharma, Kharma, Moksha. All depends upon the acceptance of the other world as the real world, where we can get the only religion of salvation and in the material world we can get the theory of religion of adaptation.

Paras Kumar Choudhary

1

The Pilgrims of Baidyanathdham (Jharkhand) A Study of Genesis of Sacred Rituals

B.N. Sahay

Introduction

India is very much popular for different sacred centres. Many of them are traditional *Pauranic Tirthas,* which includes different ancient temples, *Kundas* (ponds), *Koopas* (wells) and rivers. Besides these among sacred centres a few stones and trees are also worshiped. Related to these sacred centres, hundreds of sacred rituals like bathing of the deity, decoration of the deity, *Arati* (Moving of a type of lamp) around the deity in clockwise pattern), meditation, *Yatras* (sacred journeys) and fairs and festivals are associated.

Besides general day's rituals, many of the sacred rituals are observed on special occasions like certain time of the certain festive day or night, week, month or year according to the prescriptions made in religious texts or by the sacred specialists, the authoritarian of the sacred rituals.

Worship of Shiva deity with the offering of sacred water, specially the *Gangajal* (Ganges's water) in the month of *Shrawan* (July-August) specially on Mondays is considered very much auspicious and of much religious merits. So, in

Shrawan it is offered in almost all the shrines of Shiva, by most of the Hindus.

In recent past in a few modern and *Pauranic* Shiva temples one more ritual has been added to it, i.e., bringing of the sacred water from the Gangese or certain river flowing at a distance place (several K.Ms.) and offering of it to Lord Shiva of the respective temple. Among such Pauranic Shiva temples we may name Tarkeshwarnath temple of West Bengal and Baidyanath Dham temple of Jharkhand.

Baidyanath Dham is also one of the important *Pauranic Tirthas* like Ayodhya, Badrinath, Rameshwaram etc. Daily thousands of pilgrims and local devotees perform here different types of sacred rituals like *Sodsopchar Pooja* (worship with 16 articles of worship), *Panchopchar Pooja* (worship with 5 articles of worship), *Yagyopawit* (sacred thread ritual), *Mundan* (sacred ritual of Shaving head hairs), *Gangajal Arpan* (offering of Ganges's water) etc. Nowadays Bolbam Kanwar Yatra is also in vogue. Lacs of devotees perform this yatra every year. Baidyanath Dham temple's authority claims that in 30 days about 20 lacs of pilgrims and local devotees have visited this temple in the *Shrawan* month of 1985. (Due to Malemas, i.e., extra month as per Hindi Calender in 1985 Shrawan month was of 60 days).

All the sacred centres as well as their related sacred rituals must have the history of their origin and development. There must be certain point of their orientation and a long way of their evolution Here, we are concerned with the evolution of sacred ritual "Bolbam Kanwar Yatra of Baidyanath Dham, Deoghar."

History of Baidyanath Temple

The *Pauranic Tirtha Baidyanath Dham* is named after the Shivalingam Baidyanath. The name Baidyanath has been derived from two Sanskrit words (1) Baidya (Meaning medicine man and (2) Nath meaning Lord. According to Shiva-Puran Ashwani Kumars (Aswani Brothers/Princes) first of all bathed in *Bhawrogahar Tirtha* and worshipped the above mentioned Shivalingam for several days. By their worship Lord Shiva become pleased and gave them knowledge of Ayurved (The text of medicine 'Ayurved' is based on it) in blessing. Since then Ashwani Kumars become medicine men and Lord Shiva was called Baidyanath, the Lord of medicine men.

In 'Shivasahastra Nam' of Mahabharat also, Shiva has been known by the name 'Dhanwantari. In ancient age Dhanwantari was most famous medicine man. According to that very belief Lord Shiva is famous for curing sick. In Vaidic period *Rishis* (saints) used to call Baidyanath-Shivalingam as '*Bhishktash*' (Ayurved 2/23/4) and prayed for increasing physical efficiency of braves (Ayurved 2/43/4).

In regard to the name Baidyanath of the Shivalingam, there is a popular oral myth (nowadays which has been referred in different booklets on Baidyanath). According to this myth in ancient time a group of Brahmans migrated from somewhere settled near the Shivalingam (Baidyanath). They used to worship it regularly with offerings available to them, along with animal sacrifice. After sometime they became wealthy. Due to wealth Brahmans become idle and affluent and so started neglecting worship of the Shivalingam. To see it *Anaryas* (Tribals) of the area who earlier gave regard to the Shivalingam, started disregarding it. One of them named Baiju Bhil thought that the Shivalingam of Brahmans has become powerless, and so he decided to strike (beat) it with his stick daily and then only to take food and water. One day in the nearby contemporary *Daiwat* forest his cow was lost. He searched it for whole day and in evening returned home with his cow. As soon as he sat to take meal he remembered that on that very day he had forgotten to strike the Shivalingam. So he left his meal and come out of his house to strike the Shivalingam. To see his ignorance, and promise fullness Lord Shiva became pleased and gave him *Darsan* (presented Physically before him). He reminded him, "To strike the Shivalingam". He told, "You have forgotten even to eat and drink. You stand to your promise. I am pleased over you. You may ask for blessings. Baiju Bhil replied, "*Prabhu* (O Lord) I have sufficient wealth. I am king of my community. So, I do not have any desire of wealth and Kingdom. I have only one desire that people should recall me along with your name. Lord Shiva told *'Tathastan'* (let it be). Since then the

Shivalingam is known as Baidyanath. In regard to Baiju Bhil different other myths are also popular.

The temple of Baiju Bhil (in a north south lane near the tower) near Baidyanath temple also indictates its some relevance with the Baidyanath Shivalingam.

It is also possible that the term Baijnath of Baidyanath may have been derided from the name Baidyanath or vice-versa like Baidya Nath to Baijyanath to Baijnath as per linguistic rules and changes in pronunciation.

Regarding the establishment of the Baidyanath Shivalingam there is a story referred in the volume *Patal Khand* of the Padam Puran. According to it *Wamdeo Rishi* (Saint) describes the conversation between Parvati and Shiva (wife-husband). Parvati asks Shiva to tell her the story and the *Mahatmya* (religious merits) of Baidyanath Dham.

Shiva Describes: Rawan the king of Lanka once sitting on the thrown thought over his deeds in his life. He found every with him like wealth, kingdom and anything whatever he desired, but in the course of whole life he never found any *sat karma* (good works of religious merits, from which he could had achieved *moksha* (salvation). So, he decided to please Lord Shiva by his hard *Tapa* (meditation).

He left for Kailash Parwat (a part of Himalaya) the seat of Lord Shiva and there by meditation he got pleased and agreed Lord Shiva to come with him to Lanka, with the plan that being Shiva at Lanka he will be able to do his detail worship conveniently and regularly. Shiva instructed him to take *Manokamana Shivalingam* (symbolic form of Lord Shiva which has the power to fulfil all the desires) with him. To know about this decision of Lord Shiva, Lord Vishnu become very anxious. He thought that if Rawan takes the *Manokamana Shivalingam* with him to Lanka and worship it regularly he will become immense powerful and as he is a notorious person, he will give more trouble to *Dewtas, Rishis* (saints) and other good people. So, with the idea, to create problem or obstacle to Rawan in carrying the Shivalingam to Lanka, Vishnu suggested Parwati to give the sacred water affected with *Mantra* (magical words) for *Achman* (personal purification) to Rawan before taking the Manokamana Shivalingam. Parwati did accordingly. After *Achman* when

Rawan was carrying the Manokamana Shivalingam to Lanka on the way due to effect of magical water he felt much pressure to pass urine. But he was unable to keep the Shivalingam on land, as he was instructed by Lord Shiva that wherever he will keep it on land, it will be fixed there and nobody will be able to move it from that place. In the mean while in the pseudo form of a poor Brahman Vishnu appeared before him. Rawan requested him to hold the Shivalingam and sat to pass the urine which continued for hours. During this period Vishnu kept the Shivalingam on land where it got fixed. When Rawan stood up after urination he saw the Baiju Bhil worshipping Shivalingam. He asked about it. Baiju Bhil then narrated the whole story. Rawana become angry and tried much to take away the Shivalingam once again but all gone in vain. As per an oral myth then Rawana hitted it with leg and due to this heavy pressure hit the Shivalingam is pressed from one side.

Later Rawan dug up a well there named Chandrakoop and put into it sacred water of different Tirthas. He bathed the Shivalingam with its sacred water and did *Sodsopchar Pooja* (worship with 16 articles) in detail. At the end of worship in devotion he decided to offer his head to the Shivalingam. To see it Shiva become pleased and again appeared before him and suggested not to offer his head. He told him that in *Treta* (After certain period according to religious texts) Lord Rama will kill you by which you will get salvation. To hear it Rawana become pleased and established there other idols of other deities also including Ganesh around the Baidyanath Shivalingam and worshipped them with sacred water of Ganges brought from Haridwar and *Belpatra* (Leafs of 'Bel' tree used in worship of Shiva). To see it Shiva in pleasure announced that whoever will worship him with the sacred water of Ganges and *Belpatra,* will have the night to enter into his *Dham* (the Adhore/kingdom). To hear it Rawana in pleased mood left for Lanka.

As the Baidyanath Shivalingam has been brought by Rawana, it is also known as Rawaneshwar Shivalingam.

Presently besides the Baidyanath temple, there are other twenty two temples located around it, which are as follows :- (1) Parwati temple, (2) Jagat-Janani temple, (3)

Ganesh temple, (4) Chatur mukh Brahma temple, (5) Kal Bhairav temple, (6) Hanuman temple, (7) Mansa temple, (8) Sandhya temple, (9) Saraswati temple, (10) Surya temple, (11) Ma Bagla temple, (12) Ram, Lakshman and Janki temple, (13) Ganga-Jahanvi temple, (14) Anand Bhairav temple, (15) Gauri-Shankar temple, (16) Narmadeshwar Mahadeo temple, (17) Tara temple, (18) Kali temple, (19) Annapurna temple, (20) Laxmi-Narayan temple, (21) Nilkantha Mahadeo temple and (22) Nandi temple.

Besides above mentioned temples there are eight more sacred centres located within the area of about 30-40 k.m. from the Baidyanath temple which are (1) Baiju temple, (2) Tapowan, (3) Shivaganga, (4) Mansarowar, (5) Dolmanch, (6) Trikut, (7) Harilajori and (8) Jugal-Mandir (temple).

Historical Perspective of Kanwar Yatra

The word 'Kanwar' is derived from the term 'Kanmar' Kanmar-Ari means end of evil desires by which mental purity comes and the work done with mental purity gives 'Punya', i.e., religious merits. By accumulation of 'Punya' one gets *Moksha* or *Mukti* (salvation).

In Pauranic context 'Kanmar' means to earn punya by offering sacred water to Lord Shiva carried from certain distance place. In Purana it has been said:

SKANDHE CHA KAMRAM DHRITWA BAM-BAM PROCHYA CHHANE CHHANE PADE-PADE ASHWAME DHASHYA AKSHYAM PUNYAMASHNUTE

i.e., whoever keep 'kanmar' (the device to carry sacred water to be offered to Lord Shiva) on his/her shoulder and every moment pronounce the sacred word Bam-Bam (related to Lord Shiva) got the religious merits of *Ashwamedh yagya* (a specific ritual).

As per other verse of purana :-

DHUPE DEEPAIS TATHA PUSPAM NAIVE DYAIR WIDHAIRAPI NA TUSWATI TATHA SAMBHURYATHA KAMAṚ-WARINA.

i.e., Lord Shiva becomes more pleased with the offerings of sacred water of Kanwar than with the flower, *Belpatra, Dhup, Deep* and *Naiwaidya,* etc.

Due to religious importance of water of Ganges on the advice of Narad (a Pauranic saint) Rawana had brought the sacred water from the Ganges flowing at Haridwar to *Kailash*

Parwat (a part of Himalaya) by Kanwar and had offered it to Lord Shiva. According to a sacred myth mentioned in Anand Ramayan: *RAMASTUTE VMBHANEN GATSWAUTTAR WAHINIM NAMNAPURI TATHA GANGA YATRASTU PARMATTHADA PARWATI YATRA GANGAYAMASTI BIL WE SHWAROAPI CHA TATAH SHRI VAIDYANA THE SHAM NATWA RAWANNIRMITAM.*

(JAHNAKSHETRA, Page 17)

i.e., earllier Baidyanath Dham was the seat of Bilweshwar Shivalingam and king of Ayodhya Lord Ram after sitting on thrown did a pilgrimage to this place along-with his wife and brothers. He had brought the sacred water of the Ganges flowing at Sultanganj and offered it to the above mentioned Shivalingam.

Regarding Kanwar Yatra is a story. About 500 years ago in Sultanganj, two saint brothers named Harnath Bharati and Kedar Nath Bharati lived. Saint Harnath Bharati used to bath in the Ganges, take its sacred water and offered it to Baidyanath Shivalingam at Deoghar. One day when he was on the way to Baidyanath Dham a very thirsty Brahman came before him and requested him to give him the worship water to drink. To see the pity condition of the thirsty Brahman Harnath Bharati decided to give him worship water: and with this decision as soon as he bowed down to give the sacred water to the Brahman, Lord Shiva becam pleased over him and so, he appeared before him. Lord Shiva informed him about the presence of a Shivalingam under his meditation seat (now in the Ajgaivinath temple located at Sultanganj in the mid of Ganges). Later Harnath Bharati searched it out and started worshipping it. This Shivalingam was named as Ajgaivinath Shivalingam.

The above mentioned story indicates that in the period of Harnath Bharati the Kanwar Yatra was on start, or on regular basis he was to start it. In later periods till about 1960 no such case of regular Kanwar Yatra has been reported.

In recent past about 3-4 decades earlier, Kanwar Yatra was confined only to groups of a few saints, local aged devotees and the rich Marwaris of nearby cities and towns, all of male sex. The footpath between Sultanganj and Deoghar was very much tuff. There was no good road. On the way there was fear of forest animals including tiger as it was full of deep forests. Only at a few places thinly populated villages were located.

But at that time villagers used to give much regard and services required to the devotees performing Kanwar Yatra. They helped them by cooking and assisting in cooking their food and by doing arrangements for their might halt. Local people considered their services to the devotees as an religious act. The devotees were on the other hand very much orthodoxy, religious minded and morally high. It was out of their religious dignity to take free meal or anything from the local people, to whom they met on the way of Kanwar Yatra. At that time no case of crime has been reported. People living in the villages were also morally high.

Kanwar Yatra Present Context

Nowadays, Kanwar Yatra is not limited only to the groups of saints and aged religious people. With the development of good reads, *Dharamsalas,* hotels, shops and clinics on the way of Kanwar Yatra, the number of *Kanwaria* (devotees performing Kanwar Yatra) increased several times. Earlier this number was few but most of devotees were much religious and devoted. Nowadays, this number has increased by lacs but devoted pilgrims number is only a few. Now it has become general practice to undertake Kanwar Yatra and individuals of all age groups are participating in it.

This does not mean that Kanwar Yatra has lost its religious sanctity. There are several devotees who are very much religious minded, orthodoxy and full of devotion towards Lord Shiva. Such devotees due to devotion and mental concentration on god and pronouncing Bol-Bam, Bolo-Bam, Bam-Bam, etc. slogans pass the whole journey of about 125 kms. of Kanwar Yatra on foot without facing any or much physical trouble. Contrary to it devotees having less or no devotion towards god, face much physical trouble in covering the long tedious journey of Kanwar Yatra. Generally they suffer with high pain in the knee, body and sole; and some times headache due to hot sun.

To highlight the devotion of good devotees a few cases of them are being given below :-

On the last *Shrawan Somwar* (Monday) the Baidyanath temple was full of crowd. There was no place to move freely in and around the temple. Its floor was not visible even outside the temple. At about 10 A.M. it had rained heavily. All the neighbouring drains water came on the streets due to which mud and dirt spread in all the streets and floors in and outside the campus of the temple complex. In such circumstances a kanwaria was performing *Dand-Parikarma*, i.e. he was doing circumambulation of the temple by lying down ventrally on the floor, spreading feet and hands in straight way, marking the distance by middle finger or a small piece of stick in front covered by the whole body length, i.e., from the toes to the tip of the middle finger of the hand. Then he stood on the marked place, and again repeated the whole process. Thus he completed circumambulation of the temple and repeated it for 3 or 5 times. Due to crowd several devotees during his *Dand-Parikarma* unknowingly kept their foot on the body parts of the Kanwaria. Ofcourse as soon as they realised this mistake they expressed apology ad bowed before him and purified the *Dandi* Kanwaria by sprinkling sacred water over his body. Such incidents were very frequent. Due to crowd sometimes the hands of the *Dandi* Kanwaria was coming between the two legs of the ladies including young ladies and it made their position very awkward. But as soon as they realised it they took side. The remarkable thing here is the devotion and concentration of the Kanwaria which was never disturbed. Certainly he might had some *Manauti* (promise to perform certain hard ritual) for the fulfillment of his certain desire. With devotion concentration he was fully absorbed in the performance of the *Dand Parikarma* ritual.

Similarly on the same day there were a few Dandi-Kanwaria who performed whole Kanwar Yatra by performing *Dand*. Such *Dand* Kanwar Yatra can be performed only by having high level mental concentration on God, otherwise he/she may feel much physical trouble. Their skin at the lateral sides of their body and knees comes out and takes the shape of wounds. In the beginning these wound are very much painful, but later on they overcome it by acclimatization as well as after two days wounds also start healing besides the continuation of the *Dand* by the Kanwaria. In such cases Kanwarias pass their hard time only due to concentration and devotion towards Lord Shiva.

The high grade of devotion may be understood by considering their mental status at the time of their *Danda*-Yatra in the Baidyanath temple lane. The lane was full of 4-5 inches dirty water of the side drains due to heavy rain. Besides this dirt which included even cough, mud, night-soil etc. the *Dandi* Kanwarias were continuing their Dand in this lane. The lively feeling of Kanwar Yatra is certainly due to mental purity, devotion and concentration of these Kanwarias. People once observing these Kanwarias cannot forget them but on other hand certainly they will propagate and popularize this Yatra more in future.

As described above due to developments of modern facilities like road, Dharamsala etc. number of devotees has increased several times. Baidyanath temple authority claimed that in only *Shrawan* month of 1984 about 20 lacs devotees visited this temple. Bihar State Transport Corporation, Deoghar Branch reported that the above transport corporation earned rupees seventeen lacs in 1984 *Shrawan* month and about 50 lacs in 1985 *Shrawan* month of 60 days (due to Malemash extra month, this *Sharwan* month was of 60 days). Thus the earning of this transport corporation in 1985 was about three times of 1984. On this basis the number of devotees visited Baidyanath Dham temple may be estimated which will come around 60 lacs. In one day last *Somwar* (Monday) *Ekadasi* festive day of this *Shrawan* month about 50 thousand devotees worshipped in this temple.

TableI
Composition of Devotees in Kanwar Yatra
Sex Wise Composition of Devotees

No. of Devotees	Total Percentage	Male No.	Male Percentage	Female No.	Female Percentage
500	100%	385	77%	115	23%

The Table I shows the higher number of male devotees participating in this religious journey. Their number is 77% which is about 3 times more of the percentage number of the female devotees. The number of females may be less due to difficulties being faced in covering this long distance of this journey. Because of it very few females of higher and middle economic class participate in it. As they are not hard working they might be facing more difficulties in covering this long distance of Kanwar Yatra. A few of them cover it by Bus, Truck, Jeep or Car.

Table II

Age Group Wise Composition of Devotees

Sr.No.	*Age Group*	*No.*	*Percentage*
1.	Up to 3 years	10	2%
2.	Above 3 years to 10 yrs.	15	3%
3.	Above 10 years to 25 yrs.	125	25%
4.	Abive 25 years to 50 yrs.	330	66%
5.	Above 50 years to 60 yrs.	15	3%
6.	Above 60 yrs.	5	1%
	Total	500%	100%

Table III

Composition of Devotees on Regional Basis

Rural		*Uraban*		*Total*	
No.	*%*	*No.*	*%*	*No.*	*%*
385	77%	115	23%	500	100%

On the contrary to it rural female folks are seen frequently. Among the total female devotees rural females are 74%.

The table II shows the highest number of devotees of the age group above 25 yrs to 50 yrs, which is 66 per cent. Next comes the age group above 10 years to 25 years the percentage number of which is 25 per cent. Then comes the age groups up to 3 years, above 60 years which is 2%, 3% and 1% respectively. This indicates that the Kanwar Yatra is a sacred ritual for the physically fit age group only. It demands physical fitness. So during the course of the whole journey of about five days no disabled person was seen performing it. Very few children below 10 years and aged above sixty years participate in this ritual. Many of them move in vehicles. Rarely, babies below 2 years are seen in lap or shoulder of their mother, father or relative. Once a baby was seen being carried in a *Bahangee* (a device to carry load in the villages, made of bamboo sticks, ropes and baskets). *Bahangee is carried by a labour on his shoulder.*

The Table III above shows 77 per cent of rural people and 23 percent urban people in the Kanwar Yatra. This may be due to less religious feeling as well as lesser physical fitness among the urban people. Physical fitness is the need of this tedious long journey. Modernization, including scientific developments have also weakened the religious believes in the towns and cities. As well as less social binding in the urban area makes people more free from religious performances in comparison to the village people.

On other hand the villagers being hard working people face less difficulties in covering this long distance of Kanwar Yatra on foot, so they participate in it in much higher number.

Besides local devotees pilgrims from distant parts of Bihar, Bengal, Orissa, U.P., M.P., Maharashtra and Gujarat States and Nepal also perform this Yatra-Ritual. Of course their number is very few in comparison to the pilgrims of Bihar. Coach buses, mini buses, trucks and taxis in high number are seen carrying pilgrims to Deoghar and Sultanganj. Sometimes a few vehicles specially trucks, jeeps or cars move along with its Kanwarias carrying their food and other luggage's. On the stops respective devotees cook their meal, take it and rest on these vehicles. Such facilities makes this journey more pleasure some. But in general case Kanwarias take meal in hotels and rest in *Dharamsalas,* available at all main stops of Kanwar Yatra. Peasant Kanwarias carry with them dry food like *Cheera* (made of rice), molasses, *Salt,* Sattu (powder of fried grain like gram, maize or rice) etc. and eat it at stops. Generally Kanwarias take rest on the plastic sheets and bed sheet spread over the cemented floor of the *Dharmasala.* Very few Kanwarias engage cot available in hotels for sleeping.

Food pattern of Kanwarias vary from individual to individual as per their *Manauti* or desire or liking and the money available to them. Some Kanwarias does not take salt and rice during Kanwar Yatra.

Dharamsalas at the Stops of Kanwar Yatra

With the increase in the number of Kanwar Yatris (pilgrims), new types of occupations and business have come up, which includes several trustee and private *Dharamsalas*. Private *Dharamsalas* are seasonal and are opened only in the month of *Shrawan* (July, August). Such *Dharamsalas* are private, houses which are vacated during *Shrawan* month for giving it to the pilgrims on rent basis. Usually from each devotee one rupee was taken in 1985. Seven or eight devotees took one cemented room jointly for one might. The number of devotees and the charge of the room may vary as per size and condition of the room. Near Darsania stop of Kanwar Yatra one college lecturer used his two storied residential house as *Dharamsala* in *Shrawan* month. During this month there is a great demand of rented cots. Such cots are used in hotels and for each cot daily rupees five to ten is charged as its rent by its owners. Cots are taken by sweet shops also.

Hotels and Shops at the Stops of Kanwar Yatra

During *Shrawan* month when Kanwar Yatra is on peak there is great demand of food articles like milk-sweets and other sweets, puri, *kachauri,* rice, pulse and vegetables in Deoghar, Sultanganj and on the way of the Yatra. So, at stops of Kanwar Yatra many big and small hotels are seen who engage several cooks and sellers in their hotels. Besides many shops are found who sell *Cheera, Sattu, Murhi,* Molases, sugar, curd and milk also. The sell of seasonal fruits also increases.

Jajmani System: With the origin and development of the sacred centres a relation between priest and devotee specially regularly visiting devotees also developed. This relation after years become permanent and named as *Jajmani* relation. Its organisation i.e. structure and function is known as *Jajmani* system. Devotees who have relation with such priest are know as *Jajman* and the priest, as *Panda.*

Nowadays, a *Panda* takes all types of care, i.e., does arrangement of lodging, fooding and assists in worshipping.

At Baidyanath Dham there are several *Panda* families who are originally migrants from Darbhanga. Now their family member is more than hundreds. Each such family has maintained their register of their *Jajmans,* who are local or of different districts of Bihar or other states. Any new devotee whose name is not registered in any of the *Panda's* register may be made new *Jajman* by any of the *Panda* approaching him for the first time. Thus the number of *Jajmans* of a *Panda* increases day by day. The *Jajmans* are traditional source of income of these *Panda* families. Of course nowadays several members of the *Panda* families are taking other types of jobs also. At the time of family partition the *Jajmans* being the source of income are also distributed along with other family properties among the members of the family. During division location of residence and economic status of the *Jajmans* are also considered, as nearer the location of residence of *Jajmani* it is easier to approach them frequently and the higher economic status of *Jajman* the *Panda* gets higher payment by them.

When any devotee/pilgrim reach the temple gate *Pandas* approach him and ask about his family *Panda.* If he tells the name of his family *Panda* he is directed to meet the respective *Panda* and it fails in it he is made new *jajman* by the panda approaching him first. His name is entered in the register of the *Jajmans.*

At the time of worship *Panda* tries to extract maximum money from the *Jajman.* In different stages of worship *Panda* suggest this client to offer some money and besides it at the end of worship they demand *Dakshina* (the remuneration for assisting in worship). In Sharwan, temple-precinet is so much crowded that it is not possible for *Panda* to assist the devotees in doing *Sankalpa* rituals for worship within it. So, they complete it outside temple-precinct it. Then the devotees are advised to offer the worship articles like Flower, *Belpatra, Gangajal* etc. to the respective deities by entering into the respective temples. But due to heavy rush in and around the Baidyanath temple it is very difficult for the devotees to enter into this temple. It takes much time and labour to enter into the *Garbha Grih* (inner precinet) of this temple. In such case most of the devotees offer their worship articles including *Gangajal* by throwing over this temple from outside. Crowd is increased specially on the *Shrawan* Monday.

To give the facility to enter into the Baidyanath temple to each and every devotee the temple authority and the government administration are jointly doing their best effort. Beside thousands of devotees are not able to enter into the temple. Police engaged in controlling the crowd near the entrance of the Baidyanath temple beat the devotees with sticks mercilessly for maintaining line. Due to much crowd every year a few devotees die within the temple precinct being crushed by the crowd. The Baidyanath temple which is the main temple has only one door of entrance and exit due to which not possible to control the heavy crowd of *Shrawan* month specially on Mondays. There is a need of making another door in the *Garbhagriha* just opposite to the presently existing door.

With the development of good roads, hotels, clinics etc. on the route of Kanwar Yatra, on the one hand where it has increased the number of Kanwarias several times, on the other hand this has given good scope to the criminals to do crimes. During Kanwar Yatra season specially in *Shrawan* month every day crimes like pick-pocketing, stealth, dacaoity, loot, sex crimes and sometimes murder are reported. Of course government administration does the arrangement of police at different main places, besides, crimes are increasing with the number of devotees.

Kanwar Yatra and Kanwaria

As mentioned earlier in 'Historical perspective' of Kanwar Yatra and the belief prevailing among the devotees 'Kanwar Yatra' or 'Kanmar Yatra' is a religious act of performing journey with the aim of offering the water of certain distant river (being considered sacred) to the Shivalingam or the idol of Lord Shiva of certain temple.

In case of Baidyanath Dham (Deoghar) it is the journey from the Ganges at Sultanganj to Baidyanath Dham with the aim to offer the sacred water collectedf from Ganges at sultanganj to the Baidyanath Shivalingam at Baidyanath Dham. Generally, due to effect of modernization and with the increase in the number of devotees, variations has come in the performance of the sacred rituals as per the economic status, comfort, convenience and liking of the devotees and the time taking in ritual. This may be seen in case of Kanwar Yatra also. The increase in the number of Kanwarias brought variations in the way of performing Kanwar Yatra, in regard to the physical strength, economic capacity, comfort, liking and convenience of the Kanwaria (i.e. devotee performing Kanwar Yatra). The facility of good road between Sultanganj and Deoghar has also worked as stimuli in bringing variations in Kanwar Yatra. Due to it Kanwar Yatra is being covered on different types of vehicles also.

Types of Kanwar Yatra at Baidyanathdham

Presently at Baidyanath Dham following types of Kanwar-Yatra are in vogue:-

(1) *Paidal* (on foot) Kanwar Yatra, (2) *Dak* Bam (or running) Kanwar Yatra, (3) *Dandi* Kanwar Yatra, (4) Cycle Kanwar Yatra, (5) Motor Cycle Kanwar Yatra and (6) Bus, jeep, Truck, car or bulllock-cart or any other vehicle Kanwar Yatra. In this Kanwar Yatra generally the devotees cover the long distance of about 80 miles between Sultanganj and Baidyanath Dham on foot by walking, in more or less five phases in five days.

Devotees reach Sultanganj a day or night before the commencement of this Yatra. In early morning they bath in the Ganges and take the Ganges's water in both the tin containers. Before, taing this scared water it is *Sankalpped* (promised) to complete the sacred Kanwar Yatra. This *Sankalpped* ritual is performed with the assistance of a *Panda.* Then they start and complete the journey.

The stops or intervals of journey where they take night rests or night halt are Rangaon, Tarapur, Rampur, Belhar, Suiya, Chandan Katoria (Kanwaria Dharamsala), Gorhiyari, Patania Dharamsala, Darsania, etc. The number of places of rest is not fixed. It depends on the individuals desire and tiredness on the way Kanwaria gives the slogans of Bam-Bam, Bolo-Bam, Kanwar Bam etc. Sometimes they engage themselves in social, political and family talks also. At the time of rest also they are found in these talks. Rest activities of Kanwarias have been described in the rules of Kanwar Yatra.

(2) Dak Bam (or running) Kanwar Yatra: As its name indicates, it is the express, not-stop Kanwar Yatra. It is performed only by energetic youths. They cover the distance of Kanwar Yatra of about 80 miles by running continuously from Sultanganj to Baidyanath Dham. The record of *Dak Bam* Karwaria shows minimum time taken in it, is eleven hours. It is the record of a young police man of Gaya. About three years ago two girls (sisters) from Nepal covered this distance by fourteen hours. But unfortunately one of them died of heart failure due to tiredness and exertion as soon as she offered the Gangajal to Baidyanath Shivlingam. There are several devotees who have completed it within 24 hours. Generally to a medium pace runner it takes about 16 to 18 hours. But several devotees complete it by 34-35 hours also.

In the beginning the *Dak-Bam* Kanwarias were given priority to offer the *Gangajal* and to worship the Shivalingam Baidyanath (at Deoghar) by restricting the crowd waiting for worship outside Baidyanath temple. But later on a few Dak-Bam Kanwarias brought corruption in it. Such Kanwarias after completing the distance upto Rampur stop (i.e., about 18 km.) or earlier caught bus and got down a few kilometres earlier to Deoghar stop. After sometime of this practice, temple administration came to know about it. Since then this facility to *Dak-Bam* Kanwaria has been stopped.

A *Dak-Bam* Kanwaria needs much energy, mental concentration and physical purification to complete this tuff journey. There for certain rules have been formulated which must be followed before start of this journey.

A *Dak-Bam* Kanwaria leaves his general solid diet two days earlier of the commencement of this yatra. During these two days he takes fruits, fruit-juice, milk, etc. By the last night of the start of this Yatra he decreased the quantity of drinking water considerably, so that he may not feel or face the problem of urination during journey. During midnight or about one or two hours earlier of start of this journey they take about 50 or 100 grams of honey. By it they do not feel much thirst as well as get much energy which is required in running such a long distance.

After physical purification, i.e., passing of latrine, tooth brushing and bathing they put on the dress of an usual Kanwaria, i.e., yellow pant and shirt. The colour of the dress may vary a little. They hang on their back with the help of cloth belts an approximately one or half litre tin container which contains water of the Ganges. It is closed with its covering and sealed with soil of the bank of Ganges. Then it is *Sankalpped* (promised) with the help of *Panda* available there to complete in one phase.

At the time of *Sankalpa* they stand in such a pause as if they are in the line of running competition. Their one leg remains on top ladder and the other on the next lower ladder of the Ganga Ghat. As soon as the *Panda* completes the *Sankalp* ritual and receives *Dakshina* (remuneration for assisting in worship) for it, the *Dak-Bam* Kanwaria starts running. Their aim is to complete the journeying as early as possible. Completion of it in short time gives them prestige in the society and among the Kanwarias.

On the way to Baidyanath Dham they are offered drinking water, milk, fruits, fruit-juice, etc. by local people, shopkeepers and general Kanwarias, as per their requirement, free of cost or by charging its costs. They may purchase also eating articles mentioned above. Sometimes if they need they are bathed also by the shopkeepers or local devotees. But unique thing is this that they do each and every act maintaining running continuously. Once they start running from Sultanganj Gangese's Ghat they stop it near Baidyanath temple (at Deoghar) and complete their worship in the temple. With this ritual Dak-Bam Kanwaria ends this Dak-Bam Kanwar Yatra. Then he starts taking light meal and slowly adopts usual routine.

(3) Dand Kanwar Yatra : Among different types of Kanwar Yatras. *Dand* Kanwar Yatra is the Most difficult one. The word *'Dand'* express the meaning of salutation to Lord Baidyanath by lying on the ground ventrally. *Dand* Kanwar yatra is the journey between Gangeses Ghat at Sultanganj to Baidyanath Dham by performing *Dand* ritual on the whole way. As described earlier for *'Dand'* the *Dandi Kanwaria* (Kanwaria performing *Dand)* lies down ventrally spreading his legs and hands in strait way covering maximum distance by his whole body length, i.e., from his toe to the tip of his middle figure of his hand. This distance is marked by a small piece of stick (of size about 4'). Then he stands on the marked place and from there again repeat the whole process. Its repetition continues till he does not reach the stoppage or he does not feel tired himself. In covering the whole distance of Kanwar Yatra a *Dandi* Kanwaria takes about one and half months. A team of three *Dandi* Kanwaria complete it in one month and eleven days. On the last *Shrawan* **Somwar** (Monday) of 1985 five *Dandi* Kanwarias were seen in and around the Baidyanath temple. During fifteen days of *Shrawan* month 15 *Dandi* Kanwarias were seen on the way of Kanwar Yatra.

During this period as they need nutritious diet their diet pattern contains milk, curd, fruits including dry fruits also. All *Dandi* Kanwarias to whom this scholar could meet were of middle or higher economic class. For purity of meal *Dandi* Kanwarias cook their meal themselves. *Dand* is not performed between 10 P.M. to 2.30 A.M. night.

(4) Cycle Kanwar Yatra : In it Kanwaria completes his Kanwar Yatra on Cycle. By cycle, he takes one or two days in covering this distance.

(5) Motor-cycle Kanwar Yatra : Kanwarias have been seen covering this distance on Motorcycles. Generally groups of two or more Kanwarias are seen completing this journey on it. They complete this journey in 2 or three hours.

(6) Bus, Truck or any other vehicle Kanwar Yatra : A few Kanwarias cover the distance of Kanwar Yatra on bus, truck, jeep, car, billock-cart, etc. The number of such Kanwarias is very few and it includes mostly invalid old, children or persons facing much physical trouble in covering this distance on foot.

Prescribed Rules and Procedures of Kanwar Yatra

During Kanwar Yatra Kanwarias lead a very simple life. They neither use oil, soap or cream nor comb the hair. They wear yellow clothes. Gents wear half pant and shirt white ladies wear yellow *Sari* and *Blause.* But a few poor Kanwarias are seen in their usual folk dress also. Underwear, banian etc. of the most of the Kanwarias are yellow or Kesharia colour. Nowadays they carry side bag as well as towel also of yellow colour. Every Kanwaria tries his best to use yellow clothes. Shoes and *Chapal* (Sandels) are prohibited during Kanwar Yatra.

From the food point of view Kanwarias are of three types (1) *Falahari- Kanwaria* (Kanwaria taking only fruits), (2) *Anona-Kanwaria,* i.e., taking meal without salt during the whole journey period and (3) Nona Kanwaria, i.e., Kanwaria taking meal with salt. In no case Kanwarias take garlic, onion or non vegetarian meal. In a few cases Kanwarias leave taking garlic and onion a few days earlier of the commencement of this Yatra. A team of Kanwarias from Nepal told that they had left it since fifteen days earlier of the start of this Yatra.

To be safe from the physical trouble of knee and sole many Kanwarias practice walking on naked-foot daily for few miles for few days before the start of Kanwar Yatra. A day or night before the start of the Kanwar Yatra Kanwarias reach Sultanganj, purchase the Kanwar (the device do carrying the water of Ganges) if they do not have brought it and decorate it as per their pocket allow with different colours of plastic strips, brass-bells and *ghunghroees* (a type of bell) and small plastic-images of Ganesh, Parwati, Shiva and snakes, etc. In the early morning of the first day of the Kanwar Yatra, Kanwarias take bath in the Ganges, wash the containers and collect into it the sacred water of the Ganges from the Sirhi Ghat at Sultanganj. Sacred water of only this ghat is taken in the container for offering to Lord Baidyanath. After covering both the tin containers with its coverlids these are sealed with the soil of the bank of the Ganges. Then the containers are again covered with red cloth and is tied with thread (suttri) properly. Each container is hanged by each end of Kanwar by help of a *Sikka* a part of the Kanwar.

Besides these two containers (of size about one litre), a small container called as *Sudhi-Jal Pattri* of capacity about 250 or 300 mililiters is also filled with sacred water of the Ganges and is hanged on one end of the Kanwar.

The sacred water of Sadhi-Jal-Pattri is used as purifying water on the way of this sacred journey, when one breaks it for rest, fooding or to pass urine etc. by sprinkling this water on himself before starting this journey again.

After sealing of the containers *Sankalpa* ritual is performed with the assistance of *Panda* available at the bank of Sirhi Ghat, the place to start the Kanwar yatra. At the end of *Sankalpa* ritual the containers are hanged on the both ends of the Kanwar and the Kanwar is kept on the one of shoulders in such way so that weight of its both the ends may be balanced. During journey Kanwaria is not allowed to keep his/her Kanwar on land. Here we find a sense of sacredness. To protect it from impurity or profane things such precautions are taken. Kanwar is always kept on stand made of woden four poles and two parallel bars.

Each Dharamsala and hotel has hundreds of Kanwar stand made in front of it or within its campus. Each stand can accommodate about 15-20 Kanwars. Thus each *Dharamsala* or hotel can accommodate thousands of Kanwar. Number of stands in a hotel or *Dharmsala* varies as per their capacity to accommodate Kanwarias. In Dharamsalas thousands of Kanwarias take rest specially during night. Kanwaria Dharamsala which has about 100 rooms and several big Varandah can accommodate about five thousand devotees at a time. Nowadays it is under the management of government. Sometimes on the way if a Kanwaria needs to keep his Kanwar in such a place where there is no stand, he keeps it on the suitable thick branch of some trees.

On the way whenever a Kanwaria passes urine or eats anything (not *Kachcha Khana)* he has to purify himself by sprinkling a few drops of sacred Gangese's water being carried in *sudhijal pattri.* If one eats *Kachcha Khana* (boiled rice or pulse) or sleeps or passes stool he has to take bath before touching the Kanwar again. Urine or stool can be passed only at a distance of about ten yards or more from the Kanwar.

After reaching Dharmsala or any stop for night rest Kanwaria is required to wash his foot, hand and face. A few of them bath also. Then they do *Sandhy Poojan* (evening worship) or *Arti.* In *Arti* a flamed-Deep (a type of worship lamp) is moved in clock-wise direction around their Kanwar kept there. Maximum number of Kanwarias burn *dhup*-stick (incense-stick) and move it around their Kanwar or show it to their Kanwar. During this worship ritual Kanwarias may sing Shiv Arti (special verses written in praise of Lọrd Shiva). Before or after it they may sing religious songs also.

After *Sandhya poojan,* in night about 7 to 9 p.m. generally Kanwarias take their supper and engage themselves in talks of the current journey, agriculture, family or in social or political matters.

In the early morning at about 3.00 a.m. Kanwarias generally get up, do their morning activities including bathing and do *Pooja, Arti* of their Kanwar. Then they start their journey again. After walking of 3-4 hours they take their breakfast or meal etc. on the way. This routine of walking and rest continues till one reaches Darsania stop. From here each Kanwaria does the *Darsan* (visualization) of the peak of Baidyanath temple, which is visible from here and salute it. *Darsan* is the act of seeing and saluting sacred objects like temple or idol of the deity, with a sense of regard.

Act of *Darsan* vary from devotee to devotee. Some one does it by performing *Dand* once or five times, some one by sitting on knee and touching the land with his head, and some one only by folding his hands jointly and touching with its finger his head. After saluting, worship of the Kanwar is done by burning *Dhupbati* (Dhup-strick) and moving it round the Kanwar in clockwise and by reciting some verse of Shiva or pronouncing or remembering simply his name. One unique thing is marked here is that as soon as the Kanwarias reach near the Darsania stop one more *Dholakia* (Drumbeaters) beating their drum approach and accompany then till they reach Darssania stop and perform there above mentioned rituals. At the end of which each of the *Dholakia* takes some money like 50 paise or more from each Kanwaria or head of the team of the Kanwarias.

Then the Kanwarias proceed onward and reach Shivagana pond. Here they take their sacred bath. Sometimes a few urban devotees who are habituated to bath with fresh water hesitate to bath in to it because its water is dirty green. But generally their religions bindings does not allow them to bath outside. In exceptional cases a few devotees are seen bathing with the municipal tape water available on the side of Shivaganga-pond. The bath in cold water makes the tired devotees free of their tiredness to a much extent.

Now the devotees purchase flower, *Belpatra, Prasad, Dhup-deep* etc. and reach Baidyanath temple campus. Many devotees do purchasing of the above mentioned articles from the shops of Baidyanath temple lane. In the temple campus, with the help of *Panda,* who approaches them, they do *Sankalpa* ritual once again, do *Parikrama* (circumbulation) of the Baidyanath temple complex five times and then enter into the inner precinct of the Baidyanath temple and do worship of Lord Baidyanath by offering the sacred water of Ganges (being carried from Sultanganj) and other articles brought for offering. Here four five *Pandas* who are deputed by the temple management request and some time force the devotees to offer more and more money to the Shivalingam Baidyanath, which is taken by them. Sometimes here they help a few devotees in worshipping by pronouncing the *Mantra* (verse used in worship) and for it they charge separately as *Dakshina* which may be Rs. 5/- or more.

In case of any *Manauti* (demand/desire) of the devotee, the concerned devotee at the time of worship remind Lord Baidyanath about it. For example, if there is any *Mundan-Manauti* (promise to get head hair shaved in case of fulfillment of certain desire) the respective devotee or devotees get his/their head hair shaved outside Baidyanath temple, bath and do the worship in the above said temple. Many Kanwarias get their hair shaved outside, near the main gate of the Baidyanath temple complex or on the bank of Shivaganga pond or near it. Worship of the deity also may vary as per the Manauti of the Kanwaria. After completion of worship here, the devotees do worship and offering in other neighbouring temples of the campus including Parwati and Ganesh temples. In all these temples priests remain sitting. Generally they insist the devotees to do maximum offering of the money to the deity or deities of the respective temple. With the worship in these temples the long tedious but devotional Kanwar Yatra ends.

Devotees then do marketing in the lanes of Baidyanath temple, take their meal as per their choice, see mela (fair) around the temple-complex and in pleasing mood return home with the proud of completing Bolbam Kanwar Yatra.

Conclusion

The rituals which are being performed here today have their story of their origin. Here, the historical perspective of sociopsycho-religious situations of the ritual "Bolbam Kanwar Yatra" is being analysed to understand the origin, establishment and evolution of the sacred rituals, which has been termed as "the genesis of sacred Rituals". It may be defined as the socio-psycho-religious situation in which some one performs a new type of sacred ritual. In the beginning it suits a few people of the society, who come to know about it and its religious merits. These people follow it in their life. By observing which others also do it. Thus slowly it comes in vogue of the society. Such sacred rituals get propagated by the pilgrims/local devotees, media like newspaper, radio, T.V., texts, cinema, etc.

Regarding the origin of Kanwar Yatra, it is said that in *treta yuga* (Ramayan period) on advice of Narad, a Pauranic saint, Rawan took the sacred water of Ganges from Haridwar and offered it to Lord Shiva at Kailash Parwat (part of Himalaya Mountain).

In Anand Ramayan, it has been mentioned that Lord Ram, the king of Ayodhya, after sitting on thrown did a pilgrimage to Baidyanathdham along with his wife Sita and brothers. In connection with this pilgrimage 'He' had brought the sacred water of the Ganges flowing at Sultanganj and offered it to Baidyanath Shivalingam.

According to an oral sacred myth, about 500 years ago, two saint brothers namely Harnath Bharati and Kedar Nath Bharati lived in Sultanganj. Harnath Bharati used to bath in Ganges there, take its sacred water and offer it to Baidyanath Shivalingam at Deoghar. One day, on way to Baidyanath dham he met a thirsty *Brahman,* who requested him to give him the worship water to drink. To see the pity condition of the thirsty *Brahman,* Harnath Bharati gave him the worship water to drink. To see it Lord Shiva became pleased and gave *Darsan* to him (physically appeared before him).

He was Harnath Bharati, who for the first time performed this Kanwar Yatra regularly that may be fortnightly, monthly or yearly. Due to long distance of about 125 km. it does not been possible to had been offered the Ganges water to Baidyanath Shnivalingam daily taking from Sultanganj.

Later other pilgrims and local devotees also started to practice it on annual basis in the months of *Shrawan* and *Bhado* (July-August) of rainy season. In rainy season, farmers by end of *Shrawan* month generally get free from traditional transplantation of paddy crop. So, they might had preferred to take this sacred journey during *Shrawan* and *Bhado* months. As well as *Shrawan* month is considered more auspicious and sacred for Shiva worship. So, this journey is performed specially in *Shrawan* month.

Till about 1972, or before the release of the picture" "Ganga Dham" (Hero-Arun Goel and Heroine-Sadhana Singh) very few gangs of farmers and business-men used to perform this Yatra annually. But, the release of "Ganga Dham" picture propagated the religious merits of this Kanwar Yatra to a great extent. The number of pilgrims which was earlier in thousands, increased into lacs. Present by it is about sixty-seventy lacs only in *Shrawan* month, the most auspicious month for this Yatra. In this month Monday is considered to be most auspicious day for worship of Shiva. So, on Monday, the number of pilgrims is seen much increased here.

Thus, *Bolbam Kanwar Yatra* a new type of sacred ritual originated, got established and now evolved in a much complex form.

This Kanwar Yatra at its beginning was very simple. In metallic pot sacred water of Ganges was simply filled up and offered to Baidyanathdham Shivalinga. Slowly much compexities have been added to it. Nowadays, a general devotee starts preparation of this Yatra about 15 days or a week ago. He starts walking daily on naked foot for about an hour or more. This gives him less physical problem in the said journey covered on foot. There are fixed stops on the way of journey where devotees may take night rest. At such stops there are so many hotels and shops. At Sultanganj water container and Kanwar are purchased and decorated.

Thus, nowadays, during *Shrawan* month a big sacred industry is seen in Sultanganj, Deoghar and an stops of Bolbam Yatra. Thousands of persons of different castes and religions are employed in this industry. It is said that in one month of *Shrawan* alone they earn the livelihood of the whole year.

Present day Bolbam Kanwar Yatra is much organised. At journey stops even clinic (private/Governmental), vaccination facility and police arrangements are seen.

As in other popular sacred centres, here also we see some anti-social elements. But, this do affect the believe of mass devotees. Day by day the crowd of pilgrims increasing. In about a decade future if *Baidyanath temple* organisation and administration works properly, and the believe of devotees is not affected adversely, the number of pilgrims/ devotees may cross the number of a crore in month of *Shrawan* alone.

References

Betty, R. Scharf, 1970 The Sociological Study of Religion (London).

Chakrabarti, P. 1974 "Some observations on the Pilgrims and their Pilgrimage : A case study at Tarkshwar", *The Journal of Socila Research*, Vol. XVII, No. 1, (Ranchi).

Jha, Magna Nand1974 "Sacred Performances at Kaslin". The Journal of Social Research, Vol. XVII, No. 1, (Ranchi).

Mathur, K.S. 1964 Caste and Ritual in a Malwa Village (New York).

Narayan, Sachindra 1972 The Sacred Complex of Deoghar unpublished Ph.D. Dissertation, Ranchi University, Ranchi).

Redfield, Robert 1956 Peasant Society and Culture: An Anthropological Approach to Civilization (Chicago).

Sahay, B.N. 1974 "The Sacred Geography of Kashi." *The Journal of Social research* Vol. XVII, No. 1, (Ranchi).

Sahay, B.N. 1981 Sacred Semlar Continuum in the Tirthas of Kashi. (Unpublished Ph.D Dissertation, Ranchi University, Ranchi).

Sinha, Arvinda Kumar 1974 "Specialists in sacred performances at Kashi," *The Journal of Social Research*, Vol. XVII, No. 1, (Ranchi).

Tylor, E.B., 1874 Primitive Culture, 2 vols. (New York).

2

Managers of Pilgrimage to Kashi-Tirtha

Sharad Kumar and
Monika Sahay

Kashi is not only an oldest city of the world, but is also an ancient and one of the most important Hindu Tirthas. The Hindu religious texts are full of its religious merits. According to a famous religious proverb, i.e.,

Ayodhya Mathura Maya Kashi Kanchi Awantika
Puri Dwarawati Gaya Saptaita Mokshadayika

which means Kashi is one of the salvation giving cities like Ayodhya, Mathura, Puri etc. Again *Skanda* Purana an ancient Text of Shaiva sect describes Kashi's special merits of salvation giving power. It says that when in other mentioned cities one dies, in next life he takes birth in Kashi and when he dies here he does not required to take birth in other *Tirthas:* Lord *Vishwanath* here chants is Tarak Mantra (Salvation giving Magical words) in his ear, by which he attains Moksha (Salvation, i.e., cessation from the cycle of death and birth). In words of *Skanda* Purana it is like this-

Anyani Mukti Kshetrani Kashi Praptikarani Hi
Kashim Prapta Vimuchyante Nanyatha Tirthakoti mah

In *Bana Parba* of Mahabharat it has been said that even on *Darshan* (observation) of Lord *Vishwanath* of Kashi—one is absolved from all sins of his life, even killing of a Brahman, which is considered as highest level of sin. So, he gets salvation on giving up his physical body.

In *Matsya* Purana it has been said that even a women of loose character gets salvation by residing in Kashi. Further it has been said that without *Yoga* (Meditation) salvation is not possible. But who resides in Kashi *Yoga* and *Moksha* (Salvation) both are sure to him.

Thus in several Hindu religious texts importance of Kashi has been highlighted. In this way in Hindu religious tradition Kashi occupies the place of an important *Tirtha*. Due to this reason and faith pilgrims from all over Hindu universe come to do the pilgrimage of Kashi with the belief that they will be free from all the sins of their life and get salvation.

The pilgrimage of Kashi is managed by different groups of people of different social status. These all people are commonly known as *Tirtha yatra Prabandhak*, i.e., managers of pilgrimage.

Managers of pilgrimage (Tirtha Yatra Prabhandhak)

There are several classes of persons for assisting in sacred performances, for taking pilgrims round the temples, for arranging their residence and making other necessary arrangements for them, they are called *Tirtha Purohit, Panda, Yatrawal, Bhaddar* and *Gumasta*.

Tirtha-Purohit

The word *Tirtha-Purohit* is the combination of two words (i) Tirtha meaning traditional sacred centre and (ii) *Purohit* meaning *Poojari* i.e. who assists pilgrims in worshipping. Thus, *Tirtha-Purohits* are the person who assist in worship at traditional sacred centres. The *Tirtha purohits* of Kashi are the traditional *Tirtha* worshippers (pujaris). They call themselves the local *Pandas* of Kashi.

The *Tirtha Purohits* of Kashi claim themselves as the descendants of Rhishi (saint) Vashistha. It is said that Lord Brahma has made Vashistha the principal *Pujari* of the world, and since then *Tirtha Purohits* call themselves the descendants of Vashistha (in the Hindu caste system the entire duty of worshipping) in the world belongs to them. They also claim to be the ancient residents of Kashi. 20-30 years back these *Tirtha Purohit's* opinion prevailed upon the pilgrims hailing from all the parts of India. Their management and income were very good. When asked about their forefathers, they claimed to have descendants from *Nava* (nine) Kanyakubja Brahman *Kul* (family) who have got the following titles—Chaturvedi, Trivedi, Dwedi, Pathak, Tripathi, Upadhyay, Mishra, Shukla and Pandey. Of these, the three Kuls are completely extinct today. Of the remaining six the two families has no issue. Each of the widows of the two families had a daughter who were married with Mahabir Tiwari and Gayanand Tiwari, Local Saryupari Brahmans respectively. Thus we find these two Brahman subcastes namely Kanya-Kubja and Saryupari doing the profession of *Tirtha Purohit* and time to time in professional competition quarrelling among themselves.

Among the *Tirha Purohits* there is also a Sarswat Brahman family, who was a servant of some *Tirtha Purohit* before. As he knew some of the South Indian languages also, he gradually became the *Tirtha Purohit* of the South Indian pilgrims independently.

Now some South Indian Brahman have also entered into this profession and slowly they are trying to establish the relation of *Tirtha Purohit* with the pilgrims of South India. In this way different Brahman communities are joint in this profession of *Tirtha Purohit* today.

All the *Tirtha Purohits* of Kashi belong to the Shaiva sect. The eldest member of their family manages the work of the *Tirtha Purohit*. The younger members co-operate with him.

With the increasing competition some *Tirtha Purohits* changing their profession as well as taking interest in education. In 1974 one person was graduate in arts and law, two were Sanskrit Shastris, 3 middle passed and others have read upto secondary level. This number must have increased by now.

The number of the *Tirtha Purohits* is less but from the economic point of view they are well to do.

Out of the Kanyakubja *Tirtha Purohits* one has a coal mine and both the *Tirtha Purohits* of Saryupari have sufficient cultivable lands in Kashi and its vicinity. These properties they got from the rich and kings of the local and other areas by way of *Dan-Dakshina* (gift on occasion of assisting in worship). Their income has decreased these days. Now those kings (Rajas and Maharajas) arc not in existence who used to make heavy gift over them. Now these *Tirtha Purohits* do not get gift according to their will, so they try to extract gift by putting pressure on the pilgrims.

With the increasing communications and hotel facilities nowadays the pilgrims do not care for the *Tirtha Purohits.* Without their any assistance pilgrims come Kashi, stay in Hotels/*Dharmasalas*, visits temples and do worship of deities at different *Tirthas*.

On the other hand their servant communities namely *Yatrawal* and *Bhaddar* who earlier used to assist *Tirtha Purohit*, nowadays have taken up this business as their own. They help the pilgrims in going round the temples and doing sacred rituals, without the help of *Tirtha Purohit*. In this way the income of the *Tirtha Purohit* has been affected adversely due to much competitions in this profession.

Panda

The word *Panda* in Kashi is very commonly used for the experts of sacred rituals (Karmakandis) as well as for the *Tirtha* managers. Sometimes *Ghatia* who assists in performing simple rituals at the Ghats (Bank of Ganges) is also called *Pandajee.* But the Tirtha Purohits and Karmakandis (who performs sacred rituals according to the texts) are specially and literally called *Pandajee*. The pilgrims know them to be *Pandas* who help them in going round the temple and doing sacred performances. As well as helps them by giving a shelter or managing for their accommodation. From tradition point of view that class of people is called *Panda* which helps the pilgrims or their *jajmans* in performing pilgrimage to Kashi. They catch the pilgrims at different places in Kashi. They keep them at their own Ghat, in the *Dharamsalas,* hotels or at their own residence and arrange for their going round the temples and performing rituals. They maintain the ancestral relationship of *jajmanika* with their *jajmans*. For this they maintain a register in which they record the name, address, caste, date of visit etc. of their *jajmans* (pilgrims). They always attempt to keep a permanent relationship with the pilgrims. Thus while the relationship of the sacred ritual performers like *Pujari, Ghatia* or *Karmakandi* with the pilgrims is temporary, the relation of *Pandas* with their *jajmans* (pilgrims) is ancestral and permanent.

Since last 3-4 decades the *Tirtha Purohits* and *Karmakandis* are doing the work of the *Panda* in Kashi. This is specially seen with the Maharashtrian and South Indian *Karmakandis* who being conversant with the South Indian languages establish relationship with the South Indian pilgrims very easily. There is an union of these South Indian *Tirtha Purohits* today who are engaged as guides of South Indian pilgrims.

The *Panda* institution has given birth to the three different classes which are related to each other :- *Yatrawal, Bhaddar* and *Gumasta.* These three classes have got the right today to take the pilgrims to different sacred centres of Kashi or to *Pandas.* Thus different from Gaya and Deoghar the *Panda* class of Kashi is of different sub-castes of different linguistic groups.

Yatrawal

That class of the pilgrims-guide is called Yatrawal which catches the pilgrims in the Vishwanath temple lane or in its vicinity and help them in visiting round the temples for *Darshan* (Look) and sacred rituals related to the concerned deities. Nearly 80 *Yatrawals* are seen in Vishwanath Lane engaged in this profession. They almost take their stand near the temple of Dhundhiraj Ganesh and use to roam about in this street, because all the pilgrims primarily and necessarily go to the Dhundhiraj Ganesh temple first. From this place they take the pilgrims to gold plated Vishwanath temple, Annapurna temple, Gyanvapi *Koop* (Well), Kashi Karwat etc. where the pilgrims do *Darshan* (Look)- *Poojan* (worship) of the deities according to their choice.

Among the *Yatrawals* are the Saryupari, Joshi, Kanyakubja and Kashmiri Brahmans. The number of the Saryupari Yatrawal is very large among the Yatrawals.

Bhaddar

Just parallel to the yatrawal there is another class of pilgrim guides who do not catch the pilgrims near the Golden Vishwanath Temple Lane, but they catch the pilgrims at the Kashi Railway station or at the bus-stand and make arrangements for their stay and visit round the different sacred centres, are known as *Bhaddar*. With a view to catch the pilgrims they go also beyond the Kashi Railway station, i.e. upto Mughalsarai or other stations. They bring the pilgrims to Ganga Ghat and with significant words sell them to the *Ghatia* on getting some money. The pilgrims are not aware of this. According to the economic status of the pilgrims their prices are fixed which may vary from Rs. 40 or 50 to Rs. 200 or 300 or more. The *Bhaddars* have rare necessity for doing sacred performances. They are little educated. Their knowledge of *Karmakanda* (sacred rituals) is nearly nil. Still some of them are seen assisting the pilgrims of lower castes in worship. Such examples may be seen in the Kashi Karwat temple which generally remains lonely. This class of people may be called endogamous professional pilgrim guide.

The *Bhaddars* call themselves Joshi Brahmans. They claim to be the descendants of Maharashtrian Brahman, but the later do not admit their claim. Their dress is also different from that of the Maharashtrian Brahman. Their number in Kashi is approximately 4,000 out of whom about 850 are the registered members of Joshi Brahman *Sangh* (Union). It is said that *Yatrawal* and *Bhaddars* both were the servants of *Tirtha Purohits* who have adopted the profession of *Pandagiri* afterward, independently. Once the U.P. Govt. wanted to issue identity card to the real *Pandas* of Kashi and an enquiry was being made in this connection. At that time *Bhaddar* also began to raise their claim for *Pandagiri* which was challenged by the *Tirtha Purohits* and many were killed in this dispute. Afterwards on production of sufficient proof these *Bhaddars* also got the identity cards of real *Panda* alongwith the *Tirtha Purohits*. Since then they are in this profession independently.

The *Bhaddars* take the pilgrims to hotels, to the shops of *Benarasi sarees* and utensils also, from where they use to get some commission. There are some *Bhaddars* only who do the work of real *Pandas* as to bring the pilgrims from railway station or bus stand, to lodge them in their own houses or *Dharamsalas* or hotels to take them round sacred centres and to maintain the relationship of *Jajmanika* with them.

As they catch the pilgrims and sell them to others it will not be an exaggeration to say that they are the "pilgrim hunters". Besides this profession they also engage themselves in extra works such as wholesellers of betel leaf, sewing, to sell tickets in cinema hall and to practice homeopathy etc.

They differ from the *yatrawal* in the respect that they marry within their own *gotras* (clan) and also depend on other professions besides *Pandagiri* and are of different sects, whereas all the *yatrawals* belong to the same *Shaiva* sect and are entirely dependent on their own profession.

Gumasta

The class of the pilgrim guides which is a paid servant of the *Titha Purohit* or *Panda* bring the pilgrims from railway station or bus stand, take them round the sacred centres, give them shelter for staying and help them in performing sacred rituals according to the order of their master *Panda* is known as *Gumasta*. They also fill up the registers concerning the pilgrims. Occasionally they go to the village of the *Jajmans* and encourage them to undertake the pilgrimage to Kashi. Sometimes on some festivals or ceremonies they bring the pilgrims according to their programme and take them round the sacred centres of Kashi.

The *Gumasta* differ from *Yatrawal* and *Bhaddar* in the respect that they do not work in this profession independently rather they work as servants and they may belong to the caste of a *Brahman* or to any higher caste of middle class. The pilgrims know them as *Pandaji*. Their number is less than any other class of the pilgrim guides.

Thus, the pilgrimage to Kashi and the guides related to it are vary complex in Kashi in comparison to Gaya and Deoghar (Baidyanath Dham) regarding assistance to the pilgrims during their pilgrimage, every work is done by the same class of Panda, at Kashi there are several classes of Pandas, whose ways of assistance to the pilgrims, life styles and their family inheritance varies from one another.

References

Bose, N.K., "Organization of Services in Bhubaneswar Temple", *Culture and Society in India* - (Calcutta, 1967).

Chakrabarti, P., "Some observations on the Pilgrims and their Pilgrimage :A case study at Tarkeshwar", *The Journal of Social Research.* Vol. XVII, No. 1 (Ranchi, ·1974).

Dhrkheim, E, *The Elementary Forms of Religious Life* (New York, 1968).

Goswami, B.B. and S.G. Morab, "Temple as civilizational centre" :A case study of Chamundesari Temple in Mysore", *The Journal of Social Research,* Vol.XVII.- No.-1 (Ranchi, 1974).

Hill, Michael, A Sociology of Religion (London, 1973).

Jha, Magna Nand, "Sacred Performance at Kashi", *The Journal of Social Research,* Vol. XVII, No.1 (Ranchi, 1974).

Jha, Makhan, "Pilgrims and centres of Pilgrimage in Chhatisgarh", *The Journal of Social Research,* Vol. XVII, No. (Ranchi, 1974).

Jindel, Rajendra, *Culture of Sacred Town :A Sociological Study of Nathdwara* (Bombay, 1976).

Narain, A.K., "Varanasi", Sonvenir 55th Session of Indian Science Congress (Varanasi, 1968).

Narayan, Sachindra, "Pilgrimage to Kashi", *The Journal of Social Research,* Vol. XVII, No.1 (Ranchi, 1974).

O'Ddea, Thomas F., *The Sociology of Religion* (New Jersy, 1966).

Otto,R., *Idea of the Sacred* (New York, 1950).

Sahay, B.N.., "The Sacred Geography of Kashi" *The Journal of Social Research,* Vol. XVII, No.1 (Ranchi, 1974).

Sahay, K.N., "The Sacred Geography of Rameshwaram and Tirupati", *The Journal of Social Research,* Vol. XVII, No.1 (Ranchi, 1974).

Sarswati, Baidyanath, *Kashi : Myth and Reality of a classical cultural Tradition,* (Simla, 1975).

"The Holy Circuit of Mimsar", *Bull of Anthropological Survey of India,* Vol. VI, No. 3-4 (Calcutta, 1962).

"Studying sacred complex in Kashi", *The Journal of Social Research,* Vol. XVII, No.1 (Ranchi, 1974).

Sinha, Arvinda Kumar, "Specialists in Sacred Performances at Kashi", *The Journal of Social Research,* Vol. XVII, No.1 (Ranchi, 1974).

Srinivas, M.N., Religion and Society Among the Coorgs of South India (Bombay, 1952).

Upadhyay, Basudeva, "Some Bibliographical Notes on Sacred Kashi",

The Journal of Social Research, Vol. XVII, No.1 (Ranchi, 1974).

Upadhyay, V.S., "The Sacred Geography of Dwarka". *The Journal of Social Research*, Vol. XVII, No.1 (Ranchi 1974).

Vidyarthi, L.P., The Sacred Complex in Hindu Gaya (Bombay, 1961).

"Sacred complex as a dimension of Indian civilization", *The Journal of Social Research*, Vol. XVII, No.1 (Ranchi, 1974).

Wqeber, Max, *The Sociology of Religion* (London, 1966).

The Religion of India (Illinois, 1956).

Ram, P.R.N.D.S. Pandey, Mahabharata, Vol. 4 to 6, Translated in Hindi (Gorakhpur, Sambat, 2026).

3

Pilgrimage to Our Lord of Chalma, Mexico : Landscape as Text and as Context

Leslie Ellen Straub

This paper concerns the role of landscape in two pilgrimages to Our Lord of Chalma (El Senor de Chalma), whose Sanctuary, the Basilica de San Miguel, is located in the country and state of Mexico.[1] One of these pilgrimages was made by members of the community of San Juan Tlautla, Puebla, Mexico, in 1988. The second was made by the author, together with another anthropologist, Dr. Enya Flores-Meiser, in 1993. Comparison between the pilgrimages indicates that for pilgrims who are strangers to their destination and to the traditions embedded in the journey to the sacred place, the topography of both the route and the pilgrimage centre has a significance different from that for pilgrims who know the customs, symbols, and the terrain involved. In these two pilgrimages, the landscape along the routes followed and at the Sanctuary, was read accordingly by pilgrims either as text infroming experience or as context for that experience; the shifts from one reading to another having at their core the meaning of topographical descent. The paper will highlight the moments of descent while noting the readings of the landscape as either text or as context.

In order that the study may contribute to the written history of the pilgrimage to Chalma as well as to the methodology of the study of pilgrimage and landscape, attention will be given to ethnographic description as well as to analysis.

Landscape and Pilgrimage

This study of landscape in pilgrimage is fundamentally anthropological. Data are drawn from the 1993 pilgrimage; and from research in the literature on Chalma available to me, with special reference to the study of the pilgrimage from San Juan Tlautla, by anthropologists, Robert D. Shadow and Maria J. Rodriguez V. (1990), who participated as novice pilgrims. Other sources in the literature reduced confusion related to continuity and change in the landscape over the years; and placed both the San Juan Tlautla traditions and the 1993 pilgrimage of Dr. Flores-Meiser and myself within the framework of the history and lore regarding both Our Lord of Chalma and pilgrimages to the Sanctuary made by people coming from other points of origin and at different periods of time. These references included studies by Silvia Benuzzi (1981), Luis Reberto Galanes (1991), Alejandra Gonzalez Leyva (1991), Erich Gottlieb (1971), John Hobgood (1964), Miguel Othon de Mendizabal (1946), Javir Romero (1957), and R.P. Fr. Joaquin Sardo (1984 [c 1810]).

The focus on landscape and place, reflects not only my own sensitivity to these features, but also a growing interest in them within Anthropology in general. Note, for example, the analysis of the sacred landscape of Peruvian shrines and pilgrimage in the Andes, from an ethnographic and ethnological perspective, by Michael Sallnow (1987); the inclusion of landscape in the consideration of built environment and spatial from in the *1990 Annual Review of Anthropology* (Lawrence and Low 1990 :443-506), which consideration influenced development of academic curricula and research in the discipline; and the appearance of the Anthropology of Landscape as a newly defined area of interest within the field (Hirsch and O'Hanlon 1995).

To Anthropology, geographers, philosophers, and architects have contributed insights, reminding us that landscape, as a natural place, is the environmental level which has material substance, shape, texture, color, and, as its distinctive quality, extension. How the landscape extends—this is, what variations there are in its surface relief, or topography—determines its spatial properties and contributes to its character, or Spirit of Place—its *Genius Loci.* Within it, there are subordinate places, as well as natural things—such as a named tree—in which the meaning of the natural environment is condensed. Superimposed on natural place is the built environment of settlements, connecting paths, and other transfroming elements, together with the names and lore, out of which a cultural landscape emerges (Norberg-Schultz 1980 : 6,8,10. 32-35).

My decision to analyze landscape in terms of text and context in the study of the Chalma pilgrimage was certainly influenced by these ideas. It was also shaped by Milton Singer's (1972) investigation of the reading of literary texts and ritual perfromances belonging to the Great Tradition of Hinduism within the context of modern, urban life in Banaras, India. With this methodology, Singer sought to bring textual and contextual studies of Hinduism closer together (Singer 1972 :40). It seemed to me that the concepts, "text" and "context" could be used in the analysis of pilgrimage in more than one way : in this study of the sacred journey to Chalma, I suggest that pilgrims either read environmental features as texts, or simply negotiated topography as a context in which their pilgrimage unfolded.

Finally, reflection on specific topographical elements associated with terrain broken by ages of geological activity; and on the perceptual, cognitive, and evaluative concomitants of encountering such landscapes, was inspired by Simon Schama's (1995 :7) description of Yosemite National Park, in the United States, in which he referred to the "strangely unearthly topography of the place, with brilliant meadows carpeting the valley flush to the sheer cliff walls of Cathedral Rock" and remarked that "the fact that visitors had to descend to the valley floor only emphasized the religious sensation of entering a walled sanctuary". In the two pilgrimages to Chalma, the predominant, environmental features were the *barrancas* ("ravines", or "canyons") en route to, and at, the Sanctuary. Going down into those canyons was a more striking experience than coming out of them; and while ascent to sacred places—which we expect to find in the pilgrimage process—was not totally absent, it was eclipsed by descent. In our pilgrimages, the Sanjuaneros, Robert Shadow, Maria Rodriguez, Enya Flores-Meiser, and I experienced some kinds of descent differently en route; but, at the end of our journey, we all arrived at the cliff-walled Sanctuary on the canyon floor of Chalma.

Pilgrimage to Chalma : 1993

During the pilgrimage made by Dr. Flores-Meiser and myself on August 5, 1993, I became conscious of topographical descent when the bus which took us from Mexico City toward Chalma stopped at a small settlement named El Ahuehuete. There we entered a ravine identified as the Canyon de Chalma, or the Canyon de Ocuilan (Hobgood 1964 : 115; Shadow and Rodriguez 1990 :53). On either side of the paved road, the tree-covered, steep sides allowed little space for the line of one-and two-storied buildings, most of which were intended for the refreshment of pilgrims or for the sale of items which they might need. These included crowns of fresh flowers to wear as badges to Chalma and plastic bottles in which to collect water, which flowed through the roots of the Ahuehueted tree, or cypress, dominating the scene.

The Ahuehuete stood close to the road and marked the point at which the ravine deepened; the descent hidden in a tangle of trees and bushes. There was a high, iron railing around the front of the tree and an equally high, red brick wall to the rear and side. Because of these, people could not reach the tree itself; but they did have access to the water at its foot. Hanging from a low branch of the tree were cloth bags. I did not know at that time that the cloth bags contained umbilical cords, or that the water was thought to have physical and spiritual, healing properties. Sensing that the water was considered sacred, I blessed myself with it, but I did not drink, collect, or bathe with it; for, I had set out on a pilgrimage in which traditional symbols and practices were as unfamiliar to me as was the terrain.

The purchase of floral crowns marked Dr. Flores-Meiser and me as serious pilgrims. Once placed on our heads, the crowns would not be removed until we were about to enter the Basilica de San Miguel.

On the side of the road opposite the Ahuehuete tree and placed at a slightly higher elevation, stood a chapel under construction. It was a grey, cinder-block structure at the top of a flight of stone steps—the roofless shell of a building. The entrance was a wide arch flanked on either side by an arched window. A small, cement roof jutted out to provide some protection from the elements. Above it, was a second row of four arched windows. The iron gates were opened to give entry to the space enclosing a large crucifix, which stood on a wooden platfrom raised off the ground by cinder blocks. A sheet of clear plastic protected the Crucifix from the dust of construction. The backdrop was a marine blue hanging. Behind and to one side of the image, stood a small, blue-painted, wooden shrine. It must have been the altar to which the place for ritual dancing was transferred from in front of the tree, when the asphalt road was constructed (Benuzzi 1981 :95). Here I was directed to dance for the Lord of Chalma, by a workman who explained that usually there was accompaniment for the dancing. No one, however, was available to play at that time. Out of respect for the tradition, I did dance-a few restrained steps executed to a tune which I remembered in silence.

While Charles Hobgood (1964 : 115), writing in 1964, designated the Ahuehuete tree as the beginning of the sacred precincts of Chalma, the construction of the chapel, together with the development of El Ahuehuete as fromal stopping place for pilgrims, with signs which identified the site and explained the tree, crowns, water and their use; suggests that the place had since then become an intermediate shrine along the route to Chalma. In the chapel where pilgrims danced, the Crucified Christ bore the special advocation which linked Him with that locale : "Gran Senor del Ahuehuetey del Peregrino Chalmero" ("Great Lord of Ahuehuete and of the Pilgrim to Chalma"). Thus, the chapel, the clustering of stalls and kiosks, the spring, and the cypress tree, all enclosed by the walls of the ravine, marked a place which gathered meaning from the natural environment and the cultural symbols concentrated there.

Hobgood (1964 : 115) also called the Ahuehuete tree the beginning of "the road of pardon," but Dr. Flores-Meiser and I did not know that when we opted to walk the rest of the way to Chalma. Almost immediately, we left the main road and started down what must have been the old, pilgrimage path, regularly taken from El Ahuehuete before the asphalt road was completed from Mexico City through San Pedro Atlapulco to Chalma, sometime after 1971. Still used by some pilgrims, the dirt path, topped with broken stones and wide enough for a cart, wound deeper into the ravine. It had beauty, mystery, physical challenge, and a seclusion which facilitated focus on the pilgrimage process itself. From time to time, there was evidence in things built or left behind, that other pilgrims had passed that way : a stone hearth; garlands of flowers festooning the high branches of trees; or a green, wooden, commemorative cross, decorated with strands of paper flowers and nailed on a trunk of a tree. At a point where the path took us to higher ground, an opening in the tree tops revealed a small settlement in the distance, with the rugged cliffs of the canyon towering over it. The route continued to follow the uneven contours of the landscape downward, passing a building whose stone and brick walls showed the signs of age and partial restoration. Two white stacks visible above the roof as the path took an upward turn, suggested that the building was a factory or mill; while other aspects of the architecture, such as the courtyard open to the path, long windows, and accompanying, small balconies, suggested a residence, or an inn, from an earlier period of time—the effect marred only by the TV dish-antenna on the roof. The path later crossed the asphalt road at a bus stop called "Las Cruces-Chalmita", about one kilometre to the north of Chalma (Gottlieb 1971 :20; Sardo 1984 [c. 1810] :11). Here, the segment of the path going down again deeper into the ravine was identified as the "Bajada al Santuario 100 mts" ("Descent to the Sanctuary 100 metres").

Nearing the pilgrimage centre, Dr. Flores-Meiser and I were on ground still much higher than the Sanctuary of

Our Lord of Chalma itself, which sits on the floor of what seemed to the eye to be the lowest portion of the canyon near its mouth. Hence, to reach it, we had to continue to descend. We chose the first approach that presented itself. This was a short cut indicated by a sign, placed on the roof of a kiosk and painted with an arrow and the words, "Bajada Corta al Santuario"—the "Short Way Down to the Sanctuary". This was located at the edge of the cliff, where a complex landscape, open to multilayered interpretation as text, was spread out before and below us—a text which offered something familiar and much that was not. The Bajada Corta would begin high above the Sanctuary and close to the section of Chalma comprised of a compact cluster of buildings on a hillside, varying in colour and style, many of which appeared to be hotels. These buildings faced the plaza, or atrium, immediately in front of the Basilica itself. We followed the arrow to a well constructed, artistically designed, stone entranceway whose beautifully wrought, iron gate was open. Through the opening, the dome of the Sanctuary and the tops of tree were visible directly below; while secular dwellings and open green spaces on the opposite side of the ravine provided a backdrop. The gate opened onto a stone staircase protected by stone and cement railings, zigzagging down to the Basilica de San Miguel. It was a portal which to the welcomed pilgrims not to an ascent to the sacred—such as that experienced when climbing the sacred mountains to shrines in Japan;[2] but, rather, to a descent to the sacred, similar in kind, if not in difficulty of traverse, to the descent to the underground cavern of Balankanche in the Yucatan Peninsula. The move through this gateway and down the extraordinary staircase would be par excellence my liminal experience—the experience of threshold—framed by precisely defined space and time.

Beginning the walk down, I saw the intense shades of colour of the flowering vines on the stairway; the facade of the Basilica, with its two stone pillars; the twin bell towers; and the plaza in front of it, with a stone pavement where generations of Indian pilgrims danced, and stone benches built along its enclosing wall on which those same generations could rest, as visitors were resting that day.

The people in the plaza appeared to be tiny figures. Behind them, on the far side of the Sanctuary, where the walls of part of its lower structure about it, the River Chalma flowed to its waterfall and beyond. On the other side of the river, the wall of the canyon rose abruptly; small houses seeming to cling to its side. To my left, the staircase utilized the foundation of a house built above it for its support and rear wall. Following the line of vision of that wall, I came to the full view of the crowded settlement and a principal street winding down the hillside between the buildings to where the atrium of the Sanctuary began. Except for the lowest portion, the street itself could not be seen: it was hidden beneath canopies of many different colours stretched across the narrow thoroughfare and fastened to the facades to provide roofs in continuous succession.

Dr. Flores-Meiser and I continued the descent until we reached the plaza. From that level, we could appreciate the architecture of the grey stone hospice situated at the side of the plaza opposite the river. The first floor of the building was reached by a double staircase into which a fountain was built, providing water for pilgrims and other visitors. Having two stories of colonnaded porticos, with rooms having doors—but no windows—opening from them, the hospice was reminiscent of Santiago de Compostela, Spain-in its from, in its aesthetic quality, and in the ambience which the architecture helped to create.

Having deposited our crown of flowers on the posts provided for them at the entrance to the Basilica, Dr. Flores-Meiser and I went inside. Within its walls, the Sanctuary was spacious and filled with light. The eye was drawn upward to the Crucifix of Our Lord of Chalma, located above the tabernacle at the main altar. Behind the altar, was a staircase which we did ascend in order to be close to the sacred image.

Upon leaving the Basilica of San Miguel and its immediate surrounding on the canyon floor, Dr. Flores-Meiser and I again began an ascent; this time via staircase and walkway to a cave in the right wall of the ravine (as one faced the front of the Basilica). We did not know then that centuries earlier, when the Augustinian missionaries to the Indians of Ocuila[3] climed up with their native companions and found the image of Tezcatlipoca, bloodthirsty god of the cave, toppled and replaced by an image of Christ Crucified, the ascent to this cave from the floor of the ravine had been very dangerous (Sardo 1984 [c.1810] :23; Romero 1957 : 58). Neither did we realize that we owed a debt of gratitude to a seventeenth-century Augustinian, Fr. Bartolome de Jesus Maria, who was the first friar to reside there, living as a hermit in one of the caves in the wall of the canyon. He built the hospice and constructed a staircase behind it with steps and rail of stone, to give pilgrims easier access to the cave which held the original Crucifix of Our Lord of Chalma (Sardo 1984 [c. 1810]: 67-68; Othon de Mendizabal (1946:516). In 1993, the opening of the cave was closed off by the front part only of a small, white chapel with twin bell towers built against the wall of the system of staircases (which incorporated the Bajada Corta). A grating in the centre of the facade, flanked by two side entrances provided entry when unlocked. Above it stood a rose-hued image of St. Michael Archangel stepping on a white dragon-an appropriate figure; first, because the Crucifix of Chalma was found on the feast of San Miguel (or, close to it) and second, because this archangel is considered victorious over the powers of hell (Sardo 1984 [c.1810] :23; Gonzalez Leyva 1991:104). Dr. Flores-Meiser and I arrived at the grating when an official of the sanctuary came to collect offerings which had been left inside. We were permitted to go in with him; stepping down to the floor of that sacred place, which enclosed an altar and two images. Sylvia Benuzzi (1981 :93) reported that at the time of her field research in 1981, the cave existed only in folklore for most pilgrims, and was visited as an important site only by those who knew the history of Chalma. I had much to learn about the history of Chalma and the pilgrimage; but, on that day, the chapel front uniting the natural and cultural landscape, together with the imposing cave behind it, were my introduction to the founding tradition of Our Lord of Chalma. The multilayered topographical and built environmental text was beginning to take on new meaning.

After our visit to the cave, Dr. Flores-Meiser and I left the immediate precincts of the Sanctuary, and walked up the street on the hillside facing the atrium. We moved under the canopies of coloured cloth and plastic, and between the stalls lining the narrow way on either side, where vendors were selling food and religious articles. Without realizing it, we were probably retracing the steps of pilgrims, who came down that path for the place of the penitential crosses to the atrium of the church, many traveling the distance on their knees (Turner 1974 :199; and Galanes 1991 :82-83). This space, too, was part of the landscape of pilgrimage, read by me as a place where pilgrims could obtain sustenance and buy religious articles as offerings or as souvenirs of their sacred journey—a place—where the secular pursuits of manufacture, sale, and purchase mingled with holiness of intent and action. The character of the path, thus, was integral to the character of Chalma : in Christian Norberg-Schulz' (1980 :17) terms, it was one of the meanings gathered to itself by the canyon. It fromed the last piece of the whole which came to be Chalma for me.

Pilgrimage to Chalma : 1988

What was, for the most part, a different pilgrimage route and interpretation of the landscape was recorded by Robert Shadow and Maria Rodriguez V. (1990), who made the pilgrimages to Chalma with descendants of the Otomi from San Juan Tlautla. The Sanjuanero pilgrimage was governed by a tradition which enhanced the route, dictated the actions required at various stops along the way, and encouraged recognition of a mythological topography when traversed. These anthropologists, too, described the pilgrimage with sensitivity to the landscape and to its significance for themselves and for the Sanjuaneros.

As the pilgrimage began, the landscape of the three-day journey to Chalma was contextual. Features of the natural environment, such as the volcano, popocatepetl, and the Paso de Cortes, were route markers. Cornfields, hamlets, and shells of old haciendas were familiar sights along a road travelled since prehispanic times. Changes in vegetation indicated progress in the journey. As pilgrims reached places in their itinerary where ritual activity began, however, context changed to text. A cross set into one on the trees gave a name to a space : La Cruz- "The Cross". In this place, experienced pilgrims knew that they were to elect both the authorities, who would govern the group until the conclusion of their sacred journey back home, and the godparents of the novice pilgrims. The novices, including the anthropologists, were considered ignorant; first, of the physical and spiritual character of the way to El Senor de Chalma; second, of the roads to Chalma; and third, of the teachings which those roads held. The godparents were responsible for instructing the unifromed, weak, and, therefore, vulnerable novices (Shadow and Rodriguez 1990 :65).

After the elections, the pilgrims moved on toward San Jose de los Laureles, in Morelos. At the outskirts of the pueblo, each one picked up a rock to carry up the mountain, on whose summit were the crosses which marked the entrance to the Barranca Santa (Sacred Canyon). Halfway up the mountain, the novices were crowned with flowers : these represented the crown of thorns worn by Christ and were a reminder of His three falls. They identified the pilgrims with Him and with the Passion which He endured. The flowers also designated the novices as persons nearing the first of the three central places which defined the spatial and spiritual route of the pilgrimage; namely, the Barranca Santa; the Sanctuary in Chalma; and, upon return to their pueblo, the sites of reintegration into the world of daily and profane life, (Shadow and Rodriguez 1990 :47). Still carrying the stones, the pilgrims completed their ascent to a slight crest of the mountain which signalled the threshold of the canyon—a liminal point in the journey. Here, they found the several crosses, raised on a huge pile of rocks which had been placed there as symbols of the sins of novice pilgrims. After the addition of their own rocks, by which act the novices were freed from their sins, united more intimately with a divine person, and made hopeful of protection, succor, and defense for themselves and their families, the new pilgrims were ritually beaten with branches which were then thrown on the pile as another offering to the Cross.[4] This was done to eliminate fatigue and to made the novices more resistant to the hardships of the road, so that they would not repent of having undertaken the pilgrimage. All of the pilgrims then deposited their floral crowns on the arms of the cross as a sign of their devotion and commitment. The novices danced to a popular tune, ending the penitential ritual at this place called the "Calvary of the Barranca Santa" (Shadow and Rodriguez 1990:47-48).

The pilgrims began their descent into the Barranca Santa, the Sacred Canyon. After thirty minutes of travel along the paths that wound down to the depths of the ravine, the symbolism of the name, "La Barranca Santa," became clear. At an earlier time, travellers through the ravine had imposed on its natural features the quality of witness, offering evidence of events in a narrative born of popular religious belief and piety. Thus was bequeathed to later generations of pilgrims the tradition that the Lord had fled through this canyon at the time of His Passion. Now the landscape could be read as text and its features could be interpreted in the light of faith and oral traditions : a boulder bore the scar where Christ rested the heavy wooden Cross for a moment; a stone had small holes made by the shepherd's crook which Christ used to support Himself; another rock bore the partial imprint of His hand (the rest having been cut out by an over zealous pilgrim and carried away to the Church of San Cristobal Tepontla); and, at still another site, there was evidence of Christ's having sat down to rest. At the mouth of the ravine, a semi-circular fissure in the cliff was a belfry : it was claimed that Christ was almost caught at that point, but recovered sufficient strength to go on to Chalma, where He was finally taken prisoner and crucified (Shadow and Rodriguez (1990 : 69-70).[5]

The Barranca Santa was considered a mysterious place as well as a mystical one. When, therefore, the anthropologists wanted to take photographs of the divine traces, they were told that they were not to do so, because the pictures would not turn out. The prayer leader who thus admonished them, assured them that only God knew why it happened (Shadow and Rodriguez 1990 : 50).

Besides supporting a mythology and providing a setting in which unexplained happenings were likely to occur, the landscape of the Barranca Santa taught a moral lesson to those who could read it. The enormous boulders beneath which the pilgrims had to pass at one point in their journey through the canyon, represented godparents who had wanted to violate the rule of sexual abstinence, which pertained during the pilgrimage, and the prohibition against sexual relations between godparents. As a result they had been turned to stone. (Similar stone figures could be identified in the Canyon de Ocuilan [Shadow and Rodriguez 1990 : 50]; but not knowing how to read the text of the boulders there, I did not recognize them).

People from San Jose de los Laureles and Amatlan, who lived in the vicinity of the Barranca Santa, did not recognize any of the mystical or moral signs in the natural environment : to them, the locale was simply "the canyon" or "the ravine" (Shadow and Rodriguez 1990 :50). For the Sanjuaneros and for residents of Chalma who were from Puebla, however, the Barranca Santa was a place in which contact with the sacred person of Christ through the traces of His flight, mixed with fear of the dangers which breaking tabus carried with it.

After leaving the Barranca Santa, the treasurer and his assistant counted the pilgrims to be certain that all had negotiated the canyon safely, leaving none of their companions behind in a petrified state. Certain that all was well, the pilgrims continued on their way through Amatlan—the legendary site of Quetzalcoatl's birth-and then toward Tepoztlan. The mythological topography of the route was less dramatic, but popular belief still associated specific places with the presence of Christ. At a site called *Tierra Soberbia*, identified by hardened lava, Christ stopped after His exit from the Barranca Santa. He asked a farmer working on the land what he was sowing. The farmer responded, unpleasantly, that he was planting stones. To this the Lord replied that the farmer would reap stones. Farther long the road, the Lord met another man and asked the same question. This farmer replied that he was planting wheat (or, onions, according to another version). In response, Christ instructed the farmer to find other men and come the next day ready to cut the grain. He said, further that if anyone came by looking for him, the farmer was to say that he had seen Christ, but that the Lord had passed by when the man had scarcely begun to sow the seeds. The following day, the farmer and his helpers found that the recently planted wheat was ready for the harvest.

As the pilgrims entered Santa Maria Ixcatepec, Tepotzlan, the mythological and moral topography of the canyon and its environs was left behind. They entered La Preciosita Church, which was another ritual marker : there they prayed and left offerings of money, which symbolized the leaving behind of sufferings or fatigue. Tepoztlan, and the baths along the road outside of it, would ordinarily have offered primarily a context for travel or a secular text. At the timc of the pilgrimage, however, that landscape was more fromative of experience : the baths with their lines of tourists in swimming suits, challenged the pilgrims to maintain their discipline; while the carnival in the town offered a contrast of ambience and activity which could heighten their sense of purpose (Shadow and Rodriguez 1990 : 51-52).

The shift back to landscape as context occurred as the pilgrims travelled through Cuernavaca and Buenavista to the mountain range which divides the State of Morelos from that of Mexico. The route was familiar and the names attached to specific place were merely descriptive. Before daybreak the next morning, however, the landscape became again, for the Sanjuaneros, a text. A stony trail wound its way down through a forest to the canyon of Ocuilan; the steep incline making the descent in the darkness often difficult. Below them, the pilgrims could see the twinkling lights of lanterns carried by others making the sacred journey; the lights playing on the crosses suspended in the trees. For the pilgrims from Puebla and other areas converging on this route from the North and East of Chalma, these signs that so many other pilgrims walked ahead of them were reminders that they travelled in community (Shadow and Rodriguez 1990 :53). Fires in hearths along the way and the accompanying fragrances of cooking suggested temporary camps and hospitality in the from of coffee, atole, or *cara blanca* (an alcoholic drink) offered to ward off the early morning chill; thus enhancing the path's character of pilgrimage road in a way which I could only imagine when Dr. Flores-Meiser and I travelled through the same ravine in full daylight.

When the rising sun's rays illuminated the crosses on the wall of the canyon opposite the road into Chalma, the Sanjuaneros entered the environs of the Sanctuary. Just outside the village, they fromed a procession at a small atrium beneath four large crosses. The novices were crowned once more with flowers and the double line of pilgrims made their way down narrow streets crowded with vendors' stalls to the plaza in front of the Basilica de San Miguel, singing in honor of Our Lord of Chalma as they went.

The ritual entrance of the Sanjuaneros through the atrium and into the basilica, on their knees, was the climax of their pilgrimage. After they left their banners in the cave of the basilica and deposited their offering at the altar, they left the church without further ceremony. A ritual immersion of the novices in the rapidly flowing water to cleanse them and heal any illness or pain, was followed by another ritual cleaning in the chapel of Christ Crucified. In this ritual, a candle was passed over the body of the novice and then left at the altar as an offering of the sufferings borne during the journey. Then these new pilgrims were free to join the others to visit the town, buy their souvenirs, and rest; there is no mention in the anthropologists' account, of a visit to the cave where the Crucifix of Our Lord of Chalma first appeared.[6] Early on their third day at the Sanctuary, the Sanjuaneros prepared to retrace their steps. They followed on foot the same route in reverse—but without prescribed, ritual activity—concluding their pilgrimage with their return to San Juan Tlautla three days later (Shadow and Rodriguez 1990 :54-55).

Conclusions

Analysis of the pilgrimage from San Juan Tlautla recorded by Robert Shadow and Maria Rodriguez V., and of that from Mexico City made by Dr. Flores-Meiser and me, shows that there are categories of pilgrims whose experiences in relation to the landscape along pilgrimage routes to Our Lord of Chalma differ substantially. The first category consists of persons who are knowledgeable about the topography and are steeped in traditions which have imposed on the natural and built environments a symbolism which enriches and infroms the pilgrimage experience. The second is comprised of persons who have not made the pilgrimage before, but who are guided by representatives of the community in the most crucial phases of the journey : they learn how to negotiate the landscape and read its text, carry out the prescribed rituals, and, to some degree, channel their emotional response. The third group is truly foreign to the Sanctuary and to the pilgrimage route. Its members have little, or no, familiarity with the topography of region to be traversed; they probably do not recognize locally created symbols; and may not be able to identify traditionally important places. For them, guidance is minimal and may depend largely on features of the built environment, such as signs and other available, written texts. Ritual activity is a product of personal background and of a willingness to adapt to what they learn as they go. Emotional responses are elicited largely as a result of their religious knowledge and faith; extent of involvement in the pilgrimage process; and both their intellectual and aesthetic sensitivity to their natural, built, and social surroundings.

To all three groups, there are ingredients of the pilgrimage which are common. In the pilgrimage to El Senor de Chalma, every pilgrim identified with he Crucified Christ represented by the Crucifix—at least on the universal level of significance—and shared the motivation of reaching His Sanctuary. Crosses and other icons, such as statues of the virgin Mary and of Saint Michael Archangel, could most likely be identified by all pilgrims. Person reading Spanish shared the meaning of written texts. All pilgrims encountered and moved through the landscape, which either served as a context for their pilgrimage or provided a text which directly infromed their sacred journey. The roles of text and context alternated in accordance with ritual, symbolism, aesthetics, memory, personal background, motivation, intensity of devotion, anticipation, and the circumstances of travel.

In the relationship between pilgrim and landscape, topography is influential : it contributes to the creation not only of the spatial structure of the places en route to the sacred shrine, but also of their character-their Genius Loci (Norberg-Schulz 1980-18). In the two pilgrimages to Chalma, about which this paper is concerned, deep ravines, or canyons, were the most notable topographical feature. Sometimes the canyons were negotiated as part of the context of the journeys; other times they were the pilgrims' texts. In either case, descent figured prominently in travel and at the pilgrimage centre. In a special manner, descent into the Canyon de Ocuilan incorporated an aesthetic experience which emphasized participation in a pilgrimage process involving great numbers of people and decades of time; and, while, for Sanjuaneros, entrance into the Barranca Santa was descent into a mysterious and mystical place made sacred through belief in Christ's presence there; for me, the walk down the Bajada Corta to the atrium of the Basilica of San Miguel was my movement toward the sacred—a descent which was itself a unique experience. The Sanjuaneros' interpretation of the landscape was mostly born of community tradition; mine was very much individual and personal.

To anthropologists, consideration of the landscape as text and as context offers new richness in our study of pilgrimage. It also presents a new methodological challenge in the questions that can be raised and researched, as well as the concepts needed for the ethnographic description and analysis of data regarding the route and sites, the journey, intermediate shrines when present, and the pilgrimage centre. Anthropologists can be receptive to this offer of richness and responsive to this methodological challenge, first, by being more sensitive to landscape—to the significance of topography for the pilgrimage process in the experience of others and of ourselves; and, second, by perceiving the natural and built environments with fresh attention to detail and just a little wonder.

Notes

1. This paper was given at the 14th International Congress of Anthropological and Ethnological Sciences, Williamsburg, Virginia, U.S.A., July 26, 1998-August 1, 1998. Freed from the constraints of limited time for presentation to a listening audience, I have expanded some of the discussion, enhanced description and clarified points when helpful, and improved the flow of the language for readerss.
2. Ascent to the sacred is prominent in pilgrimages to Crosses atop mountains and hills in Costa Rica, as well. Please consult, for example, Leslie Ellen Straub, (2000) for an anthropological study of pilgrimage to the Cruz de Alahuelita, at the summit of Cerro San Miguel, Costa Rica.
3. Chalma has been in the pastoral care of the Augustinian Friars since the Colonial period (Sardo 1984 [c.1810] :67.
4. The description by Shadow and Rodriguez (1990 :48) suggests that the several crosses might be representative of the three crosses at Golgatha : Christ hung on the central one.
5. When Shadow and Rodriguez (1990: 50) asked how it was possible for Christ to have walked through the canyon, if He lived and died outside of Jerusalem, in the Holy Land, the Sanjuaneros replied that that was what their grandparents taught them.
6. It is possible that some San Juan Tlautla pilgrims

visited the cave during their free time, without the anthropologists' knowledge. There was no requirement, apparently that these pilgrims, as a group, go to the cave.

References

Benuzzi, Silvia 1981: A Pilgrimage to Chalma : The Analysis of Religious Change. (Katunob .... Occasional Publications in Mesoamerican Anthropology, No. 17) Greeley, Colorado : University of Northern Colorado.

Galanes, Luis Roberto 1991: "De Toluca a Chalma" : History, Legend, Pilgrimages, and Mexican Catholic Images. A Thesis Submitted to the Graduate Faculty of the Louisiana State University and Agricultural and Mechanical College in partial fulfillment of the requirement for the degree of Master of Arts in the Department of Geography and Anthropology.

Gonzalez Leyva, Alejandra 1991 Chalma : Una devocion Agustina. Toluca, Mexico : Universidad Autonoma del Estado de Mexico. y el Instituto Mexiquense de Cultura.

Gottlieb, Erich 1971: Chalma : Persistence and Change in Its Pilgrimages. Ann Arbor, Michigan : University Microfilms, Inc.

Hirsch, Eric and Michael O'hanlon 1995 : The Anthropology of Landscape. Perspectives on Place and Space. Oxford : Clarendon Press.

Hobgood, John 1964 : Chalma. A Study in Directed Cultural Change. A Thesis to the Faculty of the Graduate School of Arts and Sciences submitted in partial fulfillment of the requirement of the M.A. in Anthropology. Carbondale, Illinois, Southern Illinois University, April 16, 1964.

Lawrence, Denise L. and Setha M. Low 1990 : "The Built Environment and Spatial From". In Annual Review of Anthropology, Volume 19, edited by Bernard J. Siegel. Palo Alto, California : Annual Reviews, Inc.

Norberg-Schulz, Christian 1980 : Genius Loci. Towards a Phenomenology of Architecture. New York : Rizzoli.

Othon De Mendizabal, Miguel 1946 : Obras Completas. Tomo Segundo: Ensayo sobre las civilizaciones aborigenes americanas. Mexico, D.F. : Talleres Graficos de la Nacion.

Romero Q., Javier 1957 : Tezcatlipoca es el Ozteotl de Chalma. Toponomia. Dibujos Edmundo Calderon. Toluca, Mexico : Talleres Graficos de la Nacion.

Sallnow, Michael J. 1987 : Pilgrims of the Andes. Regional Cults in

Cusco. Washington, D.C. and London : Smithsonian Institution Press.

Sardo, R.P. FR. Joaquin 1984 : Relacion historica del Santo Cristo del Santuario y Convento de Chalma. Mexico, D.F. : Impresos Olalde, [c.1810].

Schama, Simon 1995 : Landscape and Memory. New York : Alfred A. Knopf.

Shadow, Robert D. and Maria J. Rodriguez V. 1990 : Simbolos que amarran, simbolos que dividen : hegemonia e impugnacion campesina a Chalma, Mesoamerica 19 (Junio de 1990) : 33-72.

Singer, Milton 1972 : When a Great Tradition Modernizes. An Anthropological Approach to Indian Civilization. Foreword by M.N. Srinivas. New Your : Praeger Publishers.

Straub, Leslie Ellen, O.P. 2000 : "Pilgrimage to the Cruz de Alahuelita, Costa Rica : Imprints on Landscape, Experience, and Cultural Traditions." In Pilgrimage Studies : The Power of Sacred Places, edited by D.P. Dubey, Allahabād, India : Society of Pilgrimage Studies.

Turner, Victor 1974 : Dramas, Fields, and Metaphors. Symbolic Action in Human Society. Ithaca and London : Cornell University Press.

4

"Nationalising the Sacred : Shrines and Shifting Identities in the Israeli-Occupied Territories."

Glenn Bowman

In this article I present a reading of Christian and Muslim Palestinian uses of two West Bank Christian holy places. The first is the Greek Orthodox monastery of Mar Elyas (the Prophet Elijah) located on the Hebron Road between Bethlehem and Jerusalem; the second is the municipal shrine of Bir el-Saiyideh ('The Well of the Lady') in Beit Sahour, a mile to the east of Bethlehem. I elucidate how Palestinians of different sectarian affiliations engage the complicated processes of interpreting the significance of a holy place and defining their relationship to it. The investigation of the shrine activities around Mar Elyas on the prophet's feast day will show that the place has very different meanings to the various groups of people who attend the feast, and will set out how the members of these groups interpret the site and their engagement with it. This multivocality of place raises the issue of the politics involved in 'fixing' its meaning : moving both in space and time to Beit Sahour during the intifada, I will discuss how the Christians and Muslims who live in the town have elaborated a means of maintaining their religious relationship with a holy place they see as a central feature of their town's identity without succumbing to the pressure, imposed upon them by religious hierarchies, to fix the identity of that place (and of themselves as users of the place) in sectarian terms.

The analysis raises the issue of the central role in constituting communities played by members' perceptions of 'antagonisms' mobilised against them (Laclau and Mouffe 1985 : 93-148). During my fieldwork (made up of a number of extended visits between 1983 and 1990), Muslim and Christian Beit Sahourans were in the process of defining the activities of both religious institutions and the State of Israel as equally threatening to what they perceived as their interests. In response to this perception, Beit Sahourans elaborated a secular nationalist communal identity which allowed them to reject communalism[1] and to unite against and resist the external forces of both 'foreign' religious institutions and the 'colonial settler state'. This identity is, however, neither inevitable nor fixed and is hegemonic only as long as it appears to offer a viable solution to the dilemmas of the people it constitutes as an imagined community' (Anderson 1991 : pp. 5-7). The elements which make up communal identity—not only the persons brought together within the definition but as well the interests which are seen to join them, the strategies perceived as best serving those interests and the antagonisms believed to beset them—are labile, and redefinitions of any of these can lead to a shifting of the entire field of identity making enemies of former neighbours and allies of previous antagonists. To illustrate this I will, in closing, examine the appeal of the distinctly communalist programme of Hamas (the Islamic resistance movement)[2]. In the wake of relatively successful state activities seeking to discredit the appeal of secular nationalism and to silence its advocates, Hamas has provided many Palestinians with new images of community (images which peripheralise Christian Palestinians) and offered alternative definitions of that community's needs, the antagonisms which threaten to deprive it of its requisites, and the strategies to follow in overcoming those antagonisms.

Robert Hertz's largely disregarded *St. Besse : a study of an Alpine cult*, first published in 1913, raises the still salient issue of the way a single religious site is interpreted in very different ways by discrete communities engaging in commemorative festivities at it (Hertz 1983). Hertz stressed that the holy place speaks for and of a community and that therefore the meaning of such a site has to be analysed in terms not of the place itself, but of the social practices of the communities which revere it and the identities generated by those activities. Following the trajectory mapped by Hertz, I explore the meaning of two Palestinian Holy places in the light of the models of community brought to them by their worshippers. In doing so I consider the wider analytic domain of identity and the situations in which it is constituted.

'Identity', like 'ethnicity', became a central issue in anthropological inquiry in the wake of Frederik Barth's programmatic assertion that we need to attend "to problems of boundary maintenance" and "ask ourselves what is needed to make ethnic distinctions emerge in an area" (Barth 1969 :17). Many recent studies of ethnic and national identities (e.g., Madan 1972; Loizos 1981; Kapferer 1988; and McDonald 1989) have emphasised the issue of the 'other' who lies beyond those boundaries in defining the identity of the 'self' which lies within. In this paper I develop that work in line with Laclau and Mouffe's theory of 'antagonism' (1953)[3] in order to explore the processes through which persons come to fromulate identities for themselves and their communities in periods of radical social conflict.

In the contemporary situation Palestinians are engaged in what is in effect a national liberation struggle. Palestinians under Israeli occupation are constructing new froms of community and affiliation appropriate to confrontation with an enemy they see as dedicated to their extirpation. Significant similarities exist here between the creation of a 'Palestinian' entity in the face of Israeli antagonism and the unification by prophets of Nilotic tribes in the southern Sudan in the context of substantial foreign aggression (Evans-Pritchard 1940 : 184-91; also Lienhardt 1961). Evans-Pritchard noted that the presence of prophets in Nuer society was a "recent development" (1940 :186) and attributed "the strong tendency towards federation between adjacent tribes .... to the new Arab-European menace.

Opposition between Nuer and their neighbours had always been sectional. They were now confronted by a more formidable and a common enemy" (Evans-Pritchard 1940 :189).

Lienhardt, in discussing the origins of the divinities who possessed various Dinka Prophets, suggested that these divinities had recently come from outside the domain of the Dinka : the free divinity Deng Kur "was the Nuer prophet Ngungdeng, father of gwek who rallied the Nuer against the British" (1961 :95) and other Western Dinka prophet-inspiring divinities were believed by the Dinka to have entered Dinkaland from areas in which the Mahdi, an Arab prophet who waged holy war against the British, had operated (1961 : 72 and 164-5). Implicit in both texts is the important recognition that novel Forms of mobilization and affiliation were generated by confrontation with a powerful external antagonist. Lienhardt's recognition that the cultural borders between the Dinka and surrounding peoples' can be blurred by shared antagonisms suggests that those borders, and the identities constituted within them, were far from fixed. Nonetheless Evans-Pritchard and, to a lesser degree, Lienhardt tended in their ethnographies to present events as though they had occurred in a stable ethnographic present. Both thus understated the impact of the British occupation of the Sudan on Nuer and Dinka societies (see Geertz 1988 and Clifford 1988: 32).

In consequence, the segmentary model bequeathed to anthropological theory by these works stressed the systematicity of pre-modern societies at the expense of attending to the processes of transformation imposed upon such 'systems' by the contingencies of conflict and historical change. In focussing on the historical context of the cultural transformations effected in contemporary Palestinian society I demonstrate that segmentary opposition can be a useful model for understanding political mobilization in modern as well as in pre-modern societies. However, in using this model I shift emphasis from the systematic workings of the internal structures of society to the role of the outside enemy in forcing reformulation of the terrain 'inside'. In so doing I suggest that the inside is neither stable nor systematic but is itself a response to the assault on its inhabitants from outside. By considering changes in the meanings of holy places and traditions related to them in contemporary Palestinian society I will demonstrate how holy sites serve as monuments to imaginings of community and how such monuments prove to be as labile as are those communities themselves.

The Shrine of Mar Elyas

In *Mohammedan Saints and Sanctuaries in Palestine*, the Palestinian folklorist Taufik Canaan not only details how Palestinian Muslims in the early part of this century inscribed central moments of their individual and collective lives on the Palestinian landscape but also notes that "the various ideas described in the following pages are common to both Mohammedans and Christians among the Palestinian peasantry; where the two groups differ the differences are only superficial" (Canaan 1927 :vi). This assertion finds validation today in the practices of villagers and townspeople from the region of Bethlehem at, to take one of several local examples the Greek Orthodox monastery of Mar Elyas.

On the day preceding the saint's day, local Muslims accompany Christians to Mar Elyas, a holy place on the peripheries of Bethlehem district, both to visit the monastic chapel and to join friends, family and neighbours on the grounds of the nearly inoperative monastery. Outside the sixth century building the area is bright with small groups of men, women and children picnicking under the olive trees and listening to the music of ouds (Arab lutes) and transistor radios. In front of the church is a mass of men, women and children waiting to enter the shrine, some of whom carry loaves of bread cooked with mastic, bottles of oil, and candles (some three inches thick and as tall as the bearer). Once inside the local people struggle through the priests and monks performing the divine offices specific to the coming feast day[4] to the front of the church where those bearing gifts light their candles, leave their olive before the icons, and hand over their loaves to a novice monk who in turn distributes bits of sanctified bread—some of which is eaten on the spot and the rest saved to be given away later to family and neighbours outside and at home. The donors then join the others who have gone directly to wait their turns to place a chain attached to the wall of the church around their necks, kiss it three times, and step through it. In the meantime the resident monks and the visiting members of the Greek Orthodox Brotherhood of the Holy Sepulchre[5] struggle to amplify the Holy Word sufficiently to have it heard over the babble of thronging Palestinians and the perpetual clanking of the miraculous chain.

This cacophony of groups, contending within the same restricted space to Perform actions deemed appropriate to the place and time, is echoed in the interpretations they impose upon those actions. One priest explained to me that the chain was found in a cave beneath the monastery and that, since the cave, like the monastery, is dedicated to Elyas and believed to be the spot where the Old Testament prophet fled from the persecution of Jezebel (1 Kings 19)[6], local people see the chain as one which had bound the saint. According to an Orthodox priest I interviewed, their fervent attention to the chain is an expression of their deep devotion to the prophet : "those who enchain themselves with it—around the neck and around the waist—bind themselves to the saint and make themselves one with him. All the sacrifices, like the oil for the lamps, the bread, the candles, express this self dedication. Elyas is a mediator between God and the people, and they can talk to him when they can't talk directly to God." The priest explained, however, that this devotion, while spiritually correct, is actually misguided; the chain had bound Christians during Muslim persecutions and is associated with the monastery because in the past local Christians had hidden from their oppressors in the caves beneath it.

The priest's story was echoed in the stories of some of the lay persons. George Halweh, a leader in the Greek Orthodox Boy Scout troop which comes from the nearby town of Beit Jala to help in the ceremonies, explained to me that

Elyas was a great protector of the Christians during their persecutions, and led me inside to show me an icon of Elijah killing the prophets of Baal. This he told me, with a blithe disregard for scriptural chronology, shows Elyas slaughtering the Jews and Muslims who persecuted the Christians. The chain, Halweh said, is an ancient chain found in a cave beneath the monastery which "may have bound Elyas or .. may have bound persecuted Christians". By revering the chain people call on Elyas to deliver the Christians from their afflictions just as God delivered Elyas from his and Elyas delivered the Christians from theirs. The chain, Halweh added, is particularly useful for alleviating insanity.

Other local people, including two Muslim women who had just stepped through the chain, told me that it is 'linked' to another at the Greek Orthodox shrine of 'Khadr (St. George) in the nearby Muslim village of the same name. Cannan wrote that the chain at' Khadr was used specifically to bind, and thereby cure, the mad (Canaan 1927 :79-80). Persons approaching the Mar Elyas chain did not, however, restrict the efficacy of that chain to curing insanity but asserted that it as well alleviated a number of other afflictions : illness, bad luck, sinfulness, and even the evil eye. If the Mar Elyas chain ever had the specific function Canaan attributes the chain at 'Khadr, that function has subsequently become more general; people using it claimed they did so because it 'gives good fortune'. While the 'Khadr chain may be 'linked' to the one at Mar Elyas because Mar Elyas is dedicated both to St. George and to Elijah (icons of St. George and Elijah flank the iconostasis), this was never proffered as an explanation. People stressed only the efficacy of the chains; what they had in common was that each served to turn bad fortune to good.

The links between the chain and the saint's day, the saint and even the place were by this time seeming rather tenuous, and several constellations of conflicting interpretations were floating around the crowded interior of the small chapel. The priests and monks were involved through their ceremonies in articulating the small chapel within a nearly empty monastery into a network of religious institutions and practices they believed to be both universal and eternal. The offices of the day preceding the saint's day, and the liturgies on the saint's day itself, rehearsed the association of the Prophet Elijah with the sacred history of the Church, and, by so doing, legitimated in the eyes of God and of the worldwide Greek Orthodox community the officiants' presence and the existence of the small outpost of orthodoxy. The chain stood for them as both a relic and an emblem of the monastery's place in the general Orthodox struggle to survive and overcome disbelief and unbelievers. To the priest with whom I spoke the spectacle of the local population binding itself within the church was an emblem of his and his colleagues' mission to promote amongst the general population the same obedience to God and his agents which bound them to their service.

In Halweh's interpretation Elyas did not have the 'transparency' attributed to him by the priest; the saint, for Halweh, was a power in himself rather than an agent of God or a transmission line to Him[7]. One does not rally around Elyas in order to state one's allegiance to the god of Elyas but because the prophet protects those who are devoted to him against whatever forces threaten them, be those religious or secular. Those forces were described as having operated in the past under the banners of Judaism and Islam. However at the time of my research they were not seen to be mobilized along denominational lines and were instead seen as aligned more generally against the possibility for local people to live a decent, satisfying life. The chain both reinvoked and signified the persecutions suffered by Elyas's community at the hands of its enemies and asserted that the Prophet Elyas would overcome those who oppress his dependents. Halweh's description of the icon as a portrayal of the prophet in ancient times destroying the Jewish and Muslim enemies of the Christians asserted a communal reading of antagonism and identity in accordance with the traditions he had imbibed during his upbringing within a Christian community and his education in a Christian (Lutheran) school. Nonetheless, Palestinian Orthodox communities in the latter half of the twentieth century have come to see the interests of the Greeks of the Orthodox church as inimical to their own, in part because of the legacy of antagonism to the Greek Orthodox Patriarchate granted them by the Arab Orthodox Movement[8]. As a result, Halweh's description of the contemporary Christian community excluded the priesthood from that community, and defined the Greek Christians as enemies of the community Elyas protects. For Halweh, the priests who claimed to be the servants of the prophet and of his God were, in fact, the enemies of those who appeal to the saint for protection. Halweh and I discussed a Greek Orthodox man who thirty years earlier had come to Jerusalem from Athens on pilgrimage and settled there to work for the Church. The previous evening this resident pilgrim had told me that "religion is more important than the land; I do not care for Palestine, I am a resident of the holy land". Halweh's response to this statement was "people like this are a problem. The Greek church—like the Muslim Brotherhood' [the Muslim Brothers of Palestine]—insists on considering everything in terms of religion. Palestinian Christians are allowed no place in the Church. The condition of being a [Palestinian] priest is that one must marry so that one cannot move up the hierarchy[9]. It feels like a foreign occupation. A couple of years ago the scouts here beat up a priest."

Halweh's identifications of himself as a 'Palestinian Christian', rather than as an Orthodox Christian, indicated a formulation of identity tying him more closely to other Christians (regardless of denomination) among whom he lived than to co-religionists who were not Palestinian. After telling of the Patriarchate rules excluding Orthodox Christians from significant participation in the church, he discussed how the interests of the 'foreign' churches prevented local Christians from asserting their identities as Christians. The fireman (an edict issued by the Turkish sultan) of the status quo, a set of regulations by which the various churches keep their holy feasts separate so that questions are not raised about which church has possession of specific holy places[10], was seen by Halweh and other indigenous Christians with whom I spoke as a denial to them of Christian—as opposed to Greek, Armenian, Latin, etc.—identity. Halweh told me "the most evil thing here is that we do not have one Christmas. All over the world

Christmas is the twenty fifth except here—it is a shame for the Palestinians. We have tried to fight it by making the feast on one day, but they would not agree because of the question of who would go into the church first".

The communalism evident in Halweh's description of the icon of Elijah and the prophets of Baal shadowed an imagined community bringing together all Christians living in his homeland in opposition to Jews and Muslims, but that sensed community was not acknowledged by the church to which he owed formal allegiance. Furthermore, the activities of the foreigners who controlled that church served not only to deny fellow Orthodox Palestinians full membership of the church but also forbad expression of the wider Christian community to which Halweh saw himself belonging. Thus, for Halweh, there was a substantial conflict between his religion, which provided him with supernatural protector and granted him an identity as part of a particular people (Palestinian Christians) living in a particular land (Palestine), and that of the priests and monks dominating that religion's institutions, who saw him, his people and his people's lives as largely extraneous to their interests as Greeks in a Greek Orthodox holy land. His participation in a festival on the territory and under the legislation of the Greek Orthodox clergy therefore brought him onto contested ground. This contest was manifest in a discourse which both stressed his identity as a Christian dependent on the succour of Christian saints and distinguished between his Palestinian Christianity and the priests' and monks' Greek Christianity.

Halweh was not, however, led by this either to pull back from the religion or to withdraw from the festivities. The religion and the feast of Mar Elyas were important to him; he wore a cross around his neck which hung prominently outside his shirt and over his boy scout scarf, he frequently went to church and prayed to its tutelary saints, and he attended the feast with his fellow boy scouts—many of home are Catholic—to protect the festivities from those who might, in the name of politics, deny his people the practice of their religion : "we watch out for trouble; some nationalists may try to disrupt things because they say there is no place for celebration under occupation". Just as Halweh saw the church leaders failing to represent the Christian Palestinians by refusing to recognise any aspect of their experiences which could not be interpreted in terms of the interests of their church, so too he believed that nationalists would disallow the full expression of local Christian identities by proscribing religious ceremonials and insisting that all manifestations must be explicitly and exclusively nationalist[11]. Halweh's identity as a Christian and a Palestinian located him, then, between mutually exclusive discourses on identity; that of the foreign church which, in providing a religion, denied national identity and that of the nationalists who, in working to realize a political identity, allowed no room for the expression of religious identity.

For those, Christian and Muslim, who linked the Mar Elyas chain with the chain at the monastery of 'Khadr and thus indirectly with St. George, the association of the miraculous chain, the feast, the monastery, the prophet Elyas and the Greek Orthodox church appeared largely contingent. Stories told by Christian and Muslims attending the feast suggested that at Mar Elyas it was the wonder-working artifact which was important. There was no discussion of why the chain was empowered or whose power it mediated; pilgrims simply referred to the chain as a source of health, good luck, sanity and freedom from the evil eye. The people who ritualistically handled the chain were at the monastery not because the day was holy to Elyas or because the day was holy at all. Rather, the chain was used throughout the year whenever there was access to it; the feast day was special because on that day the church was open.

Many persons, in fact, claimed that they came to the feast to be with their 'neighbours' rather than to revere the chain or Elyas. Such assertions, which made even the devotions to the chain appear as a consequence rather than a cause of the gathering, were reiterated outside the church where people's attentions flowed from group to group rather than being channelled towards the miraculous or the sacred by the dynamics inside the chapel. In the crowed olive groves outside the monastery the strands of motives and meanings were woven into the tapestry of a multi-denominational community united by its perception of itself as a community with shared traditions and practices. The Muslim who had accompanied the Syrian Orthodox girl referred to in note seven told me that "the religious difference doesn't matter, we all come. It is for friendship and community as much as for religion." Persons circulate from small group to small group, sharing food, drink and gossip. Some of these people told me they did not go in the church at all but simply came on his day, as they always had, to be with their neighbours. One man said " we all come to be together around the saint's place".

There was, clearly, considerable heterogeneity within this apparent unity; some attend the site just to picnic, others to take a blessing from the chain, others (Muslim and Christian) to redeem promises and ask blessings of St. George and of the Prophet Elyas, and some to visit, and sacrifice to, the Prophet. Many persons seemed to attend to carry out more than one of these activities. Each person's attested motives and the identities that devolved from those motives, shifted as the person moved from context to context. Halweh, who stressed his Christian identity while serving both as guide to a foreign anthropologist within the church and as guardian of the festivities in the company of his fellow scouts, became just another member of the mixed community which constituted itself around the monastery when he joined Muslim friends and neighbours in the small groups scattered around the olive groves.

The festivities at Mar Elyas, then, seemed to serve as a 'floating signifier' [12] for the people of the region. Each individual was able to attribute to the place and the gathering meanings personal to them, and yet, because the time and the place served as a place of inscription for so many diverse meanings and motives, the feast constituted a community. People recognized that community at the same time as they recognized the multiplexity of its character; it was, in a very real sense, a concentration of the community they moved through day to day in a more dilute from. The only people excluded from this sensed community were those who would make rigorous the criteria of participation : the priests who saw the celebration as specific to their own particular sect and, hence, as antithetical to all other religious persuasions (both other Christian communities and Muslims), and the nationalists who would deny this shared sense of communal identity in calling on a 'higher' national identity exclusive of precisely that field of faith and local community which made the people feel at home.

The following day, the saint's day proper, effectively belonged to the church *per se*; there was a strong delegation present from the Brotherhood of the Holy Sepulchre, and the only local people were old women, very few accompanied by children, who quietly attended the liturgy and drifted off after the church ceremony was completed. The Brotherhood, and the liturgy with which it asserted its ecclesiastical identity and fixed the significance of the site in relation to that identity, hegemonized the time and place, and the only Palestinians who participated were those who wished to assert themselves as Greek Orthodox believers dependent on the succour of a liturgy presented before them by a foreign clergy in a language they had never been taught to understand.

Beit Sahour and the Miracle at Bir el-Saiyideh

The situation in Beit Sahour, a municipality with a mixed Christian-Muslim population of around 12,000, which gave rise to the shrine of Bir el-Saiyideh in the nineteen eighties differed in significant ways from that described for the shrine of Mar Elyas. In some ways the demographic isolation of Mar Elyascontributed to this difference. While Bir-el-Saiyideh is located immediately below the main market place of Beit Sahour, Mar Elyas stands on an isolated promontory above the Judean Desert. Palestinian houses which had, in the past, stood within walking distance of the monastery have been abandoned and for the most part bulldozed over the past decade or so because of the expansion of Israeli settlement in the area. Consequently, when Palestinians came to Mar Elyas they came from a number of discrete areas of settlement to a holy place per se rather than to a holy place at the hub of other non-sacral community defining activities. The identities at play at Mar

Elyas tended, therefore, to be explicitly linked to interpretations of the monastery and its contents, even if those interpretations mobilized other elements of the pilgrims' lives only contingently connected to religion and religious artifacts. The sort of secular community observed in the olive fields around the shrine was, in a sense, an accident of proximity. It dissolved with the occasion, perhaps leaving behind a residue of good feeling towards others of other villages and religious affiliations, but did not provide sufficient ground for the building of political identities and programmes. The shrine of Bir el-Saiyideh, in contrast, is not only a sign of the sacred but is a marker of sacrality located in the centre of a community in which sectarian and national identities are focal concerns. It is the wider field in which a shrine operates which gives the shrine both its character and its significance, and the differences of the fields surrounding Mar Elyas and Bir el-Saiyideh lead people to interpret the places and to articulate their identities in relation to those places in very different ways. In presenting a sense of the particular context in which the shrine of Bir el-Saiyideh has developed, I elaborate some of the conditions which have given rise to the Beit Sahouran project of rearticulating the place of religion in the assertion of communal identity[13].

In 1983 Christian and Muslim Palestinians who had come to the Christmas celebrations in Bethlehem to participate in what they called 'the feast of Bethlehem' spoke to me of repeated sightings over the previous three weeks of the Virgin Mary and two other figures in the shadowed depths of an underground cistern beneath the market square of Beit Sahour. At the time I did not follow up these rumours of a 'miracle' and I did not visit the site of this apparition for another five years. Nevertheless, in the interim I learnt enough about the local communities and their situation under occupation to make their reception of and response to the alleged intrusion of the sacred into the course of their daily lives seem signally important.

It was difficult to ignore the Palestinian presence at the commemoration of the Nativity of Christ. One of the more exciting aspects of Bethlehem's Christmas Eve ceremonies was the massing of Palestinian scouts in Manger Square to greet the Latin Patriarch on his arrival from Jerusalem to prepare for midnight mass. Scout processions, which despite their military demeanour were permitted by the Israeli authorities, were a common sight at Muslim and Christian feast day ceremonies throughout the Occupied Territories before the intifada. There were, however, considerable differences between the deportment of Muslim and Christian troops. Muslim scouts marched in black-and-white 'Fatah' keffiyas and bore banners on which the nationalist tetrad of green, red, black, and white was conspicuously manifest. Among the Christians, national emblems and colours were conspicuously absent, and the uniforms and banners of Christian scouts served solely to distinguish between the troops' various sectarian identities. Conversations with scouts and religious functionaries made it clear that it was the churches which restricted the public discourse of the Christian scouts to the celebration of religious identity. Church leaders, at the time exclusively foreign, were afraid of offending the Israeli authorities who maintained the 'status quo'[14] and loath to allow local Christians to denigrate the importance of the foreign-run churches by publicly asserting that their religious identities were only part of a larger national identity. At the Bethlehem Christmas procession no Muslim troops were allowed to march with the Christians, even though Muslim Bethlehemites also saw Christmas as the 'name day' of their city and despite the fact that local Muslim scout troops annually asked to participate. The Latin Patriarchate allowed Christian troops from various sectarian groupings (Catholic and non-Catholic alike) to march together, but the entire display (the order in which the scouts marched, the insignia of their costumes and the slogans on their banners) made manifest only the communal identities which distinguished between the groups; there was nothing to suggest that these young men and women shared a political identity with each other and with the excluded Muslims.

There was, however, one exception. The Beit Sahour troops, although like the others organized into sectarian groups by the different churches which sponsored them, were uniformly dressed. All wore black-and-white keffiyas and webbed military caps. On their shoulders were patches (attached by snaps or safety pins) on which the scout fleur de lis was figured out in the Palestinian national colours of green, red, black and white. The difference was striking, and one person in the watching crowd remarked : "they must be Muslims from Jerusalem". Others would not allow that—there could not be Muslims marching with the Christians-but were clearly nonplussed by the scouts' overtly political appearance but by the uniformity manifested across the groups. The Beit Sahour scouts considered the differences to be nominal; unlike the other scouts, who continually wished to know which of the troops were thought to be most impressive, the Beit Sahourans wanted only to know my impression of the town's contingent as a whole. They also wanted to know whether I would come to Beit Sahour the next day to see "the real Christmas celebration".

On Christmas Day the winding streets of the hilly town were crowded with local people and bereft of Israelis or foreigners. The focus of enthusiasm was the scout troops, as it had been the day before, but in Beit Sahour the procession was very different. For one thing, it was much more military; whereas in Bethlehem many of the scouts had seemed to be flirting with the crowd, calling out to friends and family in the audience and showing off with bravura poses and exaggerated baton tosses, in Beit Sahour boys and girls, men and women marched in disciplined formation with their faces set and fixed firmly forward. More significant, however, was the fact that the various Christian troops from Beit Jala, Bethlehem and other towns were joined by a large contingent of Muslim troops, not only from Beit Sahour but also from as far away as Ramallah, Silwan and Jerusalem. Scout uniforms were less flamboyant, and where on the previous day the bright Insignia of the various sectarian communities had stood out strongly, here all the scouts had covered the badges of their particular troops with the green, red, black and white fleur de lis patch previously worn only on the shoulders of the Beit Sahour contingent.

In Bethlehem the troops had been brought together to receive the Patriarch, and when the Patriarch had withdrawn (to meet local dignitaries, including the military governor of the Occupied Territories) the scouts dispersed. In Beit Sahour, in contrast, the Christmas parade from the Greek Orthodox church through the town to the community hall in the basement of the Latin Church was merely the ceremonial facet of what was a larger, and distinctly extra-ecclesiastic, project. In this instance religion provided the occasion-not the reason-for a public manifestation exceeding, both in duration, rhetoric and purpose, the bounds set by the ceremonial event. After the parade had ended the mingled troops gathered for two hours to chant nationalist slogans, dance with their keffiyas wrapped around their heads and enthusiastically applaud a succession of speakers (scout and civilian alike) who referred to them as "rifles for the pleasure of Abu-Ammar's (Yasser Arafat's) eyes" while discussing the complexities of organizing a united Muslim and Christian "Pan-Palestinian Scout Movement" in the face of opposition from church and mosque. The fleur de lis scout emblems which I had seen pinned or snapped onto scout uniforms were the markers of this movement, and they were removable precisely because the movement was an anathema to the religious authorities on which the troops depended both for funding and for legal status.

The central role played by the Beit Sahour scouts in uniting Muslims and Christians within a political organization explicitly intended to substitute nationalist union for sectarian divisiveness[15] was not something exceptional for Beit Sahour; the demography of the town brings Muslims and Christians together in their economic pursuits, and the strength of the town's economy (based on small factories producing plastics and various craft goods) has led local Christians to commit themselves to remaining there rather than emigrating to the Palestinian diaspora as have many Christians from other mixed towns such as Bethlehem and Beit Jala. Beit Sahour is a largely Christian town, although there is some question about the precise proportions of Muslims and Christians in the population. The most recent survey was carried out in 1984 when Father Pena of the Franciscan Order estimated that eighty-three per cent of the town's population was Christian, largely Greek Orthodox but with substantial numbers of Latin and Greek Catholics and much smaller Lutheran and Syrian Orthodox populations (Pena 1984)[16]. Christians and Muslims I spoke with in Beit Sahour in 1990 tended to quote much higher figures for the Muslim population—between twenty-five and thirty per cent—but just as Pena's interest in Christian communities and his dependence on local parish priests for his information may have caused him to underestimate the number of Muslims in Beit Sahour, so Beit Sahourans' pride in having overcome the opportunities for fragmentation thrown up by religious differences may have led them to inflate Muslim numbers. Whatever the actual proportions, in 1990 two members out of eight on the municipal committee were Muslim, and people were quick to point out that these were on the committee not as representatives of the Muslim population but as spokespersons for major family groups which happened to be Muslim. The distinction was significant; Beit Sahourans saw themselves as Palestinians who happen to be either Christian or Muslim, rather than as Christians or Muslims who happen to live in Palestine.

An alternative reading of identity, which would define people by religious affiliation rather than in terms of the place in which they live and the neighbours with whom they share that life, was promulgated then, as now, by three significant forces in the Occupied Territories : the Israeli government, the Islamic Resistance Movement (Hamas), and the foreign churches. Israeli encouragement of Palestinian sectarianism is not simply an extension of Israel's own imaging of itself as the Jewish nation for the Jewish people; it is perhaps more saliently a continuation of the policy of divide-and-rule it has used against 'non-Jewish minorities' in Israel and the Occupied Territories since 1948 (Lustick 1980; Tamari 1982). The state's covert support of the 'Muslim Brothers of Palestine' through the mid-eighties and the free rein it gave to the Hamas movement until May 1988 are widely recognized by Palestinians as facts of a general Israeli strategy of dividing Palestinians along sectarian lines so as to undermine the foundations of the nationalist movement (Litani 1989; Taraki 1989 : 31; Schiff and Ya'ari 1990 : 233-234; Dumper 1992 : 422-423).

Hamas, which opposes Palestinian nationalism and advocates liberating the entirety of Palestine from 'Jewish' rule so that it can be set up as a trust (*waqf*) for the Islamic peoples of the world, built up a strong following in Gaza after the 1982 invasion of Lebanon on the basis of welfare and education projects funded with moneys from Saudi Arabia and Jordan. Between 1982 and 1988 Hamas orchestrated a campaign of violence and intimidation against the secularist movements which effectively drove them into hiding in Gaza and severely disrupted their activities on university campuses throughout the Occupied Territories. Even Fatah (the centrist party of the Palestine Liberation Organisation led by Yasser Arafat), which had supported Hamas's Gazan campaign against the Communist Party and the Popular and Democratic Fronts, suffered the onslaughts of the movement just prior to the outbreak of the intifada[17]. Hamas's hostility is, however, directed only against nationalists (who it terms 'communists' or 'secularists') and not against Palestinian communities it is able to accommodate within its religious purview. Palestinian Christians are not attacked as Christians *per se* and would have a protected status within an Islamic state as a 'People of the Book'. Israeli attempts to isolate Christian Palestinians by leading them to think that the Muslims, led by Hamas, were turning against them were, as of January 1990, easily recognized. Christians in Bethlehem, Ramallah and Jerusalem spoke of Israelis who " dress up as Hamas" to daub anti-Christian graffiti on West Bank walls, and a 1989 ' Hamas' communique condemning the wealthy Christians of Beit Sahour "for having" drunk and danced with the Iraelis who "dress up as Hamas" to daub anti-Christian graffiti on West Bank walls, and a 1989 'Hamas' communique condermning "the wealthy Christians of Beit Sahour, for having" "drunk and danced with the Israelis since the beginning of the intifada" was identified by Beit Sahourans as an Israeli forgery.

In large part, the churches of Israel and the Occupied Territories define the land and its peoples in terms that have more in common with the vocabulary of the Islamic fundamentalists than with that of Palestinians engaged in struggling for self determination. Just as Hamas argues that Palestine is holy ground for Muslims and should be kept in perpetuity as an Islamic trust, so the foreign-dominated churches define Palestine as the 'Holy Land' and treat it as a repository of sanctity for the edification of priests and pilgrims. Since the sixteenth century, when Patriarch Germanos expelled local Christian clergy from the Greek Orthodox Church and transformed the parochial churches into monastic holy places for the Greeks (Bertram and Young 1926 : 34-78), the Latin and Orthodox churches have been for the most part indifferent to the condition and fate of local Christians. In the past when foreign churches needed 'bargaining counters' in diplomatic struggles for hegemony over the holy places they would 'buy' local Christians into their folds with offers of housing, employment and the like. This was especially true after Ali Pasha opened Palestine to increased western intervention when the western nations, for secular as well as religious reasons, engaged in well-funded programmes to court disaffected Greek Orthodox Palestinians into the protestant, Latin and Russian Orthodox churches (Tibawi 1961; Hopwood 1969; Horner 1989; Scholch 1989). The establishment of the State of Israel and the consolidation of the Occupied Territories (wherein lie most of the sites revered by foreign pilgrims) under its control changed the nature of the struggles. Subsequently the churches found that the best way to maintain and expand their property holdings, gain residence permits for monks, nuns and clergy, and facilitate the flow of their pilgrims was to nurture good relations with the state, and that meant, even more than before, ignoring the plight of Christian Palestinians[18]. One man in Beit Sahour, where over eighty per cent of the Christian population is Greek Orthodox, told me "we have two imperialisms here—the Zionists and the Greeks... They (the Greeks) are more interested in religion than in us".

While the Israeli state, Hamas and the dominant

Christian churches strive to impose religious boundaries on a land populated by people of different religious affiliations, Beit Sahourans attested commitment to the idea of unifying different religious communities within the borders of a single secular state both in interviews and in their establishment of non-sectarian organisations such as the Pan-Palestinian Scout Movement and the popular committees (the latter provided models for intifada organisation to communities throughout the West Bank and Gaza Strip) (Hiltermann 1991). One Beit Sahouran Christian told me "we are ready in our own state to live as Christians, Muslims and Jews in one nation" and this was echoed in numerous other statements such as that of a Muslim who said "we hope for liberation with one community with many religions. God is for one, the nation for all. Zionists changed Palestinian Jews to Israelis". In this rhetoric religious identity is subsumed under national identity. In an interesting temporal reversal of the segmentary system of establishing common identity by tracing genealogies back to an apical ancestor, the nationalist rhetoric posits a common identity by projecting forward to a future moment in which all persons, be they Christian, Muslim or Jew, will share citizenship in a common secular state. The only persons excluded from this process are those who see their national identity as devolving from their communalist identity and thus refuse to allow that their religious identity will be subsumed within an overarching secular national identity. Thus Zionists, who see national and religious identity as inextricably linked, are future foreigners and present day enemies. Although future developments will tell how well this rhetoric translates into political reality, at the time of my research the Beit Sahour municipality and political activists within the town had established, and were maintaining, strong links with 'non-Zionist' Israeli communists and peace activists.

The sectarian tendency to define public space and public identities in religious terms was rejected in Beit Sahour. Traditionally mixed Palestinian towns were cognitively divided into the Quarters' in which the various religious communities in large part resided; Jerusalem's

Old City, for instance, is still mapped in terms of Jewish, Muslim, Christian and Armenian Quarters (Ben-Arieh 1984 :15-16; see also Eickelman 1989 :100-107). This nomenclature is an inheritance of the Ottoman millet system wherein the various non-Muslim religious communities within the *dar al Islam* (realm of Islam) were granted relative autonomy by the state. This led their respective members to cluster around the residences of the religious leader the Ottoman authorities recognized for each :

"as long as they paid their taxes, the minorities, Christians and Jews, were left to administer their own internal affairs within the framework of Islamic law which gave them the status of *ahl al-dhimma* (protected peoples). Their religious affairs (which included laws pertaining to marriage, property and the like) were regulated by their respective heads of communities" (Asali 1989 : p. 206; see also Abu-Jaber 1967 and Cohen and Lewis 1978).

> Today most 'Quarters' tend to be integrated as the collapse of Ottoman rule has rendered the apparatus of the millet system largely extraneous, and economic and social developments have led persons of the various denominations to settle in areas traditionally populated by other groups (an exception is the Jewish Quarter in Jerusalem's old city which, because of planned developments carried out in the nineteen seventies and nineteen eighties, is almost exclusively inhabited by Jews). After the 1982 invasion of Lebanon the Beit Sahour municipality renamed the sectors of the town so as to memorialise locales the war had rendered significant as moments of Palestinian national resistance to Israel; locals now call the highest section of town Shqaif Castle (the site of an important battle) and refer to other sectors with the names of two of the most important Palestinian refugee camps in Lebanon, Tal el-Za'atar and Shatila.

Religious difference, which is not inscribed across the landscape, was also not a factor determining the character of interaction between individuals in public spheres. The following quotations are drawn from interviews with Beit

Sahour residents (both Christian and Muslim) :

> "we do not remember we are from different religious unless somebody from outside reminds us ..... we are Christians and Muslims in spirit and in our hearts, but in public we are Palestinian";
>
> "it is you outside who try to make a difference between the Christians and the Muslims. We are a people; we all go to each other's feasts, we visit with each other, we live the same life. We are one people";
>
> "my relation with my god is in my heart and my house; it does not concern the public. In the street I am Ahmed."
>
> These assertions, like numerous others recorded in interviews, signal an awareness of contextual identities and suggest that the programme of constructing a national identity, to which all of the Beit Sahourans I interviewed[19] showed a commitment, is precisely one of redefining the contexts in which sectarian identities are manifested. This redefinition creates a new public domain in which non-religious, nationalist identities can be evidenced.

The repudiation of 'public' markers of religious identity in these quotations does not signal a renunciation of religion itself; it is instead symptomatic of rearticulation of the place of a religion in the formulation of identity. From the evidence I was able to gather in visits to their houses, Beit Sahourans remained committed to the 'faiths of their fathers'. The interiors of the houses in which I listened to the most virulent rejections of sectarianism were dense with signs of religiosity; pictures of the Virgin Mary (in both Christian and Muslim houses) or of Mecca (in Muslim houses) were hung next to photographs of family members and members of neighbours' families who had been jailed or killed by the Israelis. A three foot high statue of the Virgin Mary graced a corner of the living room of one house belonging to an organiser of Local committees and a self-avowed secular nationalist. I was unable to uncover evidence of any increase in the extremely rare occurrence of 'mixed' (Muslim-Christian) marriages in the town; unlike in Ramallah, where the incidence of such marriages was perceived as having increased over the past decade (interview with Ramallah resident, April 1990), in Beit Sahour I was told that mixed marriage occur only when a Beit Sahouran emigrates and becomes involved with a member of another community 'outside'. This suggests that religion and sectarian traditions retained hegemony over areas of life such as faith, worship, and marriage and that they there determined the appropriate practices and ceremonials. Thus many of the aspects of communal identity fostered by the millet system were retained within the domain of home, family and kinship relations. What had changed, I will argue, was that another domain had opened up and had come to be seen as constituting another, supplementary yet subsuming, field of identity.

The sectarianism fostered by the Ottoman millet system provided each religious community with a space in which to operate in relative autonomy and insisted, by strictly defining the way the dhimmi (protected religious minorities) could dress and deport themselves in all contexts, that sectarian identity always be emphasized. All aspects of personal life were subsumed under sectarian identity and few, if any, alternative contexts were available in which to enunciate other identities which might allow for collaboration and identification with persons from outside one's own millet (for twentieth century examples see Joseph (1978) on the Lebanon and Webber (1985) and Bowman (1986) on Jerusalem). Even in relations between men in the market place, roles and interaction were choreographed by sectarian identities so that exchanges of goods and services could occur without separate identities being merged. The Beit Sahouran project of rearticulating the religious and the secular led to an expansion of the 'neutral' space of the market (see Gilsenan 1982 :173-177) so that space came to provide not only for economic necessities but also new modalities of identity appropriate to the situation of occupation.

Chapman, McDonald and Tonkin, following Ardener, discuss the way that the perception of some "novelty" in a community's experience can impel it to "pick up behind it a new trajectory to replace or modify the old" (Chapman *et al*

1989 : 8). Beit Sahour has a long history of Muslim-Christian interaction and, because there are traditions recounted which trace that admixture back to the town's mythical foundations, it was easy for Beit Sahourans to rearticulate their past in the light of the imagining of the present community brought about by the Israeli occupation (Bowman 1990 : 51-52). The new form of 'imagined community' constituted in the context of occupation was, however, substantially different from the identities which had proceeded it. In the past Muslims and Christians had worked together but had seen themselves as Muslims and Christians who happened to be involved in economic exchanges rather than as Palestinians who happened to be Muslim or Christian. The new identity- "We are Palestinians first, then Muslims or Christians" -came not from a market situation which brought them in to contact with each other but from a situation of confrontation which forced them to recognise that 'outside' their realm of cooperation was an antagonist equally threatening to all towns persons, regardless of their religious affiliations. In the light of the struggle against this antagonist certain elements of the town's past were rendered significant, and were memorialized in the production of a 'new' history. Various towns persons told me stories of Muslims and Christians marching together to Nebi Musa (an Islamic shrine in the Jordan Valley which became the focus of Islamic dissatisfaction with British rule) of Baathist, Nasserite and Communist demonstrations against the Jordanian occupation. They spoke, in addition, of the long history of support for the 'Popular Front for the Liberation of Palestine' and the 'Democratic Front for the Liberation of Palestine' during the period of Israeli occupation. What is significant in these histories was not that Beit Sahour had a long history of resistance to various occupiers of the land but that the fractiousness of that resistance, in which residents' allegiances to different factions of the struggles often turned the town into an arena of struggle between parties rather than a united front against the 'outside', was here elided so that the entirety of the community could be constituted as an 'us' which had always resisted the incursions of 'foreign' rule.

The Israel occupation provided a space for identification that differed from that provided by other occupiers, all of which—as Christian or Muslim regimes supporting capitalist property owners—presented opportunities to factions of the Beit Sahour population for identification and collaboration. The Israeli forces, which viewed 'Arabs' as enemies and saw 'Arab' capitalist successes as a strengthening of 'Arab' power, demonstrated to Christians and Muslims (both employers and workers) that "there is another who is enemy to us both"[20]. The portrait of a young man, Basem Rishmawi, was hug on the walls of many houses in Beit Sahour and his name was often mentioned in conversations. On the evening of 11 April 1981 Rishmawi had disappeared while returning home from his fiancee's house. A week later Israeli soldiers had returned his body, severely mutilated, its wrists cut from having been bound with wire. They claimed that he had been killed when a bomb he had been making exploded prematurely. No one had believed the story, and word had spread through the town that he had been kidnapped, tortured and finally killed either by settlers or the army. Many residents considered Rishmawi's death to have been arbitrary; they believed any Beit Sahouran could expect a similar fate at the hands of the occupation's agents : "it could have happened to anybody, and by chance the victim was Basem". Subsequent experiences strengthened that assumption. In 1989 Edmond Ghanem was killed while walking down the main street of the town when a soldier dropped a stone on him from a third floor guard post in the municipality building. The arbitrariness revealed in the tax raids, which Al-Haq has described as constituting "a sustained campaign of aggression against the town's residents under the guise of compliance with the law" (Al-Haq 1989: 1), has exposed behind the mask of occupiers' law the face of a conquering army engaged in pillage. One Beit Sahouran told me amidst the detritus of a neighbour's house which that morning had been 'searched' : "this is plunder, looting, it's indiscriminate .... All they want is money from us." It appeared to the residents themselves, there for that they were all equivalent in the eyes of the occupying forces : "We see that one day it is one person and the next day another. The following day it may be us, so we say *hellas* (enough) and begin to work to stop it". The existence of the entire community and the lives of all its members were seen as being at risk, and in that context the differences between individuals, families, religious communities and political affiliations became insignificant: "If I want to throw a stone I will not call to my neighbour to say 'become a Muslim and then we will throw stones together'. We forget our religion; we forget our political groups. The bullets do not differentiate between Christian and Muslim, P.L.O., D.F.L.P., etc."

At issue here was not the continuance of public cooperation in economic projects which had been a central feature of Beit Sahouran life for the past several centuries, but the question of the survival of any form of Palestinian community at all on the site. The 'space' of cooperation is thus transformed and extended, and in that space—which was now that in which Beit Sahourans faced an Other across a boundary which had come to mark the difference between 'the community' and 'the foreigners' intent on destroying that community-Beit Sahouran Muslims and Christians became 'Palestinians' mobilized in a struggle for survival against 'Israelis'. It was, therefore, the antagonist which provided the 'novelty' discussed by Chapman, McDonald and Tonkin (1989) and which delineated the 'boundary' Barth (1969) saw as constituting the ethnic group; Beit Sahourans 'invented' an identity which encompassed all aspects of their lives in the face of an antagonist they saw as threatening those lives in all their diversities. As a result, a political project of resistance was elaborated which went beyond the quotidian sectarian co-existence which had characterized intercommunal interaction in the past. The antagonism to the community perceived by Beit Sahourans in the policies and practices of the Israeli state and the settlers it defended had led them to reify the inter-communal cooperation which had marked their everyday life. The diffuse sense of community Beit Sahourans had shared in the past—a loose sense of the communal not unlike that described above as having taken place among Palestinian participants at the feast of Mar Elyas—coagulated, under the mobilizing threat of state antagonism, into an 'identity' which penetrated, constituted and united self, community and nation [21]. This fixing of identity transformed the elements of everyday community life into emblems of a communal self *per se* and as such all these elements—regardless of whether they were originally Christian or Muslim, sacred or secular—came to signify 'Palestinian life'. Politicisation was fundamental to the constitution of this new, subsuming, identity; the 'Palestinian' entity took form as something which had to be protected, and people envisaged in its survival or destruction not only the fate of the 'imagined community' of Palestine but also their own.

Beit Sahouran's recognition that Israeli occupation threatened the community as a whole led them to redefine the resources of the community so that these could be mobilized against that occupation. The resources of religion, so often used (by themselves as well as by others) to divide and oppose Palestinian people in the past, were appropriated and marshalled in the defence of local and national aspirations. In 1989 many Beit Sahourans sent out printed Christmas cards to churches and embassies throughout Israel and the Occupied Territories which played off the bucolic and auspicious image of Christ's nativity against the darkness of the contemporary situation. On one side of the card was written "Christmas 1989 in the Third Year of the Intifada" and on the other, beneath a drawing of a group of armed Israeli soldiers massed around a grotto in which an empty cradle stood over the prone body of a masked Palestinian, was written "Silent Night, Holy Night, All is Dark, All is Sad" and "From the City of Peace we Palestinians wish you a Merry Christmas and a Happy New Year". These cards, like the municipality-organized 'Day of Prayer for Peace' in November 1989 to which were invited Jewish, Christian and Muslim religious leaders as well as Israeli peace groups and foreign diplomats and the address to a similar audience by South African bishop Desmond Tutu on Christmas Eve of that year at Shepherd's Field Church, manifest a public face which Beit Sahourans turn to the 'outside'. In such instances the community presented itself as united in a sort of 'Popular Front' to garner support from the world outside the community. Such demonstrations, of course, might have been organized only for the delectation of outsiders and might not be intended to change internal perceptions of the lineaments of identity. As such these would be border phenomena meant to mask for external eyes the fact that the internal community was still riven by sectarian and other divides.

'Palestinian Traditions' and the Shrine of Bir el-Saiyideh

More interesting, therefore, and in the long run perhaps more significant, were transformation being effected within the ways Beit Sahourans interpreted the elements of their everyday lives. In January 1990 I was told by a Muslim schoolteacher that "we must nationalize our beliefs, should rebuild our customs so they reflect our national life". This 'nationalisation' of religion and custom involved a substantial redefinition of the field of religious belief and practice. Such a redefinition was not always fully visible on the ground because religious belief retained its saliency in personal and familial identity. Where, however, in the past communal identity—rooted in a distrust of other religious communities fostered by the religious hierarchies and fed, particularly in the cities, by financial support from the churches and the *waqfs*—had provided the core of a person's sense of social self, what was occurring in Beit Sahour and other places in Palestine in the eighties and early nineties was a tendency to subsume that sectarian identity within an encompassing nationalist identity. Part of this was a matter of the withdrawal (forced or voluntary) of the support of religious foundations as I have mentioned above and as Dumper elaborates in his studies of the *waqfs* under Israel (Dumper 1991; 1992). More salient was the recognition that , for the first time, the survival of both Muslims and Christians was threatened by a common antagonist.

At this stage I can only point to some symptoms of that change. One, which I witnessed on several occasions between 1984 and 1990 during religious festivities in Jerusalem, was the tendency of Muslim and Christian Palestinians of most denominations[22] to join members of other religious communities in publicly celebrating religious feasts. One Muslim youth, who joined the riotous march of Christians along Christian Quarter Road to the Holy Sepulchre for the Holy Fire ceremony[23] remarked : "this (the time of religious celebrations) is the only time you see the nation of Palestine on its streets; I am here to celebrate with my nation". Such a 'national' interpretation of a sectarian celebration differs substantially from interpretations evident at the Mar Elyas feast. At the celebrations around Mar Elyas groups were for the most part constituted around the particular rationales their members had for attending, and whatever sense of 'community' came into play was an accidental consequence of the fact that these motivations were focused on the same site. 'Community' was never recognised as a significant entity in itself, in large part because no antagonism threatened the whole and caused the participants to recognize their equivalency in the eyes of an enemy (the telling exception is referred to in note twenty-one). For the Muslim taking part in the Christian Holy Fire ceremony, inter-communal 'manifestations' celebrated a national identity within which particular sectarian identities were incorporated. In this discourse the Palestinian 'whole' is made up of a collocation of differences rendered equivalent by the recognition that all are equally threatened by Israeli state policies. In the context of that antagonism the feast is defined as a manifestation of 'Palestinian' tradition and the gathering seen as an assertion of the insistence of Palestinians in celebrating that tradition in the face of 'foreign' forces which would deny Palestinians the right to define themselves as members of a national community with a rich heritage of traditions.

Religious difference is not, however, elided by a nationalism insisting on full identification by all members of the nation. Difference is maintained, and, while persons of different affiliations will take part in each other's celebrations, they will not participate in other sects' liturgies or rituals when those conflict with the articles or practices of faith of their own sectarian communities. A shift in context will, in other words, lead to a redefinition of identity;

what is interpreted in a space read as 'public' as national and inclusive will be seen as religious and exclusive when participants are interpellated into subject positions (Althusser 1971) emphasizing their identities as members of a specific religious community. Thus, while Muslims will participate in public aspects of Christian ceremonies such as the procession down the Mount of Olives on Latin Palm Sunday or the Holy Fire ceremony during Orthodox Holy Week, they will not take part in the liturgical celebrations of the Crucifixion or Resurrection within the churches. Christian Palestinians, joining Muslims on the Haram al-Sharif (the Temple, Mount) to celebrate the birth of the Prophet Mohammed or the occasion of Mohammed's Ascent to Heaven, will, similarly, absent themselves when the Muslims pray. Palestinians who see themselves as active members of religious communities maintain the tenets of those communities in situations which are defined in religious terms. Distinct religious identities and practices, rather than being homogenised as equivalent forms of 'Palestinian culture', are instead given supplementary meaning by the national discourse and come to be seen not only to signify the particular ways of life of sectarian communities, but also to bear witness to one of many facets of the way of life of the Palestinian nation. In this politicised instance, as in many others witnessed during fieldwork, identities are not exclusively sectarian or national but are both sectarian and national.

Another symptom of this change, in which transformations in the field of identity are actually monumentalized on the landscape, is the aforementioned shrine of Bir el-Saiyideh. In 1988 I was taken to an underground cistern in the centre of Beit Sahour which had been the site of the visitation by the Virgin Mary in 1983. The Beit Sahour municipality had built a shrine over the cistern expressly for the use of both Muslims and Christians of all denominations. The exterior appeared distinctly modern, and, aside from the cross surmounting it, it bore less resemblance to a church than it did to a traditional Islamic *makym* (a building with a dombed chamber characterising a Muslim shrine). Inside, the walls were covered with icons and paintings of Christian subjects given by worshippers[24] but, profusely and randomly scattered among these, were a significant number of gifts, paintings and pictures which were clearly Muslim. The cross and the predominance of a Christian tone was not surprising; the site was, after all, dedicated to a figure highly revered in Christian worship (although also venerated in Islam). What seems more important than a more thoroughgoing syncretism is the fact that in the shrine the exclusion of devotional objects of other religions which would be rigorously enforced by religious hierarchies in a church or mosque owned and operated by the religious institutions had here been violated, and that no one visiting the shrine (and there was a constant flow of local people passing through it) seemed offended by evident signs that a community wider than that of their religious community used the place.

I was told by both the caretaker and the Greek Catholic priest who accompanied me on one visit to the site that religious practices at the shrine reflect this heterogeneity. As the shrine belonged to the municipality, representatives of all local religious communities were able to book time in it. Since the stories surrounding the Nativity of Jesus are celebrated by Muslims and Christians throughout the Bethlehem region as founding myths of the local communities, Muslims and Christians alike gathered at the shrine to celebrate their traditions in a place where the sacred had interacted with their locality. Sometimes these were shared celebrations, nominally organized according to the calendar of one of the religious communities, while at other times local Christian and Muslim officiants carried out ceremonies specific to their congregations. Moreover, as with the blessings available to all at Mar Elyas, water from the cistern in the back of the shrine is taken by both Muslim and Christian Beit Sahourans as a sacred substance for healing, blessing and providing good luck. I asked the caretaker why the Marian shrine was owned by the municipality and not, as one would expect, by one of the Christian churches. He indignantly replied : "we are here Muslim and Christian, and there are two Christian groups. The Municipality builds for all the people, and the people all own and use the well. *Hellas.*"

This statement suggests (as does the shrine's existence) that a new 'space' has been constituted which stands between the communalist domain of faith and family and the boundary which marks the separation of the residents of Beit Sahour from the 'outsiders, they perceive as working to destroy them. The fact that this new discursive space is articulated in nationalist rather than localist terms (people here identify themselves as members of a larger Palestinian community which stretches far beyond the municipal limits) points to the role of the enemy in constituting identity. Israeli soldiers and settlers, the most salient symptoms of occupation to the people of Beit Sahour, see and treat Beit Sahourans as 'Arabs' in line with their own constitutive logic of antagonism and identity[25]. Beit Sahourans, well aware that what they define as a war waged against their town is simultaneously being waged against other communities throughout Israel and the Occupied Territories and further afield into the Palestinian diaspora, are able to imagine a 'nation in waiting' constituted of other individuals and communities 'like' themselves in facing the same enemy. This similitude is not, however, imagined as literal; Beit Sahour residents do no imagine all Palestinian communities have the same demographic mix as does their own and realise that many of the identifications and strategies of resistance they have developed are particular to the contingencies of their own situation. The equivalence that leads them to identify themselves as Palestinians is rendered in the same discursive space as is the perception of similitude which impels them to identify themselves as 'the same' as other Beit Sahourans who, despite being Muslim or Christian, nonetheless have been forced to engage in a collective struggle for mutual survival against an external antagonist.

Conclusion

However, this particular elaboration of sectarian elements within an encompassing nationalist framework is not the only possible articulation of religion and politics available to Palestinians under occupation. Hamas, for example, manifests a drive, itself motivated by the Israeli occupation, to mobilize religion towards the pursuit of political ends. It does not present a programme for returning to traditional Islamic identity but instead, using Western modes of populist organization and demanding conformity with newly invented 'traditions' of Islamicity in markers of identity such as dress[26], organizes a particular'; post-modern' activism which attempts to replace the 'modern' project manifest in Jewish-Western political hegemony over the region with another all-encompassing reconstruction of the world, this time in accordance with a vision of a new 'pan-Islamic' order. Hamas's Islam proposes to make the political and religious coterminours through an extension of a politico-theological discipline into all domains of life, from the state to the household, and with particular positions and disciplines for non-Islamic populations. Hamas ideologues claim to draw their model for the theological hegemonization of the political from early Islamic theories of the state (Rodinson 1971 : 215-92) but are actually more determinately influenced by the particular anti-Western and anti-colonial articulation of politics and religion propounded by the Islamic revolutionaries in Iran (Mortimer 1982 : 353-8).

Ironically, Hamas's model of state and religion shares the logic of the Likud right and Gush Emunim sectors of the Israeli population which provided the agenda for Israeli politics between 1981 and the 1992 elections (Sprinzak 1991 : 300-5). Lustick describes the defining characteristic of 'fundamentalism' as the assumption that "political action dedicated toward rapid and comprehensive transfromation of society.... express(es) uncompromisable, cosmically ordained, and more or less directly received imperatives" (Lustick 1992 :431). The Israeli religious right sees the real stake of the 'redemption of the land' (the extirpation of a Palestinian presence and the full settlement of the Occupied Territories with a Jewish population) as a

> " metaphysical question of transcendental importance... whether or not the process of God's redemption of the Jewish people, and of the world as a whole, including the advent of the Messiah

himself, will be brought to its glorious conclusion in the relatively near future, or whether it will be tragically delayed or even halted" (Lustick 1992 :434).

Hamas's project of driving Jews and foreigners out of Palestine calls upon similar metaphysical imperatives; "the Islamic people has a consciousness of its duties before God in the defense of Palestine, God's blessed country and that of the prophets, eternal property (*waqf*) of the Islamic community" (Legrain 1990 :181). The cosmic certitude provided by these assumptions to advocates of each of these 'fundamentalist' movements not only ensures a passionate, and uncompromising, commitment to their respective causes but also allies them with a power far greater than anything available in the profane domain of struggle and politics. For Palestinian Muslims outraged by the constant presence of an antagonistic state and frustrated with the apparent inefficacy of secularist solutions, the appeal of a programme which is profoundly political yet draws its Plegitimacy from the word of God rather than the fromulations of men and women is powerful. The struggle against what the secularists call a 'colonial settler state' here becomes the age-old struggle of the faithful against the demonic : "religion is ... placed at the service of the anti-Israeli struggle, which is depicted as the eschatological combat between Good and Evil" (Legrain 1990 :183). There is, consequently, no need for delicate strategies of compromise and confrontation, since all that is necessary is to take a purely reductionist stance against co-habiting with the devil and his minions.

Hamas's religious definition of antagonism in items of 'pollution' of God's land extends the battlefield beyond direct confrontation with the forces of the Israeli state to encompass issues of Palestinian deportment and moral rectitude. In this struggle to purify the land of 'evil', Jews and Western powers are only one manifestation of the enemy; secular and 'westernised' Palestinians are another. Hamas's redefinition of the field of political struggle as a domain for the extirpation of 'corrupt morals' allows Hamas activists to feel fully engaged politically while taking on enemies who are far less dangerous than armed Israeli soldiers. Hammami writes that

> "those who joined (Hamas) were attracted by the possibility of participating in a political community that claims to confront the occupation without (until very recently) exposing its members to danger... Politically unaffiliated *shabab* (youth) who felt left out found harassing these (unveiled) women a safe way to express nationalist sentiment" (Hammami 1990 : 25 and 26).

Thus Hamas, in the face of a national enemy which shows little sign of having weakened after six bloody years of intifada, has rearticulated the confrontation and its appropriate strategies by contending that the reason Palestinian Muslims have not been able to wrest Palestine from the hands of the infidels is that it has allowed itself to be weakened by internal pollutants. The first stage of struggle thus becomes the moral purification of the 'inside', and only after that goal has been achieved can the 'outside' be confronted successfully.

Hamas's redefinition to the struggle is as well a redefinition of the imagined community engaged in that struggle. This shift in the field of identity causes Christian Palestinians to query what sort of role they might play in a Palestinian entity in which a movement which tends to consider 'Palestinian' as synonymous with 'Islamic' has substantial influence. Christian Palestinians, whose religion can in that discourse be seen as a betrayal of their national identity, can take little comfort from *The Covenant of the Islamic Resistance Movement* which cites a Hadith (written tradition alleging a statement or action of Mohammed) to assert that

> "The people of (Greater) Syria are Allah's lash in His hand. He wreaks His vengeance through them against whomsoever He wishes among His slaves. It is unthinkable that those who are double-faced among them should prosper over the faithful. They will certainly die out of grief and desperation" (Hamas 1988:12).

Thus a recent survey showed that 34.9 per cent of Christian Palestinians in Jerusalem and the West Bank intended to emigrate in the near future (Kreutz 1992 :271) and, although most gave lack of job opportunities and a dearth of housing as their primary reasons for leaving, growing anxiety about the increasing influence of Hamas was voiced.

Tamari argues that a central weakness of the late nineteenth and early twentieth century Arab Nationalist movements in Greater Syria (the area which is now Lebanon, Syria and Israel and the Occupied Territories) was their failure to develop a popular culture in which images of secular identity could be celebrated (Tamari 1992). In the absence of such a domain for the recognition of trans-sectarian identities, the identities foregrounded in periods of political struggle can only be those that arise from realms of personal and familial life and these, in a context like that of the Middle East in which religious confession plays such a central role, are almost exclusively sectarian. Antagonists, at such times, need only to exploit the differences between confessional groups in order to fragment and disperse the forces they oppose[27]. One of the most telling strengths of Israel, a national community constituted out of a wide diversity of potentially conflicting communities (Paine 1989), has been its state's success in programmatically constructing precisely such a domain of popular national identity (Handelman 1990 :160-233) which, by overarching and subsuming the multiple sectarian identities of its Jewish population, holds the nation together in times of stress.

I have argued that the shrine of Bir el-Saiyideh must be seen as a manifestation of a similar programme, elaborated by a mixed Palestinian community, of creating public spaces in which residents of Beit Sahour can recognize and celebrate a binding image of a trans-communal identity. I have focussed on the shrine in part because it is one of many salient manifestations of Beit Sahour's 'national' programme. More central however is the fact that a contemporary inquiry into the social significance of holy places connects with the work of Durkheim (1915), Halbwachs (1980) and Hertz (1983) elucidating the dialectical process through which social groups reify their sensed community in monuments and markers on the landscape they occupy and in turn recognize the spirit and power of that community when looking upon those edifices. In contrasting the interpretations imposed by Palestinian communities on Mar Elyas and Bir el-Saiyideh, I have shown how the multivocality of a holy place in the interpretations of the diverse communities which approach it can become 'fixed' in periods of intense social conflict by the recognition of the members of those various communities of an external antagonism which endangers the survival of all of them. At such times, a shrine like that of Bir el-Saiyideh not only reifies the new sense of community constituted through antagonism but also stands as a sign of the power of that new 'national' identity to impose its vision of community on the social and political landscape.

Endnotes

Biographical Sketch : Glenn Bowman trained in social anthropology at Oxford. His doctoral fieldwork (1983-1985) focused on Jerusalem pilgrimage and led to his subsequent interest in Palestinian communities under occupation. He has carried out field research in Yugoslavia on nationalist mobilization and the production and dissemination of contemporary art in Belgrade. He currently teaches in the anthropology department of the University of Kent (Canterbury, U.K.) where he coordinates the MA programme in the Anthropology of Ethnicity, Nationalism and Identity.

This article was first published in Man : *the Journal of the Royal Anthropological Institute.* (XXVIII :3) in September 1993 between pages 431 and 460.

1. Louis Demount, in an important article setting out the genealogies of nationalism and communalism, defines the latter as 'that ideology which emphasizes as the social, political, and economic unit the group of adherents of each religion, and emphasizes the distinction, even the antagonism, between such groups' (Dumont 1970 : 89).
2. The 'Islamic Resistance Movement' or Hamas (the acronym of its Arabic title, Harakat al-Muqawama al-islamiyya) was known, from the late seventies until the opening months of the intifada, as the 'Muslim Brothers of Palestine' (an offshoot of the Egyptian

'Society of the Muslim Brothers'). During this period it engaged in political and educational work around mosques, schools and universities designed to educate youth in their moral responsibility as Muslims and to draw them away from the secular influence of the Palestinian nationalist parties. Through the 1980s, student members of the Islamic Resistance Movement attacked secular nationalist demonstrations on West Bank and Gaza Strip campuses. In 1988, as popular support for the nationalist uprising became irrefutable, the organization changed its name to Hamas and entered into open struggle with the Palestine Liberation Organization for leadership of the intifada. Its 'nationalism' is, however, actually 'communalism': Lisa Taraki, summarizing the "Charter of the Islamic Resistance Movement', writes that Hamas sees 'the land of Palestine (a)s an Islamic trust (waqf), to be held as such for generations of Muslims until the Day of Judgement. No one has the authority to give up any part of Palestine. Nationalism is a function of religious belief, and the defense of Muslim land is the duty of every Muslim' (Taraki 1989 : 31). The strategy which devolves from this religious interpretation of 'nationalism' is onc of stcadfast allegiance to perceived divine will rather than one of compromise and debate. In its assumption that Palestine is a divine trust granted to the Muslims in perpetuity, the membership of Hamas has much in common with Israeli settlers from fundamentalist movement such as Gush Emunim who say the same about the link of the land of Israel,' God and the Jews (Taraki 1989 :31; Lustick 1988). Hamas, like the settlers, has steadfastly opposed the U.S. sponsored peace negotiations, and its attack on Israeli soldiers and Israeli secret police operatives in December 1992, which resulted in the expulsion to Lebanon of 415 of its alleged supporters, were meant to stall the negotiations.

3. "In the case of antagonism... the presence of the "Other" prevents me from being totally myself. .... (it is because a peasant cannot be a peasant that an

antagonism exists with the landowner who is expelling him from his land). Insofar as there is antagonism, I cannot be a full presence for myself" (Laclau and Mouffe 1985 : 125).

4. Although the saint's day in the Greek calendar is nominally on one day (25 August), it stretches over two days because of the saint-specific vespers of the preceding day and the saint-specific liturgy of the saint's day itself. The popular ceremonies, with some variations which will be described below, cover these two days. This description is based on my observations on 24 and 25 August 1984.
5. The Brotherhood of the Holy Sepulchre, the ruling body of the Greek Orthodox Church in Israel and the Israeli Occupied Territories, is made up of Greek and Cypriot monks, and resides in the Patriarchate of the Greek Orthodox Church in Jerusalem. It has full control over the activities of the church in the region (as well as in Sinai and Jordan) which include not only liturgical and pastoral activities but also maintenance of considerable properties.
6. There is no sign in the Bible, Old Testament or New, of Elyas (the Prophet Elijah) having been enchained. The use of 'Elyas' for 'Elijah' is interesting as a moment in the diacritical process whereby Christians mark themselves off as other than Jews; 'Elyas' is the New Testament from of 'Elijah' and is used by both priests and lay-persons to refer to biblical events prior to the period rendered by the New Testament.
7. A Syrian Orthodox girl, who walked from Bethlehem to Mar Elyas (about 5 miles) with two co-religionists and a Muslim, told me that she had asked a favour of the saint and had promised to walk from Bethlehem to Mar Elyas and back in return. I asked : 'you have walked here to ask a favour of God?' and she rapidly and firmly corrected me, saying 'No, of St Elyas' Canaan, discussing Palestinian Muslims, confirms, this : 'According to Palestinian Arabic belief God is the Almighty One.... But the saints are preferred.

They are easier of access and stand nearer to men—as they all were once human beings. At the same time they know human needs, ailments and weaknesses very well. Therefore the belief in them and the fear of them has spread so widely among the Palestinians that gradually they have taken the place of God' (Canaan 1927 :132).

8. One of the consequences of the pre-revolutionary Russian Orthodox church's attempts to extend its influence in Ottoman Palestine was that it systematically fomented dissatisfaction within Greek Orthodox Palestinian communities with the Greek church's failure to provide Palestinian congregations as well as with representation in the church, education and other froms of pastoral and social service (Hopwood 1969). Increased awareness of discrimination led to the lay creation of the Arab Orthodox Movement, an organization dedicated to wresting control of the church and its substantial properties from what it defined as a 'foreign' priesthood. After the Russian church's intervention was abruptly ended by the revolution, the Movement was strongly supported by the British mandate government (Bertram and Young 1926) and, after British withdrawal in 1948, by thc Jordanian government which then appropriated the West Bank and Jerusalem. After the Israeli government took control of the West Bank in 1967, the Israeli state came to work closely with the Greek Church (Nachmani 1987) in an attempt to subvert the Greek government's opposition to the Israeli occupation. As a result, the Movement became in large part quiescent since the church-state alliance made it evident to many Arab Orthodox activists that any gains that might be made by the Christian Palestinians would only be made after the Israeli occupation was ended (interview with Arab Orthodox Movement member, Bethlehem, March 1987). Nonetheless, one of the outstanding legacies of the Movement is the awareness among Christian

Palestinians that the interests of the hierarchy of the Orthodox church are foreign and antagonistic to their own.

9. Official Patriarchate policy is that one must be a Greek or Cypriot national in order to be a member of the Brotherhood of the Holy Sepulchre. Christian Palestinian men are allowed to become priests in the church but are forced to marry as a condition of being made priests. As a result, they cannot subsequently become monks and are therefore excluded from joining the powerful Brotherhood. This policy was overturned by the British during the mandate period and as a consequence two Palestinians had joined the Brotherhood. These had since died of old age, and Israeli support of the church had ensured that the old exclusionary policy had been reinstated and that no new Palestinians had entered the Brotherhood to replace them.
10. The status quo agreements, finalized by an Ottoman firman in 1852, legislate over the conflicting claims of the various churches to rights and privileges within the holy places. The firm an, adopted in turn by the British, the Jordanians and the Israelis, establishes the reigning government as perpetuator of the status quo fixed in 1852, and withdrawal by the Government from its role could lead to an open-ended struggle between the churches over which would control the shrines.
11. "Salim Tamari points out that the Palestinian left, which dominated political activism along the Ramallah-jerusalem-Bethlehem axis, maintained until the early 1990s 'venerable tradition of divorcing the political from the cultural and social spheres in the agendas of socialist parties' (1992 : 17-18). While on the one hand this meant that the left in large part failed to address issues of women's rights and the personal status code forbidding civil marriage, it meant on the other hand that its programme could encourage activists to define the domain of public expressions of identity such as festivals in purely political (i.e., national) terms.

Whether or not this was actually the case, what is significant is that it was defined as such in Halweh's discourse.

12. The term floating signifier', drawn from Levi-Strauss' introduction to the work of Marcel Mauss (Levi-Strauss 1987 :63), is proposed by Jacques Derrida as an alternative to the classical idea of an essence which is held to stand at the centre of any discursive structure and which constitutes and determines the signification enabled by that structure. Derrida provides several examples of such 'transcendental signifiers' from the history of Western metaphysics such as eidos, arch e, telos, en-ergeia, ousia (essence, existence, substance, subject), aletheia, transcendentality, consciousness or conscience, God, man, and so forth' (Derrida 1972 :249). Derrida contends that Saussure's insight that all signs take on signification through opposition to other signs in a diacritical system invalidates the idea of such extra-linguistic essences standing outside of semantic structures and giving rise to these structures. The constitution of all meànting within language undermines all assertions of referentiality; things 'outside' language only come to have significance in language. Since there is no meaning outside of language which language elaborates and describes, all definitions of a field of discourse are effectively 'unfixed' and 'up for grabs' : '(t)he absence of the transcendental signified extends the domain and the play of signification infinitely' (Derrida 1978 :280). By extension, we can understand that 'objects' of/in discourse, such as the festivities at Mar Elyas, are constituted in the way people talk about them and through the meanings they attribute to them. Unless the process of interpretation is stabilized or hegemonized by an uncontestable act of power, the 'object' itself 'floats', taking on a number of meanings from the ways it is read by the people who engage it.

13. Systematic research on Beit Sahur took place in January 1990, while Beit Sahur was under siege by the Israeli Defense Force, and was funded by the Middle

East Research Infromation Project. Some of this material has already appeared in Bowman 1990 :50-3.

14. In 1987 Michel Sabbah, a Palestinian from Nazareth, was appointed as Latin Patriarch because, lay persons and priests said, the Catholic church had decided in the face of growing antipathy to the church by Catholic Palestinians to make a significant concession to local Christians. On the outbreak of the intifada Sabbah announced that he was cancelling the Christmas Eve procession in Manger Square and restricting the ceremony to the midnight mass, out of sympathy with the Palestinian people. In response, Israeli officials warned that if the procession was not held as usual 'it might result in the erosion of some of the rights of the Roman Catholics in the Holy Land' (Jerusalem Post 24 December 1987). Al-Tali'a, a Palestinian weekly, reported in the same week that Shimon Peres had contacted the Vatican and threatened that the Israeli government would stop carrying out its obligations as the ruling authority in the holy land in maintaining the status quo agreement. In consequence, Sabbah withdrew his threat. At present the Christmas Eve procession is fromally carried out, but scouts and local people do not attend.

15. Between 1983 and 1987 I maintained contact with the 'Pan-Palestinian Scout Movement' which, in that period, expanded considerably. In March 1987 it was working in close collusion with Mubarak Awad's 'Centre for Non-Violence' in organizing a West Bank boycott of Israeli goods (a forerunner of intif ada strategies of non-co-operation and resistance). In January 1990 I asked about the scouts and was told by a young man taking me around Beit Sahur that 'the scouts have closed up their building.... They made the connections, and will open again when they are needed'.

16. Pena estimates that Beit Sahur in 1984 had a population of 8,900 of which 7,400 were Christian (6,000 Greek Orthodox, 670 Latin Catholics, 500 Greek Catholics, 200 Lutherans and 30 Syrian Orthodox).

17. The protected status enjoyed by Hamas was reversed in May 1988 when the government outlawed the organization after Hamas activists claimed responsibility for the kidnapping and execution of two Israeli soldiers. The high media profile that Israel had granted the movement in presenting it as a rival to the United Leadership of the Uprising, along with the immunity to prosecuting its activists had enjoyed prior to its banning, meant that the Israelis had no trouble pinpointing its leadership when the arrests began; in the last two weeks of May 1988 more than 250 Hamas organizers were jailed.
18. There appears to be a close correlation between properties maintained for the delectation of pilgrims and lack of interest in the local peoples. The Greek Catholic and Anglican churches have few holy monuments to maintain for foreign visitors and have strongly supported their Palestinian congregations under the Bishoprics of Lutfi Lahan (Lebanese) and Samir Kafity (Syrian). The Lutheran Church, which divides its powers in the holy land between three delegations (German, American and Palestinian), supports Christian Palestinians unless such support interferes with the privileges of its foreign members. In 1985 the Lutherans shut down the 'Austro-Hungarian Hospice', which had served since 1948 as the only hospital in Jerusalem's old city, in order to refit it as a hotel for well-off Lutheran pilgrims.
19. It is important to stress here that, as a foreign anthropologist engaged in research during conditions of what is in effect a national liberation struggle, I created a particular context for the persons I interviewed. People were keen to present an impression of unity to someone who, they rightly assumed, would be presenting Beit Sahur to the world outside. I suspect that an extended stay in the town, such as that upon which I am about to embark, would reveal moments of disharmony and conflict which might show that the nationalist project in Beit Sahur

is precisely a project and not a fully realized and sutured new identity.

20. Yehoshua Porath, who wrote a meticulous study of Palestinian mobilization leading up to the 1936 Revolt (Porath 1977), was quoted in the Jerusalem Post of 12 March 1988 as saying of the intifada that 'this is the first time that there has been a popular action, covering all social strata and groups'.
21. The closest thing I saw to this at Mar Elyas occurred on 24 August 1984 when Israeli police began to break up the market in children's toys which had fromed along the edge of the road, claiming that the dealers were not properly licensed. Only at this moment did persons in the crowd speak of themselves as Palestinians and of their traditional practices, then threatened by the incursion of representatives of the Israeli state, as manifestations of a Palestinian national identity. When the police withdrew, the fromulation of identity in 'Palestinian' terms ceased.
22. Among the Christian exceptions were some Armenians—both Orthodox and Uniate—who saw themselves as Armenian nationals rather than as Armenian Palestinians, and Protestants of fundamentalist and mi Uenarian groups which defined the future in chiliastic rather than nationalist terms. Fundamentalist Muslims were also, as Lustick asserts, unlikely to wish to pollute their God-given identities at a time when all hope was resting on divine intervention (Lustick 1992 :431). Furthermore, various people who were still substantially patronized by the religious institutions were not likely to see their interests served by violating the terms of that support.
23. The Holy Fire ceremony is a Greek Orthodox ritual which has been recorded as occurring as early as 870 AD (Peters 1985 :261-7). It takes place in the Holy Sepulchre in Jerusalem at approximately I p.m. on Holy Saturday and is alleged to signal the passage of Christ from hell to heaven. It stands, for Christians, as a sign that Christ's resurrection is promised on the following day. Interviews with attending Muslims revealed that

it was also interpreted, by them and by participating Christian Palestinian youths, as an opportunity for Jerusalem Palestinians to welcome their foreign guests to their city. Massive crowds of local Christians and foreign pilgrims collect for the ceremony with occasionally disastrous consequences as Arthur Stanley recorded for 1834 (Stanley 1889 :464-9; see also Williams 1849 : 533-5; Canetti 1973 : 185 -93).

24. Icons, which present well-established representations of religious phenomena in traditionally fixed froms and styles, are signs of Orthodox froms of devotion. Paintings tend to be freer and more realist in their desire to inspire a mental 're-enactment' of the scene portrayed, and are most often Latin and, in this area, Franciscan devotional artefacts (Bowman 1991).

25. I would argue that the threat of disintegration to Israeli unity which Paine saliently points out in his study of Jewish identity in a national state (Paine 1989) is held at bay by a general consensus among Israeli Jews that an enemy (the Palestinian entity) exists 'outside' the fissile national community which is far more threatening than any other community within the nation.

26. Reema Hammami writes that Hamas 'endowed that hijab with new meanings of piety and political affiliation. Women affiliated with the movement started to wear long, plain, tailored overcoats, known as shan'a (Islamic law) dress, which have no real precedents in indigenous Palestinian dress. Supposed to represent a return to a more authentic Islamic tradition, it is in fact an invented tradition in both from and meaning. Here the hijab is fundamentally an instrument of oppression, a direct disciplining of women's bodies for political ends' (Hammami 1990 :25). She notes the failure of a belated attempt by the United National Leadership of the Uprising to halt attacks on women for not wearing hijab and comments that since February 1990 the "hijab campaign" has been renewed with even greater force than before. Now that the imposition of the headscarf has been accomplished, a

new goal seems to have been set : the imposition of the jilbaab (full length dress or coat)' (Hammami 1990 :28).

27. Porath points out that the British were able to sow discord between the various Palestinian groups (rural and urban, Christian, Druze and Muslim, radicals and moderates, Husseini and Nashashibi) fighting against them in the Arab Revolt by emphasizing the antagonism of other factions to the particular interests of each (Porath 1977 : 249; see also Johnson 1982).

References

Abu-Jaber, K. 1967. The millet system in the nineteenth century Ottoman empire. In *The Muslim world.*57 (3). 213-223.

Al-Haq. 1989. *Illegality of Israeli Tax Raids in Beit Sahour : Infromation Update.* Ramallah : Al Haq (Law in the Service of Man.

Althusser, L. 1971. Ideology and ideological state apparatuses (notes towards an investigation). In *Lenin and Philosophy and other Essays.* London : Verso. 121-173.

Anderson, B. 1991. *Imagined Communities : Reflection on the Origins and Spread of Nationalism.* London : Verso.

Ardener, E. 1972. Belief and the problem of women. In *The Interpretation of Ritual : Essays in Honour of A.I. Richards.* (ed.) J.S. La Fontaine. London :Tavistock. 135-158.

Asali, K.J.1989. Jerusalem under the Ottomans (1516-1831 AD). In *Jerusalem in History.* (ed.) K.J. Asali. London :Scorpion. 200-227.

Barth, F. 1969. Introduction. In *Ethnic Groups and Boundaries : the Social Organisation of Culture Difference.* (ed.) F. Barth. London : George Allen and Unwin. 9-38.

Ben-Arieh, Y. 1984. *Jerusalem in the Nineteenth Century : the Old City.* New York :St. Martin's Press.

Bertram, S.A. and J.W.A . Young . 1926. *The Orthodox Patriarchate of Jerusalem : Report of the commission appointed by the Government of Palestine to Inquire and Report Upon Certain Controversies Between the Orthodox Patriarchate of Jerusalem and the Arab Orthodox Community.* London : Humphrey Milford.

Bowman, G. 1986. Unholy struggle on holy ground : conflict and its interpretation. In *Anthropology Today.* VI (3). 4-7.

Bowman, G. 1990. Religion and political identity in Beit Sahour. In *Middle East Report.* XX (3-4). 50-53.

Bowman, G. 1991. Christian ideology and the image of a holy land : the place of Jerusalem pilgrimage in the various Christianities. In *Contesting the Sacred : the Anthropology of Christian Pilgrimage.* (ed.) J. Eade and M. Sallnow . London : Routledge. 98-121.

Canaan, T. 1927. *Mohammedan Saints and Sanctuaries in Palestine.* London : Luzac and Co.

Canetti, E. 1973. *Crowds and Power.* Harmondsworth : Penguin.

Chapman, M., M. McDonald, et al. 1989. Introduction : history and social anthropology. In *History and Ethnicity.* (ed.) E. Tonkin, M. Mc Donald and M. Chapman. London :Routledge. 168-82.

Clifford, J. 1988. *The Predicament of Culture : Twentieth Century Ethnography, Literature and Art.* Harvard : Harvard University Press.

Cohen, A. and B. Lewis. 1978. *Poppulation and Revenue in the Towns of Palestine in the Sixteenth Century.* Princeton: Princeton University Press.

Derrida, J. 1972. Structure, sign and play in the discourse of the human sciences. In *The Structuralist Controversy : The Languages of Criticism and the Sciences of Man.* (ed.) R. Macksey and E. Donato. Baltimore : Johns Hopkins Press, 247-265.

Derrida, J. 1978. *Writing and Difference.* London : Routledge and Kegan Paul.

Demont, L. 1970. Nationalism and Communalism. In *Religion/Politics and History in India.* The Hague : Mouton. 89-110.

Dumper, M. 1991. *Muslim Institutions and the Israeli State: Muslim Religious Endowments (Waqfs) in Israel and the Occupied Territories, 1948-1987.* Ph. D. Dissertation. University of Exeter.

Dumper, M. 1992. Forty years without slumbering : *waqf* politics and administration in the Gaza Strip, 1948-1987. In *Democracy in the Middle East : Proceeedings of the 1992 Annual Conference of the British Society for Middle East Studies.* University of St. Andrews. 408-427.

Durkheim, E. 1915. *The Elementary Froms of the Religious Life.* New York : George Allen and Unwin.

Eickelman, D. 1989. *The middle East : An Anthropological Approach.* Englewood Cliffs, New Jersey : Prentice Hall.

Evans-Pritchard, E.E. 1940. *The Nuer : A Description of the Modes of Livelihood and Political Institutions of a Nilotic People.* Oxford : Oxford University Press.

Geertz, C. 1988. *Works and Lives : The Anthropologist as Author.* Stanford : Stanford University Press.

Gilsenan, M. 1982. *Recognizing Islam.* London : Croom Helm.

Halbwachs, M. 1980. *The Collective Memory.* New York : Harper and Row.

Hamas. 1988. *The Covenant of the Islamic Resistance Movement.* Mimeographed circular.

Hammami, R. 1990. Women, the Hijab and the Intifada. In *Middle East Report* . XX (3-4). 24-28. Handelman, D. 1990. *Models and Mirros : Towards and Anthropology of Public Events.* Cambridge : Cambridge University Press.

Hertz, R. 1983. Saint Besse : A study of an Alpine cult. In *Saints and Their Cults : Studies in Religious Sociology, Folklore and History.* (ed.) S. Wilson. Cambridge : Cambridge University Press 55-100.

Hiltermann, J. 1991. *Behind the Intifada : Labor and Women's Movements in the Occupied Territories.* Princeton : Princeton University Press.

Hopwood, D. 1969. *The Russian Presence in Syria and Palestine 1843-1914 : Church and Politics in the Near East.* Oxford : Clarendon Press.

Horner, N. 1989. *A Guide to Christian Churches in the Middle East : Present Day Christianity in the Middle East and North Africa.* Elkhart, Indiana : Mission Focus.

Johnson, N. 1982. *Islam and the Politics of Meaning in Palestinian Nationalism.* London : Kegan Paul International.

Joseph, S. 1978. Muslim-Christian conflict in Lebanon : a perspective on the evolution of sectarianism. In *Muslim-Christian Conflicts :Economic, Political and Social Origins.* (ed.) S. Joseph and B. Pillsbury Boulder : Westview Press. 63-97.

Kapferer, B. 1988. *Legends of People/Myths of State : Violence, Intolerance and Political Culture in Sri Lanka and Australia.* Washington, D.C. : Smithsonian Institution Press.

Kreutz, A. 1992. Arab Christian communities in the holy land : a minority in crisis. In *Democracy in the Middle East : Proceedings of the 1992 Annual Conference of the British Society for Middle East Studies.* University of St. Andrews. 263-278.

Laclau, E. and C. Mouffe. 1985. *Hegemony and Socialist Strategy : Towards a Radical Democratic Politics.* London : Verso.

Legrain, J.-F. 1990. The Islamic movement and the Intifada. *In Intifada : Palestine at the Crossroads.* (ed.). J. Nassar and R. Heacock. New York : Praeger. 175-189.

Levi-Strauss, C. 1987. *Introduction to the Work of Marcel Mauss.* London : Routledge and Kegan Paul.

Lienhardt, G. 1961. *Divinity and Experience : the Religion of the Dinka.* Oxford : Oxford University Press.

Litani, Y. 1989. Militant Islam in the West Bank an Gaza. In *New Outlook.* (11-12). 40-42.

Loizos, P. 1981. *The Heart Grown Bitter A Chronicle of Cypriot War Refugees.* Cambridge. Cambridge University Press.

Lustick, I. 1980. *Arabs in the Jewish State : Israel's Control of a National Minority. Austin* : University of Texas Press.

Lustick, I. 1988. *For the Land and the Lord : Jewish Fundamentalism in Israel.* New York : Council on Foreign Relations.

Lustick, I. 1992. Gush Emunim : the meaning and impact of Jewish fundamentalism in Israel. *Democracy in the Middle East : Proceedings of the 1992 Annual Conference of the British Society for Middle Eastern Studies.* University of St. Andrews. 428-447.

Madan, T. N. 1972. Two faces of Bengali ethnicity : Muslim Bengali or Bengali Muslim. In *Developing Economies.* X (4). 74-85.

McDonald , M. 1989. *'We Are Not French' : Language, Culture and Identity in Brittany.* London : Routledge.

Mortimer, E. 1982. *Faith and Power : the Politics of Islam.* London Faber and Faber.

Nachmani, A. 1987. *Israel, Turkey and Greece : Uneasy Relations in the East Mediterranean.* London : Frank Cass.

Painer, R. 1989. Israel : Jewish Identity and competition over tradition. In *History and Ethnicity.* (ed.) E. Tonkin, M. Mc Donald and M. Chapman. London : Routledge . 121-136.

Pena, G. 1984. *Christian Presence in the Holy Land.* Jerusalem : Christian Infromation Centre.

Peters, F.E. 1985. *Jerusalem: the Holy City in the Eyes of Chroniclers, Visitors, Pilgrims and Prophets from the Days of Abraham to the Beginnings of Modern Times.* Princeton : Princeton University Press.

Porath, Y. 1977. *The Palestinian Arab National Movement 1929-1939; From Riots to Rebellion.* London : Frank Cass.

Rodinson, M. 1971. *Mohammed.* Harmondsworth : Penguin Press.

Schiff, Z. and E. Ya'ari. 1990. *Intifada : The Palestinian Uprising-Israel's Third Front.* New York : Simon and Schuster.

Scholch, A. 1989. Jerusalem in the nineteenth century (1831-1917 AD). In *Jerusalem in History* (ed.) K. J. Asali. London : Scorpion. 228-248.

Sprinzak, E. 1991. *The Ascendance of Israel's Radical Right.* Oxford : Oxford University Press.

Stanley, A. 1889. *Sinai and Palestine in Connection with their History.* London : John Murray.

Tamari, S. 1982. Factionalism and class fromation in recent Palestinian history. In *Studies in the Economic and Social History of Palestine in the Nineteenth and Twentieth Centuries.* (ed.) R. Owen. London : Macmillan.

Tamari, S. 1992. Left in limbo : Leninist heritage and Islamist challenge. In *Middle East Report.* XXII (6). 16 -22.

Taraki, L. 1989. The Islamic Resistance Movement in the Palestinian uprising. In *Middle East Report.* XIX (1). 30-32.

Tibawi, A.L. 1961. *British Interest in Palestine 1800-1901.* Oxford : Oxford University Press.

Webber, J. 1985. Religions in the Holy Land : conflicts of interpretation. In *Anthropology Today,* V (2). 3-10.

Williams, G. 1849. *The Holy City : Historical, Topographical and Antiquarian Notices of Jerusalem.* London : John W. Parker.

5

Pilgrimage for Salvation of Ancestral Souls : A Case Study of Gaya

Paras Kumar Choudhary

From pilgrimage point of view, Bihar is an important state of India. Gaya is the most important sacred place of pilgrimage in Bihar, where pilgrims come from different parts of Hindu Universe to offer *Pindas* to their passed ancestors. Thus Gaya is very famous place for offering *Pindas* to the ancestors and *Shraddha-Sanskar* (death ceremony). It is believed that the dead ancestors, who have not got *Pinda* after death, they do not get salvation and, contrary to it, those who have got it, get salvation. The *Pinda* should be offered either by the son or by the relatives in the name of their ancestors.

The Gaya City

Gaya has been identified by different names in various times. The list includes such names as Brahma Gaya, Vishnupuri, Kikata, Alamgirpur, Sahibganj, and Gayapuri.

Gaya as a city formed a part of the district of Bihar and Ramgarh till the year 1865. It was subsequently carved out as an independent district with Gaya, Nawada, Aurangabad and Jehanabad as its subdivisions. In January 1972 the subdivisions of Aurangabad and Nawada were also given the administrative status as independent districts.

The entire region was under the influence of Buddhism, Jainism and Hinduism. Gaya and Bodh Gaya played very significant role in maintaining an enlightened zone of peace and understanding.

Bodh Gaya is known as the most revered place for the Buddhists of the world. Gautam Buddha attained his supreme enlightenment at Bodh Gaya.

Besides Vishnupad temple, other important places are monasteries of Japan, China, Tibet, Burma, Bhutan, Thailand and ASI (Archeological Survey of India) museum, the lotus tank, the Birla Mandir, the large marble statue of Buddha and numerous spots associated with Buddha's life.

The place is well connected with metropolitan cities of the country. The grand chord section of the eastern railway covers this place. Besides, the grand trunk road touches Gaya at Dobhe connecting Delhi and Calcutta.

Vishupada Temple

The Vishnupada temple is the most important traditional sacred centre, made of blackstone has been built by Ahilya Bai Holkar, a Maratha widow queen of Indore. It was built in between 1782 to 1852 A.D. Before it the temple was made of bricks. The temple was constructed at the cost of Rs. 3,00,000. The top of the temple looks like tomb which is very decent. At the top of the temple a donor of Calcutta city named Gayapal Balgobinda Sen placed a flag of gold weighting approx. 40 Kg.

Inside the temple there is an eight cornered silver *Kund* (boundary). In the middle of which the foot-print of Lord - Vishnu lies. In the middle of boundary one big bell is hanging. Outside of this varandah another big bell is also hanging. There is varandah on the east of the temple which is used as worship place by the devotees. A silver umbrella lies beautifully on the top of the said foot-print. This umbrella and some silver utensils have also been gifted by above mentioned Balgobinda Sen.

Pilgrimage of Gaya

At Gaya, according to the pilgrims Act of 1920, a Committee consisting of the representative of the government, the priests, the city municipality, and the public has been organised to look after all the affairs concerning the pilgrims as well as the religious buildings. During the last twenty years the Lodging Housing Committee has completed several constructions and repair works, like the construction of a large *Dharmashala* or pilgrims rest-house. According to Lodging Housing Committee the numbers of pilgrims visiting Gaya in the year 1995, 1996 and 1997 are approx. 14 lacs, 15 lacs, and 16 lacs respectively. In 1997 out of 16 lacs, 7 lacs pilgrims came in *Pitripaksha* (in October month), 7 lacs pilgrims came in *Ganga Sagar Mela* (fair) (in between 1 January to 25th January) and 2 lacs in other days. Pilgrims use to stay in *Dharmashalas,* Hotels, rest house and *Panda* houses. Pilgrims came from different states of India like Rajasthan, Maharashtra, Gujarat, Madhya Pradesh, Punjab, Haryana, A.P., Tamil Nadu, Kerala, Karnataka, West Bengal, Bihar and Uttar Pradesh and neighbouring Hindu country like Nepal.

Sexwise composition of pilgrims consists of 30% female and 70% males. So far their literacy rate is concerned 12% of the pilgrims were illiterate and 88% were literate. Among the literates the educational status of the pilgrims is as follows :- Up to Matriculation 45%, upto graduation 35% and upto Postgraduate and above 20%.

So far economic status is concerned 50% of pilgrims were with the yearly earning range of Rs. 35,000 to 50,000. 20% within Rs. 51,000 to 750,000 and 30% within 76,000 to 1,00,000.

Out of total number of pilgrims 65% were of rural background and 35% urban background.

As per profession 22% of pilgrims were peasants, 30% businessman, 20% doing private jobs, 18% holding higher posts in Govt. Department like Doctors, B.D.O., Lawyers, teachers etc. and 10% were from other professions.

Earlier Study Related to Gaya Tirtha

The reference of Gaya *Shraddha* and *Pinda-Dan* is found in the pauranie literature viz. the "Vishnu Sutra" (chap LXXXV Ves 4,22,40) and then in the Vayu Purna (n.d. Chaps 105-12), which are believed to be approximately of first century. Manu Smriti (n.d. Chap 111 VSS 122.285) also makes an elaborate reference to the rules that are to be followed in the observance of different types of *Shraddha.*

The Gaya *Tirtha* was, first of all, anthropologically studied by late L.P. Vidyarthi in 1961. He has given more emphasis on the sacred centres of Gaya, the sacred performances at Gaya, the sacred specialists, the orthodox style of priestly life, the sacred specialists: Extension and the sacred specialists : Heterogeneity and phases of change. The present author has tried to marked the changes which have occurred since last four decades as follows :-

The factor of social change has affected social structure of society. These changes have affected Gaya *Tirtha* too. But basic fundamental principle of sacred ritual performance at Gaya *Tirta* has not been change so far.

It has been observed that numbers of pilgrims are increasing every year. According to Lodging Housing Committee, since 1995 every year approx. One lac pilgrims increases. Main reason behind it is the development of Road Transport and Railway facilities.

Rate of literacy is also a factor which effects Gaya *Tirtha.* Literacy rate has been increased in India. Literate people (Pilgrims) generally go through religious text and they communicate importance of the *Tirtha* to the illiterate people. Thus the increasing rate of literacy has also effected the number of pilgrims visiting Gaya *Tirtha.*

Another reason behind it, is a process of *Sanskritization.* During British period people, who were in contact of Britishers and followed their life style. But after independence they are following their traditional religious activities also which, includes performance of *Shraddha* and *Pindadan* at Gaya. This indicates their strong belief related to salvation of soul.

Keeping in view very busy daily life engagements, most of pilgrims nowadays seek to complete all the sacred performance related to Gaya *Tirtha* (Shraddha, Tarpana, Pinda-dan) in a few days instead of 15th days as prescribed in the religious text.

It has been observed that life style, thinking and behaviour of *Panda* (specialists) has been changed. Once upon a time their were 1984 *Pandas* living at Gaya region. Nowadays it has decreased to 945. Previously, *Pandas* depended for their subsistence mainly on pilgrims. But nowadays several of them have took up Govt. and private jobs. This shows a process of change in their traditional occupation.

A *Panda* is always not satisfied with *Dakshina* (gift or remuneration paid by the pilgrims) given by the pilgrims, that is why they try to cheat and misguide the pilgrims. So many such cases have come before the District Magistrate. Therefore in 199 5 district magistrate fixed the *Dakshina* for the *Panda*.

It has been observed that due to modern life style nowadays most of the pilgrims don't want to get head hair shaved. Instead of it, they like simply haircutting and beard shaving. Traditionally purity in food (vegetarian) and avoidance of sexual act, were essential for all pilgrims. But today pilgrims are not maintaining these seriously.

It has observed that, *Panda* has changed their food habit and dress also. Previously they don't eat non-vegetarian food and use to wear *Dhoti-Kurta* (traditional cloth). But today a few *Pandas* use to take non-vegetarian (like meat and fish) food also and a few are weaning shirt and pant.

Above mentioned changes have been observed by present author and he hopes that these changes will lead to a new system of ritual performance (Shraddha and Pinda-dan) in near future.

Textual Importance of Pilgrimage at Gaya

Once Narda (a very popular saint described in Hindu religious texts) approached Sanat Kumar Maharaj alongwith *Rishis* Saunaka and other's requested him "*Swami* (Lord) please let us know the stories of such *Tirthas* (traditional sacred centre) whose greatness is such as that by hearing it one may bestowed with internal happiness".

Sanat Kumar Maharaj replied 'O' Narad, Gaya is prominent among the *Tirtha*. If people perform *Shraddha* and give *Pinda-dan* to their ancestors they can get internal happiness. Further, he narrates the story as follows :-

Once a *Daitya* (demon), named Gaya-Asura performed severe *tap* (penance). Being afraid of his *tap*, all *Devas* (gods) approached Brahma, the creator, for solution. The Brahma, with the suggestion of Lord Vishnu, asked Gaya-Asura his body for performing a *Yagya* (sacrificial ritual). The Gaya-

Asura accepted Brahma's suggestion and the performance of *Yagya* started. At the end of *Yagya,* the body of Gaya Asura was moving. Then Dharamaraja placed a *Sila* (holy stone) on his body. Even then he was able to move his body.

The Lord Vishnu sat on the *Sila* with his conch and *Chakra* (moving powerful spiritual disc) mace and lotus in his hands along with other Gods. Then Gaya Asura could not move his body. Then he became happy and prayed Lord Vishnu, that this place will be renowned after my name. Accordingly Lord Vishnu blessed him and the area is named as "Gaya *Kshetra* (Region)".

If the son visits this holy place, the soul of his dead father will be pleased. Those who perform *Pinda-dana* and *Shraddha* here will go to *Vaikuntha* (Heaven) at the end of his life. However sinful one may be will be liberated of his sin by visiting Gaya *Kshetra* (region).

Narada asked Sanat Kumar Maharaj please let us know the story of Gaya-Asura. So, he narrates further the story as follows :-

"The Gaya-Asura performed severe penance on Kolahala mountain for several years. Gods were afraid of his severe penance. So, Bhahama along with Shankara approached Lord Vishnu for relieving their tension. So, Lord Vishnu gave *darsan* to the Asura and asked him to have a boon. Then Gaya-Asura prayed Vishnu- "Oh my Lord make my body as holu as if however touches it will get a place in *Vaikuntha* (heaven)". Lord granted him the aforesaid boon and disappeared. Since then people are getting *Mosksha* (Salvation) by touching him.

Gradually it so happened that the number of sinners in *Yomoloka* (hell) decreased. Then *Yama* (the god of death) along with other gods informed Vishnu about the disbalance of sinner's souls in the *Yomoloka* (hell). Then Lord Vishnu asked Brhma to get Gaya-Asura's body for Yagya. AccordinglyBrahma asked Gaya Asura to give his body for Yagya. So listening it Gaya Asura laid down keeping his feet towards the south.

Then Brahna performed *Yagya* upon his body. Even after *Yagya* was over Gaya-Asura was able to move his body. Then Brahma asked Yamraj to keep Sila (holy stone) upon his body. Yamraj did likewise. Even then he could move his body.

Then Gaya-Asura told that if Gods will sit on my body, it will not move. So, as per boon of Lord Vishnu Gods sited on his body and will remain on it as long as the sun and moon are in the sky.

Again Narada questioned Sanat Kumar Maharaj "Oh great one". Please let us know where from Yamaraj got that holy stone. Sanat Kumar Maharaj replied. Dharmaraja has a daughter named Dharmautra. Having observed that she had grown up he asked her to do *tapas* (penance) for getting husband. A sage by mane Maricha considering her to be pious, approached Yamara to give Dharmautra to marry. Dharmaraja gave her to him. After sometime one day sage Maricha returned home very much tired and said his wife to massage his feet. Accordingly she was attending him. After few minutes he slept. Later on father of Marich came there. So, she came out leaving the service to her husband and attended her father-in-law. Meanwhile Maricha woke-up having observed her missing. So he cursed her to become a stone.

Later she penanced for her sin Lord Vishnu appeared before her and asked her to have some boon. She asked him to regain her original human form. Lord Vishnu replied "It is not possible to go against the word of a sage and asked her to have some other boon "she prayed to Lord" I must be treated as a holy stone. All Gods should reside on me. By Lord Vishnu she was blessed accordingly. Whosoever comes in contact with this sila gets relieved from the sins and gets *Moksha* (salvation). With a condition that whenever this sila will be kept on the body of Gaya Asura. This boon will be effective. He then disappeared.

Sanat Kumar continued the story of the greatness of that very sila. He told by seeing and touching it people will get liberated from birth and death cycle as well as by performing here *Shraddha* by their aneestors will attain salvation. If one performs *Shraddha* in Matanga *tirtha* one's ancestors get salvation. Whoever crosses Brahmayoni mountain will cross the *Sansara* (worldly life).

He further said 'O' Narda listen the story of pilgrimage to holy place attentively. Before coming to Gaya on pilgrimage one should observe celibacy some time. After reaching Gaya on the first day he should bath in Falgu river. Then he should perform *Sraddha* and *Tarpana.* On the second day after taking bath in Brahmakunda (pond), he should give *Pinda* with *Tilas* for his dead father. Then he should speak the name of the dead ancestors. He should also remember Gods name. By this action concern ancestor get salvation. By performing the said ritual in this manner one should do charity by offering food to his friends and relatives. By doing this the ancestors get relieved from the bondage of birth and death.

Sanat Kumar said once a King named Gaya has performed a great Yagya in Gaya region. Pleased by his *Yagya* Lord Vishnu gave him *darsan* and asked him to have a boon. He requested to Lord Vishnu that the curse of Brahma upon *Brahmaloka* may be lifted. Lord Vishnu granted him the said boon.

Also a King named Vilasa of Vilasapuri had no son. *Brahmins* (caste) advised him to go on pilgrimage to Gaya and by visiting Gaya *Tirtha* he was blessed with a son.

Once a soul of dead person gave his money to blindman and asked him to do *Sraddha* ritual for five days in Gaya for his salvation. By that very ritual he got relieved from his *pretayoni* (Ghost life).

Sanat Kumar added once Lord Shiva was pleased upon Vasishta and asked him to have boon. Vasishta replied that Lord Shiva should always reside in Gaya *kshetra* (region). And he was blessed accordingly. So this Gaya *kshetra* (region) is holier (place) among such places and of greater importance.

Contextual Part of the Pilgrimage

On the level of observation author found the *Shraddha* sacrifice being modified to accommodate the regional practice as well as the economic status of the sacrifices on the level of analysis of the motives and expectations for making such a sacrifice, author noted immense variations. Now the important features of the Gaya *Shraddha* in the being describe.

The day a sacrifice embarks on the Gaya pilgrimage he begins a period of austerity, self mortification, restrictions, and prescriptions, which continues until the sacrifice is successfully completed. He avoids certain food that may pollute him, he abstains from sexual acts: and he must not be in a hurry or shed a tear. He is anniversary of ancestor worship (annual *Shraddha*) is performed on *Mahalaya* or *Jitiya*. While there are several common elements among the four forms of ancestor worship, the very fact that Gaya *Shraddha* is observed at a public sacred ground rather than at domestic and local sacred centre and its success brings final emancipation to the ancestors and happiness to the survivors. So it is performed with seriousness, and sacredness. It is then a sacrifice (yagya) to which a name, pushkara, has been given (vishnu sutra no chap LXXXU VS-1) and it should be distinguished from and compared with the *Mirtyu Sanskar* (death sacrament) anniversary, ancestor-worship (Varshik Shraddha) and annual calendric ancestor worship (known by different names like Mahalaya, Jitiya, Kanagat etc.). Again the person, who perform a Gaya *Shraddha* of his father and other relatives is a sacrificer *(Yagya Karta)* and not a main Mourner *(Karta)* as in the case of the death sacrament or a *Shraddha* worship (Shraddha pujak) as in the case of the annual *Shraddha* worship. River Falgu and is usually guided by the ritualist (acharya) who acts as a secondary priest under the direction of the local ritualist (Gayawal). The acharya recites hymns from the ritual book. Gaya *Shraddha Paddhati* which are appropriate for the various stages of the ritual and directs the sacrificer to make appropriate offerings and prayers.

The *tarpana* ritual lasts about five hours and consists of four main stages. In the first stage, called *devatarpana* (refreshing of the Gods) water is taken in the right hand and poured over the sacred *Vishu-pada*. Special hymns recited and water offerings (tarpana) are made for Brahma, Vishnu, Mahesh and then for other Gods of the Universe. In the second stage *tarpana* is offered to the ten ancient holy sages, Maricha, Atri, Angiras, Pulastya, Ratu, Pullaha, Gautama, Kasyapa, Vasistha and *Vihvamitra*. Evidently the name of the last three rishis are later appendages, are they do not constitute a part of the traditional constellation of supposed to purify himself by avoiding wrath and banishing evil and impure thoughts. When he reaches the place of pilgrimage. Gaya-*Tirtha,* the process of purification becomes further intensified and before he starts the actual performance of the ritual, he observes fasting for a day, undergoes ritual of hair shaving and bath in river Falgu and then puts on a sacrificer's ritual garments, i.e., new white *Dhoti* (popular Indian traditional dress approx. of 5 metre length 1 metre breadth it is wrapped around the waist and its end hands on shoulder). He now invokes his priest as the representative of his ancestors. Worships his feet by making offerings of flowers and gifts and thus seeks his blessings for the successful completion of the sacrifice.

Having completed the ritual of feet worship (Charan Puja), he starts the long series of water offerings *(tarpana)* dedicated to the divinities (Devi-Devta) and the ancient sages (rishi). The *trapana* ritual is always performed at the seven sages represented by the seven stars. In the *Deva Tarpan* and *Rishi Tarpana* the sacrificer faces the east.

In the third stage, *Tarpana* is offered to *Yamaraj* and his accountant Chitragupta. Chitragupta keeps on account of the activities of the mortals according to which they are placed in appropriate situations, i.e., heaven or hell, after their death. Special offerings are made to Yamaraj and Chitragupta for consideration of the ancestors. In the end *Tarpana* is offered to all the *pitris* (ancestors). In both the stages of *Yamatarpana* and *pitri-tarpana,* the sacrificer faces the south and puts on a *Kusha* (a type of sacred grass) ring on the right hand ring finger and keeps sesamum seeds and sacred water in the middle of the right plam which is poured down by the inner side of the root of the right thumb.

In respect to the *pitri-Tarpana,* the immediate paternal ancestors, i.e., father, grandfather, great grandfather and other progenitors are invoked, one by one, at the first instance. Next, the female relative of the paternal lineage and then the immediate relatives on the material side are invoked. Special *tarpana* is offered to those relative who have died of some accident or suffered a premature death. In many cases *tarpana* is offered also to such neighbours or distant relatives whose ghosts might be harmful to the sacrificer. It is believed that an offering of water will satisfy their thirst, refresh them and this lead them to peace.

The second type of ritual known as the *Pinda* offering follows the next day - a *Pinda* is a tiny ball (of 1" approx. diameter) usually prepared with the wet rice powder. In addition to this offering of cooked rice is also offered to the money at some sacred centres. *Pinda* offering is an elaborate ritual which is performed by a sacrificer under the guidance of the ritualist of the *Shraddha* Shrines. The first and the most elaborate *Pinda* offering is usually performed in the neighbourhood of the Vishnupada temple. It consist of several stages of worship like vedic recitation (Gayatri Mantra) symbolization of gods and mons (Sthapit Karma), joining of gods and (Sapindikarana), and finally, *Pinda* worship (Pinda Pujan).

Through the *vedic* practice of *sankalpa* the sacrificer invokes his mones by their names and clan (gotra) which discloses his identity and he defines the purpose of the sacrifice with the ritualist, then a few hymns from the *veda,* known as *gayatri* are repeated by the sacrificer. Next comes the stage of symbolization or enshrinement of the Vishnu deva and the *pitri.* The first is represented by a betal leaf to which offerings of nuts, flowers fruits and coins are made one after the other under the guidance of the ritualist. An earthen pot with offering of barley, butter, honey, tulsi-leaves etc., is also enshrined to represent the gods of the universe. Then the rice balls are enshrined to represent the paternal and maternal ancestors. Another small earthen pot *(Chukka)* is enshrined to represent the manes along with offerings of barley, Sesamum, honey, tulsi leaves and clarified butter. Thus the sacrificer on the one hand has enshrined the Vishnu Deva and on the other side the *pitri.* Such enshrinements are always guided by and accompanied with the recitation of the ritualist.

After this each *pinda* representing a manes is invokes individually and offerings of sesamum, *kusha* grass, honey and white flower are made and a piece of thread symbolizing the dress of the *pitri* or manes is put on it. Such ritual offerings accompanied by the recitation of hymns, continue for each *pinda.*

The last stage *Sopindikarana,* is the combination of the contents of the manes pot with that of the gods pot. This ritual joining at the two symbols is believed to unity the *pitri* with those of the Vishnu *Deva.* The whole ritual concludes when the sacrificer has performed the ritual. Salutation by putting his head on the ground before the unified symbols. He then goes to the duty of Vishnupada temple and there makes the usual offerings and salutation. Later rice balls are collected together and are left to be eaten by crows. Sometimes they are removed to be immersed in the Falgu river or in tank.

These two types of worship *tarpana* and *Pindadan* dominate the *Shraddha* sacrifice. When a sacrificer goes to other sacred centres of Gaya *Tirtha* (noted for Sharddha sacrifice) represented by an image or rock or tree, some form of *Pindadan* is made and when he goes to other sacred centres represented by tanks, *tarpana* becomes the important form of worship. But at many of the other places, the symbol as well as other form of worship became largely oriented in terms of ghosts and spirits of hell and heaven. At Ramshila not only *Yamaraj* is worshipped but also his two infernal dogs are offered *pinda* so that they might not bark at the sacrificer's ancestors and thus torture them.

At *pretashila* the primary offerings are to the god and goddess of ghosts (pretashila and pretabhavawi). In addition to rice powder balls, cooked rice also may be offered.

At another sacred centre, *Kak Bali* (crows sacrifice) the crows of hell are worshipped. Besides *Pinda* offering, friend powdered borly (Sattu) and sesamum seeds are thrown in air so that the spirits may partake of them. At the sacred centre of *Giddhkut* (*Vulture*'s house) in earlier days *Pinda* offering was made but there days the Shrine is completely abandoned.

A *Shraddha* sacrifices also visits several tanks to offer *tarpana* among them *Baitarani* needs special mention here. The tank *Baitarani* mythologically represents the terrible river that flows between the earth and heaven. Baths and *tarpana* performed at *Baitarani* enable the ancestors to obtain emancipation from the horrors of hell. Some sacrifiers make gifts of a cow or set free a bull in the name of their ancestors in the belief that it will help them in the passage of the *Baitarani*, the Hindu style.

A sacrificer also makes a visit to the sacred centres of Ram Gaya and Sita Kund where the Ram is said to have attained Gaya *Shraddha* to his father Dashratha. Here, *tarpana* is offered in the Sita *Kund* and *Pindadan* is performed at the temple of Ram. The performances should continue on each day of the week and on each day of the dark fortnight of a month for satisfying different types of desires and for achieving many kinds of happiness of ancestors which each coming day and date are believed to offer them. In general practice, a sacrificer visits from three to ten sacred centres and completes his round in three to seven days. There are a few sacrificers however, who make the ritual more elaborate, spreading it over fifteen days and over all the sacred centres.

When the round of sacred centres marked for visiting is completed the final two rituals, *Sakshi Shravana* (witness invocation) and *suphal* (success declaration) are observed. These rituals are observed either at Akshayavat or at the residence of the Gayawal priest. *Sakshi-Shravana* is dedicated to deities like parpitamahesvar, Gadadhar, Ram, etc. who are invited to act as witnesses for the performance of Gaya Shraddha. Then according to the suphal ritual, the Gayawal priest is worshipped as the embodiment of the ancestors and all types of gifts are made to him with the belief that they would be imperishable and would be enjoyed by the sacrificer's ancestors in heaven. This ritual is marked by a sacred conversation between the sacrificer and the priest. The sacrificer ask: May you be satisfied? The priest replies. We are satisfied the gods and the manes. Then the sacrificer seeks blessings for the increase in family members as well as in wealth. The priest replies, "Thus let it be". Such a conversation with and seeking of blessing from the priest as the embodiment of the gods and the manes are made by sacrificer.

The priest is satisfied with what has been offered to him in the way of gifts and when the final blessings testifying to the success of the *Shraddha* are granted by him. The sacrifice comes to an end. The sacrificer touching the feet of the priest makes a final ritual solution and the priest in return presents the sacrificer with a ritual garland and sweets as a mark of blessing for his sacrificial deeds and future happiness. Owing to this wide choice perhaps, the flow of sporadic sacrificers to Gaya continues all the year round, but about sixty to seventy percent of the total sacrificers prefer to observe Gaya *Shraddha* during the dark of the month of *Asin.* This period known as *pitripaksha* (the fortnight of the mones) has become significantly established as the most effective period for *shraddha* sacrifice in Gaya. It is a common belief in Bihar and perhaps many other parts of India that during the month *Asin* ghosts, spirits witches and mendicants (Ojha) become very active and restless. The women take special care to protect their children from the evil spirits, and the sources and witches observe rituals and vows to attain perfection.

In Indian religious Philosophy the goal of human life is considered to attain *Moksha* (salvation), i.e., from the worldly cycle of birth and death. This believed that the souls of dead persons take rebirth to satisfy unsatisfied desires and by this way one passes his like, dies, and takes rebirth. So far *pindadan* and *Shraddha* performance specially at Gaya *Tirtha* are concerned it is believed that if *Shraddha* and *Pindadan* ritual are performed here with devotion towards liberated ancestral souls, the souls of respectives dead ancestors get satisfaction and ultimately get salvation.

In the present scenario science has done much progress. But so far existence of soul is concerned, it is not able to say anything in concrete way on the other hand a Hindu as per his religious experiences believes that after death of a person his soul takes rebirth to fulfil his unsatisfied desires, it *Pindadan* and *Shraddha* at Gaya is not performed by his inheritors. Contrary to it if *Shraddha* and *Pindadan* for salvation of a ancestral soul is performed the respective ancestor's will get salvation.

By analysing socio-psychological aspects of *Pindadan* and *Shraddha* ritual, it is beyond the approach of researcher to say "whether the souls of ancestors get salvation or not ? But it is certain that performers of the rituals get mental satisfaction. That is why performer motivates the pilgrims to visit Gaya *Tirtha*. Therefore number of pilgrims are increasing day by day.

References

Bharadwaj, S.Mohan, 1973, *Hindu places of pilgrimage* in India, Thomson Press, New Delhi.

Chakraborty, Prafulla,1984, *Social profile of Tarakeswar study of a pilgrim town in West Bengal*, Firma, Calcutta.

Jha Makhhan, 1971. *Sacred complex in Janakpur*, United Publishers, Allahabad.

— 1995, *Pilgrimage : issues, Themes, concepts and methodology*, Inter India Publication, New Delhi.

Morinis, E. Alan - 1984, *Pilgrimage in the Hindu tradition, A case study of West Bengal*, Oxford University press.

Oommen, T.K. 1992, Religious and development Hindu Society. *Social Compass*, 39 (1) March 19: 67-76. (ISN -4460).

Saraswati, B.N. 1975, *Kashi Myth and Reality of classical cultural tradition*, Institute of Advanced Study Simla.

— 1983, Traditions of Tirthas in India, the anthropology of Hindu Pilgrimage N.K. Bose Memorial Foundation, Varanasi.

Singh, Rana P.B., 1987, The pilgrimage Mandala of Varanasi (Kashi), *National Geographical Journal of India.*

— 1991, *Panckaroshi Yatra, Varanasi sacred Journey. Ecology of place and Faith scale*, Varanasi, Tara Book Agency.

Srinivas, M.N. 1952. *Religion and Society among the Coorgs of South India.* Oxford, London.

Sunderam K. 1984, The Simhachalam Temple by Simhachalam Devastanam, Andrapradesh.

Turner, V and E. Turner, 1978, *Image and Pilgrimage in Christian Culture Anthropological Perspectives*, New York: Columbia Press.

Vidyarthi, L.P., 1961, *The sacred complex of Hindu Gaya*, Asia Publishing House. Bombay.

— 1979, *The sacred complex of Kashi*, Concept Publishing Company, New Delhi.

6

Pilgrimage in Hindu India : Past and Present

(A study on two sacred centres : Puri and Simhachalam)

Sabita Acharya

A pilgrimage may be regarded as a visit to any Sacred Centre undertaken as an act of religious devotion. The study of pilgrimage is a matter of great concern for anthropologists as it is an important dimension of Indian civilization. Social anthropologists have been studying the religion of both the simple, primitive as well as complex, modern societies since the inception of the discipline. Anthropological studies of pilgrimage have sharpened the understanding of the structure and function of Indian civilization. Such studies have contributed substantially towards an understanding of the role of religious institution in maintaining and modifying the structure and function of larger social system of Indian civilization.

In Indian Anthropology, Hinduism has been studied by many anthropologists and among them L.P. Vidyarthi's *Aspects of Religion in Indian Society* (ed) (1961). Milton Singer's *When a Great Tradition Modernizes* (1972), Srinivas's, *Religion and Society among the Coorgs of South India* (1952) may be referred. Robert Redfield (1956) had developed the idea and methods for the study of civilization by anthropologists. His approach was by and large, microscopic, synchronic and socio-cultural whereas Kroebor's (1963) approach was telescopic, diachronic and culture-historical. For Redfield, civilization had both a "Social Structure' and a "Cultural Structure". Social structure is a structure of networks and centres of many different kinds, in which communities, little and great, are the unit 'points' and Social relations between them are the 'connecting lines'. Cultural structure of a civilization is the structure of its ideas and the products of ideas, i.e., of its cultural traditions (Singer : 1972). In every civilization, both the great and little traditions are the two dimensions interact with each other continuously. The media of interaction are the networks setup between them like marriage, trade, pilgrimage, festivals, etc. The practice of pilgrimage is very complex and culture specific a reflection of Indian civilization.

Anthropological research on pilgrimage has been initiated during past few decades and the literature related to this study is scattered. Vidyarthi, a student of Redfield in 1961, studied the sacred city of Gaya in ancient cultural zone of Magadha, which actually initiated the rise of "Sacred Complex" studies in Indian Anthropology. It reveals that the sacred complex is a trichotomic interrelated phenomena of "sacred geography", "sacred performances" and "sacred specialists" that reflect the great and little traditions of Hindu civilization. Jha in 1971 studied "Sacred complex of Janakpur" in Nepal and brought out how the civilizational boundary oversides the political and administrative boundaries. In his other book *Rising India* he discusses about Lord Jagannath at Puri and in another book *"Dimensions of Indian Civilizations"* Jha describes different aspects of Jagannath Cult, its origin and development, pilgrims and pilgrimages at Puri. Saraswati in 1962 in his book *"Institution of Pilgrimage in Nimsar"* of Uttar Pradesh, discusses about pilgrim networks, sacred specialists, and all. Durkheim's study in an analysis of Indian pilgrimage can not be ignored and his axiomatic sacred-profane dichotomy is quite counter productive for the understanding of Hindu Pilgrimage as well as Hinduism in general. After these major works, a number of studies were also made on Hindu Tirthas (Pilgrimage) as dimensions of Indian Civilization which have also been described and reviewed.

However, the present study is an outcome of anthropological research made on the basis of empirical data, collected through fieldwork at two sacred centres, i.e., Puri (Orissa) and Simhachalam (Andhra Pradesh), the two neighbouring states of India. At Puri, Lord Jagannath and at Simhachalam Lord Narsimha are the presiding deities worshipped by the Hindus. Both are the Vaishnavite Shrines, one from eastern India and other from southern India to which countless pilgrims (Tirtha Yatrees) come on pilgrimage from all over India even from abroad. It provides an appropriate area of research related to the study of pilgrimage.

Puri is treated as one of the most important centres of pilgrimage in Hindu India. Being the place of Lord Jagannath, Puri has been described as 'Nilachal', 'Purushottama Kshetra', 'Shankha Kshetra', 'Shrikshetra' 'Dhama' and 'Tirtha'. Puri forms one of the four great Dhamas of Hindus, renovated according to tradition at the instance of Adi Shankar (788 A.D. to 820 A.D.), the great teacher and revivalist of Philosophic Hinduism, situated at four corners of India. In North, Badrinath dedicated to Lord Vishnu, in south, Rameshwaram, associated with Lord Siva, in west Dwarika, dedicated to Lord Krishna and in east, Puri, the place of Lord Jagannath; the Krishna-Vishnu incarnate. To every Hindu, a visit to all the Dhamas (sacred place) is almost obligatory in his life. The Kshetra of Jagannath had already become a centre of pilgrimage (Tirtha) of inter - regional fame since 10th century (Kulke : 1978 : 200). The Vaishnavite name and fame of the deity made Puri famous and it became popular as an important pilgrim centre where world famous festival "Rath Yatra" (Car festival) of Lord Jagannath is held every year. To observe the occasion, large gatherings of pilgrims are seen at Puri who are from all corners of India and abroad irrespective of their religion, sect, caste, creeds, sex and age. It shows the unity in diversity in Indian Society.

Simhachalam is also an important centre of pilgrimage of Hindu India. The decorative architecture and sculpture of Simhachalam temple are very much famous in India and the temple attracts people from all over India even from abroad. The rituals of Lord Narasimha do not differ in essentials from the rituals of other Vishnu temples of South India. In the medieval times, Simhachalam and its environs grew into importance. Simhachalam - the hill of the Lion, is a famous centre of pilgrimage for great Man-Lion, Narasimha the fourth incarnation of Lord Vishnu. The hills and dens are generally conceived to be the abodes of lions, so the temple is dedicated to Lord Narasimha, placed on hill tops. The Simhachalam temple attracts a large number of pilgrims to fulfill their wishes, having different motives and purposes. Devotees visit the temple, take a drip in the Gangadhara, the bathing ghat (Tirthavari) and undergo tonsuring ceremony before entering the temple. The tonsuring ceremony is the most attractive sacred performance at Simhachalam temple for which most of the pilgrims come on pilgrimage to Simhachalam.

During medieval times, Simhachalam and its environs grew into great importance. From 4th century A.D. due to political divisions of ancient times. Simhachalam formed part of Madhyama Kalinga, and the region above it Uttar Kalinga and below it Dakhina Kalinga. Its history is connected with the past of Kalinga (Sunderam : 1969).

This study of two sacred centres will facilitate in bringing out varied features of pilgrimage in Hindu India. The present study is an exploratory and also a descriptive type of study.

The approach of study is both synchronic and diachronic. It is purely an empirical one as most of the data have been collected through anthropological field work methods. Some data have also been collected from secondary sources to know the past history.

Pilgrimage in India during Past

In Hindu India, pilgrimage (Tirtha Yatra) to holy places is an ancient and continuing religious tradition. (Bharadwaj : 90). The concept of pilgrimage is directly associated with the concept of religion which form an important aspect of Indian Society. Even during past period, pilgrimage was a practice of sacred act in India which could hold the belief and faith of people of different communities for long period. The ideology, cultural cohesion and social structure are the most important elements of society which can be studied through pilgrimage. In India, pilgrimage is an old institution and an important aspect of indigenous civilization. It traces back to antiquity and the textural evidences give an idea that even during vedic period it was also in vogue. After Vedic period, the practice of pilgrimage had gained considerably and increased its popularity as referred in epics and puranas. Among Hindus, religion provides the basis of pilgrimage by offering the reward of purification of the soul and attainment of objects related to the problem and existence.

In Hinduism, the pilgrimage (Tirtha - Yatra) does not mean only the physical act of visiting to the holy place/ sacred centres but it also implies to the mental/moral aspect of human beings. Regarding the origin and development of pilgrimage, there are varied opinions and one has to trace back to the early stage of Hindu cultural traditions. Its antiquity is evidenced by both Brahminical and the Buddhist literature. The nature and spread of pilgrimage are found in the Rig-Veda where it has been suggested that in order to wash 'evil' or 'sin' people used to undertake journey to the sacred rivers for purification and redemption from sin.

In Veda, the 'Mahatma' (religious importance) of rivers are described, known as Nadi - Stuti (river hymn) and in Smritis, the sanctity of the rivers is stressed which used the term 'Tritha' (centre of pilgrimage) in describing them. The Aryan people of Vedic period used to refer the rivers and grow the concept of tirtha. The water of mythological rivers, particularly the Ganges, the Saraswati, the Jamuna etc. were believed to have been endowed with special merit. The Vishnu-Smriti gives us an exhaustive list of the Tirthas, spread over whole of ancient India. It recommends Tirtha Yatra (pilgrimage) which is equated with Ashvamedha Yagna (Vedic form of horse sacrifice), as the effective means of expiation for all sins. The Manu-Smriti also attaches a great importance to pilgrimage. A number of epics also mention about Tirtha Yatra which were undertaken by the people.

In Mahabharat, a section of Vanaprava (Chapter 78-158) entitled "Tirtha Yatra-Prava" is exclusively devoted to pilgrimage.

The 'Puranas' and 'Upa-puranas' are the main sources of information on pilgrimage. The 'Tirthasthala' the place of pilgrimage and Kshetra-Mahatma, the importance of the centre of pilgrimage are the two important parts of Puranas dealing in great detail with the efficacy of pilgrimage and the righteous way of life a pilgrim is required to lead during Tirtha-Yatra (Pilgrimage) (Vidyarthi; Jha; Saraswati: 1976 : 126). Besides the epics and purans, the writers of the Nibandhas (Digests and Commentaries) emphasized on the types, nature and importance of Hindu pilgrimage of medieval India.

It has also been mentioned in the Indian history about the reports of the foreign travelers like Meghasthenese (3rd century B.C.), Fa-Hien (5th Century A.D.), Hieun Tsian (7th Century A.D.) who have clearly described about the various places of pilgrimage in ancient India.

Crooke (1956) observes : " The origin of the modern practice of pilgrimage may be traced back to the revival of Brahminism and its absorption of local cults. Every place where a local spirit was propitiated or worshipped soon came under the control of a body of local priests, interested in attracting visitors because their offerings formed their means of livelihood". Diehl (quoted by Bhardwaj, 1973) describes the motives of pilgrimage under two categories. First, there is commitment or vow to the deity whose blessing is sought for the solution of a problem the pilgrim is afflicted with. Here there may be improvement of such rites as the first hair cut of a male child or expiation for a ritual impurity that an individual may have acquired. The second motive is to earn religious merit, which may include a holypath, sight of a deity, or visiting holy men. Bharati believes that pilgrimage proper is not mentioned in the vedic literature but Bharadwaj believes that the Aryan people of vedic period used to rever the rivers (Nadi-stuti) which had ultimately given the concept of Tirtha.

Numerous Hindus places of pilgrimage spread all over India. Although there are a large number of sects in

Hinduism, out of them three sects, i.e., Vaishava, Shaiva and Shakta are more dominant and popular Hindu sects. The sacred centres belonging to these three sects of Hinduism are distributed all over India. Holy places of various sects throughout India have created an essentially continuous "sacred geography" in which various regional cultural diversities become less significant for the movement of pilgrims from long distances.

In India, the sacred centres have exerted a powerful pull on believers beginning from the most ancient civilization to the present time. The sacred centres of India patronised by different sects are Puri, Simhachalam, Dwarika, Prayag, Kashi, Kanchi, Rameswaram, Ayodhya, Mathura, Ujjain, Nasik, Kamakhya, etc. They are widely distributed in India which will ultimately strength the national solidarity. Both at the textual and contextual levels, the rules of pilgrimage are liberal so also democratic in nature.

In ancient times, the institute of pilgrimage was also an important part of Hindu life. People practised it with full devotion, faith and courage and faced a lot of difficulties during their pilgrimage. Earlier pilgrims used to visit the sacred centres and shrines annually or periodically on foot, preferably during dry months of the year because of lack of communication and transport system. One could rarely visit sacred places and shrines alone or in the company of family members and relatives, which were in nearby places. But to distant places pilgrims used to go in groups because such types of journeys were risky and hazardous. Roads were not there, bridges had not been constructed across rivers, portable water was not available and pilgrims were always susceptible to epidemic and way side matching. Train services were only available in India during 19th century and no other mechanical; quick public transport system was available for the pilgrims. Very few sacred centres had the provision of dharmasala or public lodging houses. There were no hotels, or other accommodation for different categories of pilgrims.

It is believed that there is a sacred aim with certain specific object behind it to fulfill the desire of obtaining

'Punya' (Pious) and to get rid of 'Papa' (Sin). In India, the sacred centres generate a complex network of socio-religious elements regulating the entire Hindu population. India is so large and the practice of pilgrimage is so popular that the entire India can be regarded as vast sacred 'Kshetras' organised into a system of pilgrimage centre of varied importance.

It would not be out of context to quote Mendelbaum who suggested that pilgrimage to sacred centres reinforce religious precepts but also impress the pilgrims with vastness, the diversity and seemingly paradoxically the oneness of the society".

Pilgrimage at present in India

To the centres of pilgrims like Puri and Simhachalam, different types of pilgrims are coming throughout the year from different social strata of Indian society. The Sacred places of India serve the local, regional and the entire Hindu Universe through sacred activities. They are the meeting places for different kinds of people and traditions, of castes and sects, of class and status, thus it nourishes a sense of unity. So the sacred centres are the places where exchange of ideas and ways of life and tradition take place.

It is observed that amongst the pilgrims at Puri, the female pilgrims outnumber the males, particularly Hindu widows who visit the temple twice daily to earn piety and ritual merit. Normally local pilgrim prefer to come to temple in the evening time and offer *deepas* (lamps), *bhogas* (edibles) with incense sticks and flowers to Deities. On festive occasions the number of pilgrims visit temple increases five to ten times as compared to normal days because pilgrims from nearby villages come to attended the festival at Puri very frequently.

At present, there are regular visits of pilgrims of all over India to Puri and Simhachalam showing their sense of religiosity and deep faith and devotion towards the Hindu deities. To Puri for Rath-Yatra (Car festival) about five to six lakhs of pilgrims come to observe the occasion irrespective of their caste, class, creeds, sect, language, religion, status and all. Similarly to Simhachalam temple, for 'Chandan

Yatra' (sandalwood paste festival) of Lord Narsimha, about forty to fifty thousand pilgrims gather to observe the occasion with full devotion.

Puri, the sacred centre, has two faces, it has holy aspect centred on Jagannath temple and other sacred places in its precincts which the pilgrims are solemnly enjoined to circumambulate ; it has also a profare aspect confined to the seashore and modern hotels and to which the holiday makers come in thousands during holidays. After making sacred performances, some pilgrims visit different places of tourist interests of Orissa. The daily activities of pilgrims, irrespective of age, sex, caste, education, profession during their pilgrimage vary from person to person. Old-aged pilgrims are more kin to spend more time inside the temple. They are more—interested to have holy bath in Swetaganga pond, in Narendra pond, in Mahodadhi (Sea) water in early hours of the day. But youths and middle aged pilgrims are having likeness to visit and enjoy different places at Puri after having puja and darshan of Lord. The activities of pilgrims at Puri are regulated by their socio-economic conditions and religious beliefs and practices.

Below are given tables on 'Pilgrims and pilgrimages' at Puri and Simhachalam

Tables showing types of pilgrims and characteristic features of pilgrims at Puri and Simhachalam.

S. No.	*Particulars of pilgrim*	*Puri*		*Simachalam*	
		No. of pilgrims N= 500	*Percent-age*	*No. of Pilgrims N= 200*	*Percent-age*
1	*2*	*3*	*4*	*5*	*6*
I.	Types of Pilgrims				
	1. Local	90	18%	24	12%
	2. Regional	115	23%	76	38%
	3. National	290	58%	96	48%
	4. International	5	1%	4	2%
II.	Characteristic Features of Pilgrims				
1.	Sex				

Contd.

Contd.

1	*2*	*Puri* *3*	*4*	*Simhachalam* *5*	*6*
	(a) Male	331	66.20%	160	80%
	(b) Female	169	33.80%	40	20%
2.	Marital Status				
	(a) Married	412	82.40%	120	60%
	(b) Unmarried	58	11.60%	72	36%
	(c) Widow	20	4%	4	2%
	(d) Widower	10	2%	4	2%
3.	Age Group (in years)				
	(a) 10 - 19	2	0.40%	12	6%
	(b) 20 - 29	108	21.60%	56	28%
	(c) 30 - 39	120	24%	32	16%
	(d) 40 - 49	109	21.80%	44	22%
	(e) 50 - 59	83	16.60%	40	20%
	(f) 60 - 69	66	13.20%	8	4%
	(g) 70 - 79	8	1.60%	4	2%
	(h) 80 - 89	4	0.80%	4	2%
4.	Occupation				
	(a) Service	188	37.60%	72	36%
	(b) Business	86	17.20%	42	21%
	(c) Farming	81	16.20%	20	10%
	(d) Priesthood	18	3.60%	8	4%
	(e) Wagelabour	32	6.40%	6	3%
	(f) Householdwork	70	14%	28	8%
	(g) Studentship	20	4%	16	8%
	(h) Nothing	5	1%	8	4%
5.	Income (Per month in rupees)				
	(a) <500	90	18%	88	44%
	(b) 500-1000	246	49.20%	24	12%
	(C 1000-1500	74	14.80%	48	24%
	(d) 1500-2000	37	7.40%	16	8%
	(e) 2000-2500	16	3.20%	6	3%

Contd.

Contd.

1	2	Puri 3	4	Simhachalam 5	6
	(f) 2500-3000	22	4.40%	8	4%
	(g) 3000 and above	15	3%	10	5%
6.	Religion				
	(a) Hindu	490	98%	192	96%
	(b) Others	10	2%	8	4%
7.	Educational Qualification				
	(a) Illiterate	20	4.40%	20	10%
	(b) Primary	48	9.60%	28	14%
	(c) M.E.	36	7.20%	20	10%
	(d) Undermatric	76	15.20%	16	8%
	(e) Matriculation	114	22.20%	32	16%
	(f) Intermediate	30	6%	16	8%
	(g) Graduate	99	19.80%	36	18%
	(h) Post-Graduate	43	8.60%	12	6%
	(i) Technical Education	17	3.40%	12	6%
	(J) Others	15	3%	8	4%
8.	Mother Tongue				
	(a) Oriya	176	35.20%	16	8%
	(b) Hindi	98	19.60%	60	30%
	(c) Bengali	82	16.40%	8	4%
	(d) Telgu	15	3%	100	50%
	(e) Marwadi (Rajasthani)	89	17.80%	-	-
	(f) Chhatishgarhi (M.P.)	6	1.20%	-	-
	(g) Urdu	2	0.40%	-	-
	(h) Marathi	11	2.20%	4	2%
	(i) Manipuri	5	1%	-	-
	(j) Punjabi	4	0.80%	-	-
	(k) Kannada	-	-	6	3%
	(l) Konkani	-	-	2	1%
	(m) Tamil	-	-	4	2%
	(n) Others	12	2.40%		
9.	Caste Category				
	(a) Brahmin	125	25%	48	24%

Contd.

Contd.

1	2	Puri 3	4	Simhachalam 5	6
	(b) Kshyatriya	50	10%	24	12%
	(c) Vaishya	120	24%	40	20%
	(d) Sudra	100	20%	60	30%
	(e) S.C.	60	12%	16	8%
	(f) S.T. & Others	45	9%	12	6%
10.	Family Type				
	(a) Nuclear	325	65%	104	52%
	(b) Joint	175	35%	96	48%
11.	Family Size				
	(a) Two	80	16%	20	10%
	(b) Three	100	20%	40	20%
	(c) Four	75	15%	32	16%
	(d) Five	60	12%	8	4%
	(e) Six	10	2%	4	2%
	(f) Seven	65	13%	28	14%
	(g) Eight and above	110	22%	68	34%
12.	Sect				
	(a) Hindu	490	98%	192	96%
	Vaishnavite	475	95%	144	72%
	Saivite	5	1%	40	20%
	Sakta	10	2%	8	4%
	(b) Non-Hindu	10	2%	8	4%
13.	Devoted Towards				
	(a) Lord Jagannath	150	30%	14	7%
	(b) Lord Vishnu	185	37%	56	28%
	(c) Lord Venkateshwar	11	2.20%	40	20%
	(d) Lord Rama	105	21%	4	2%
	(e) Lord Siva	15	.3%	40	20%
	(f) Goddess Sakti	5	11%	8	4%
	(g) Lord Hanuman	3	0.60%	2	1%
	(h) Lord Narsimha	4	0.80%	24	12%
	(i) Lord Mahavir	4	0.80%	—	—
	(j) No Specific deity	18	3.60%	12	6%

The above tables show the different types of pilgrims coming to Puri and Simhachalam for pilgrimage. Total number of pilgrims taken from Puri is five hundred where as from Simhachlam it is two hundred. Demographic characters of pilgrims of both Puri and Simhachalam such as their age, sex, marital status, occupation, income, education, family size, family type are taken. Besides these informations regarding their caste group, native place, religion etc. are collected for the present study.

At present among Hindus it is observed that the purposes and motives of pilgrims are diverse and multipurposed. The sacred centres are the places where many varieties of rituals and devotional activities are carried on. They include several types of offerings, fire rituals, prayers and recitations, observances of some sacraments and festivals, sacred baths, water offerings, etc. Vidyarthi (1961), Singer (1955) have referred such activities as cultural performances. In Indian civilization the similarity between religion and rest of the culture might be a valid consideration.

Nowadays, pilgrims have come to pilgrim centres with two types of motives First motive may be concerned with mundane existence, i.e., involvement with a commitment or vow to the deity whose blessing is sought for the solution of a problem, the pilgrim is afflicted with. It may be concerned with *mundan* (hair cutting), *Upanayana* (sacred thread ceremony), marriage or to have a son, or to get a job or quick promotion in service and so on. The second category of motive consists of earning religious merit through the holy bath, darshan of Deities, visiting holy places, holymen, etc. This religious merit of *Punya* ultimately leads to *Moksa* (Salvation) as conceived by the pilgrims.

Thus irrespective of the time period (past or present) the religious pilgrimage is undertaken by the Hindus to get Moksa or to have moksa one has to earn dharma, the religious merit. That is the universal purpose of pilgrimage which can be fulfilled only by visiting different pilgrim centres. In Hindu pantheon, various types of Gods and Goddesses are worshipped for the fulfillment of various desires by the pilgrim.

The importance of pilgrimage in the cultural evolution of the Hindu people can hardly be ignored. From remote past, this institution has preserved the spiritual aspirations of the people and created stimulation in the Hindu mind a deep love for its culture and civilization inspite of its diversities. Gradually the institution of pilgrimage has become more popular and more people visit sacred centres than ever before in the history of India. It may be the fact that people have not become more religious, rather it is because of modern means of transport systems which made it easier for large number of pilgrims to undertake pilgrimage at different centres more frequently.

Pilgrimage has increased several fold since 1950's with the improvement in road communication, development of mechanical system of transport and expansion of facilities of accommodation at different pilgrim centres of India.

Such studies have contributed substantially towards an understanding of the role of religious institutions in maintaining and modifying the structure of the larger social system. However, it has been found out that modernization has direct impact and influence on the institution of pilgrimage and in the performance of religious act. Nowadays, modern technologies are quite responsible to increase the speed of the rate of the practice of pilgrimage at various sacred centres of India. So Hindu Pilgrimage is an indigenous institution and the most popular religious practice among Hindus today.

References

Acharya Sabita 1997, *Pilgrimage in Indian Civilization* by Manak Publications, New Delhi.

Bharati Agehananda 1990-91, "Grammatical and Notational models of Indian Pilgrimage" in *Social Anthropology of Pilgimage* (ed) M. Jha, Inter-India Publication, New Delhi.

Bharadwaj, S. Mohan 1973, *Hindu Places of Pilgrimage in India,* Thomson Press (India), New Delhi.

Eschman, A, Kulke, J and Tripathy G.C. 1978, *The cult of Jagannath and Regional traditions of Orissa* (ed) published by Manohar Publication, N. Delhi.

Jha, Makhan 1971, *Sacred Complex in Janakpur,* United Publishers, Allahabad.

Jha, Makhan 1990-91, *Social Anthropology of Pilgrimage* (ed) Published by Inter-India Publications, N. Delhi.

Jha, Makhan 1978, *Rising India : An Urban Anthropological Approach to Puri,* Classical Publications, New Delhi.

Jha, Makhan 1979, *The Dimensions of Indian Civilization,* Classical Publications, New Delhi.

Redfield, Robort 1995 *The Little Community* by University of Chicago Press, Chicago.

Redfield, Robert and Singer, Milton 1956, "Cultural role of Cites" *Man-in-India,* Vol.36, No.3, Calcutta.

Sunderam, K.1984, *The Simhachalam Temple* by Simhachalam Devastanam. Simhachalam, Andhra Pradesh.

Srinivas, M.N. 1952, *Religion and Society among Coorgs of South India* by Oxford.

Singer, Milton 1972, *When a great tradition modernizes,* Praeger Publishers, New York.

Vidyarthi, L.P. (1961), *The Sacred Complex of Hindu Gaya,* Asia Publishing House, Bombay.

Vidyarthi, L.P., Saraswati B.N., and Jha, Makhan (1979), *Sacred Complex of Kashi - A microcosn of Indian Civilization,* Concept Publishing Company, New Delhi.

7

Pilgrims to Kashi Self-Organized Patterns in Space and Time

J.McKim Malville,
Rana P.B. Singh

Kashi as a Tirtha

Varanasi, the holiest city of Hinduism and Kashi, its sacred centre, have been the object of a vast collection of literature and mythology. Recent analysis of phosphates in the soils of Varanasi suggest an age of 2800 years, which makes it one of the most ancient and continuously occupied cities of the world. (Eidt 1977) Lying on the west bank of the Ganga, the city is an ancient *tirtha,* a "crossing-over" place, where heaven and earth meet, providing access for humans to the gods and a route for the gods to enter the human realm. Together with Prayaga and Gaya, Varanasi is one of the three great tirthas of India. (Singh 1987; Eck 1983)

The word *tirtha* is derived from the Sanskrit root *tr* meaning to ford or cross a river. Tirtha initially designated a place where a river was fordable, which was initially chosen entirely for its practical value. While crossing travelers might take a bath, either intentionally or inadvertently. Since the act of bathing has such great ritual significance for Hindu, many tirthas denote a spot on a river where the act of taking a bath had a very special importance. The significance of a particular tirtha, such as Varanasi, would have been established through the accumulation of historical events associated with countless generations of travelers crossing a river at a particular spot; thus travelers might camp on the banks prior to crossing; traders, merchants, priests may congregate there to provide services for the travelers. Not by coincidence, the Grand Trunk Road sweeping across northern India between Calcutta and Delhi fords the Ganga at Varanasi. Over the millennia the build-up layer upon layer of memory would sanctify the spot. With time in Hindu India, the presence of a river was not necessary, and the term tirtha was extended to any holy spot, with or without water, that affords an opportunity for crossing over between realms of earth and heaven. The gods come down and humans ascend.

The most famous descent into Varanasi was by Lord Shiva, the mountain ascetic, who needed to find a suitable home for himself and his bride Parvati, daughter of the Himalayas. He scanned the entire earth from the high Himalayan peak on which he lived, Mt. Kailash, and chose Varanasi as the most beautiful place on earth, a place of streams, springs, dense forests on the edge of the Ganga, bejeweled with palaces, gardens, and temples. The mountain god, descended to Kashi became both a family man and a city man in the Forest of Bliss. It is now difficult to imagine the former great beauty of such a crowded city, but not very many centuries ago the land was full of pools and lakes through which pure water flowed. Temples and ashrams sat on the edges of lakes and streams in the forest in quiet seclusion.

Water is a central part of the collection of memories that is Kashi. The memory of water is deep, extending back to the origins of life itself. Dark water was present before the dawn of life on our planet, and today water provides a bridge to those beginnings. At dawn on the ghats of the Ganga as pilgrims dip into the Ganga, they move back in time, symbolically die to the world and then are reborn into the light of the rising sun which is itself reborn every morning. One of the greatest bathing festivals on the ghats is on the morning of new moon following Makara Samkranti, when the sun enters the constellation of Makaram, Sagittarius, which it once did on winter solastice, when the old year dies, and the new year is starting. On that morning, major primordial events are re-enacted: the birth of the moon, the birth of the year, and the birth of the day. The birth of life in the waters of the Ganga is celebrated in the river at the place where its waters are flowing northward to the place of the river's birth.

Beyond the river's edge, beyond the walls of buildings, beyond the narrow alleyways is a network pilgrimage paths, the yatras of Kashi, the sacred and cosmic reals of Varanasi. Therein lies a complex pilgrimage landscape established by the footprints of pilgrims, shrines, temples, and memory, with interlinking alignments in space and multilayered structures of time (Singh 1991).

The Yatras of Varanasi

The *Padma Purana (Shristi Khanda, 65.14-20),* a 7th century text, describes the sacred territory of Kashi at the centre of which lies at Madhyameshvara. Madhyameshvara refers to Lord Shiva around whom the universe revolves; Shiva keeps the universe alive and energized through his dance of destruction and creation; Madhya is the centre and Ishvara is his name. The largest circumambulatory circuit covers 168 miles (296 km or 84 krosha) and is known as *Brihata Panchakroshi,* or *Chaurashikroshi Yatra.* Rarely performed now because of the lack of time of modern busy pilgrims, its exact route is not well known. In the past the journey was completed in 10 days, and it involved visiting 144 shrines.

During the past few centuries, this circuit has shrunk down to the present Panchakroshi and the three yatras that lie inside it. The Panchakroshiyatra covers a distance of 5x5 *krosha (i.e.,* 55.2 miles/88.6 km), requiring five nights and six days of walking and 108 shrines (this ubiquitous number has astronomical roots: 12 signs of the zodiac and 9 planets; or 4 cardinal directions, three realms of the cosmos and 9 planets; or 27 days of the lunar sidereal cycle and 4 directions). The circuit has two centres, the ancient centre of Kashi at Madhyameshvara and the ritual centre of Kashi at the Jnanavapi well where the initiation and concluding rites for most of the yatras take place (Singh 1991). The start of the pilgrimage starts with a ritual bath at

Manikarnika ghat, the great cremation ghat of Varanasi, followed by a vow to complete the pilgrimage at the Jnanavapi well, the current centre of the city. The first 17 shrines are along the banks of the Ganga. This is a landscape that is rich in memories. As many generations of Hindus have followed the same pathway, visited the same shrines, watched the same sun rising through the mists, and performed darshan to the same gods and goddesses.

Inside the Panchakroshi is the *Nagar Pradakshina,* covering 25 km and containing 72 shrines. The fourth level, *Avimukta,* also contains 72 shrines; the name *Avimukta* means the "Never Forsaken" zone, a place where Lord Shiva will never forsake, even a time of the dissolution of the cosmos. The journey to the "inner sanctum", the *Antargriha,* spirals seven times from Manikarnika Devi into Vishveshvara and contains 72 shrines. Among its various meanings, the number seven refers to the seven realms of the heavens and the seven visible planets. Its presence in the inner sanctum of Kashi signifies the similarity of the macrocosm and microcosm.

These five sacred routes are identified with the five gross elements (sky, earth, air, water, and fire) and the five parts of the human body (head, legs, face, blood, and heart), affirming similarity of the macrocosm, the mesocosm of the sacred realm of Kashi, and the microcosm of the human body. (Singh 1993) By means of the simple act of walking through this space, the pilgrim participates in a non-verbal lesson about the symbolic structure of the cosmos and the connections between the divine and the human realms. Another pilgrimage route in Kashi incorporating cosmic symbolism is that of the 56 Vinayakas, which contains its seven spirals and eight directions of space. All of these are examples of self-similarity, which is an important characteristic of self-organized systems.

Self-Organization of Pilgrimage Landscapes

Pilgrimage landscapes contain the cumulative memories of generations of individuals who have moved across space in search of the sacred and holy. Similar to forest and ocean ecosystems, these landscapes can develop self-organized structures in space and time with repeating constellations of fractal patterns (Mandelbrot 1977) (Appendix). These patterns will emerge from a landscape only if it is open to new energies, has a unity built of multiple interconnections of interacting entities, and is not dominated by processes striving to maintain permanence and equilibrium (Malville 2001). Fractal patterns will not appear if there are too few individuals to achieve coherence and inter-connectedness. Non-interacting individuals arrive on a landscape like random strokes of lightning and contribute little to collective memory. Random events leave few memories; there is no memory in the toss of dice just as there is no memory in the imposed geometry of circle or square. All circles and squares are alike and in spite of their geometrical elegance they carry little information.

Between these extremes of randomness and perfect order lies of the realm of maximum embedded memory, which has also been described as "lying at the edge of chaos" (Kaufmann 1995) this is the region of snowflakes, complex forest ecosystems (Levin 1999), structures in the great herds of wildebeests in the Screngeti Plains, forest fires (Malamud, Morein, and Turcotte 1998), avalanches of sand and rice (Bak 1996), and fractals (Cambel 1993). Two important characteristics of self-organized patterns are self-similarity, wherein similar patterns are repeated at different sizes, and the presence of power law distributions of sizes of patterns. There are many more small self-organized patterns than large once, and the very simple mathematical model of a power law can reproduce this behaviour. The frequency of occurrence of a particular size decreases as a power of the size of the pattern or of the structures within it.

In real ecosystems, self-similarity and power law distributions are statistical; repeated structures are never exactly alike. An actual snowflake in the natural world with its approximate six-fold symmetry is never perfect. The structure of the snowflake reflects the variations of temperature, humidity, wind, and pressure as it moved through the atmosphere, and consequently no two snowflakes, while they may be statistically self-similar, will ever be exactly identical. For those who can read them, there is a vast amount of detailed information about atmospheric conditions that is obtainable from their broken symmetries.

The power law distribution is the fingerprint of self-organization that we can use in our search for the spontaneous patterns of nature, mature ecosystems, and other fractal landscapes (see Appendix). The sizes of fords of Norway and other coastlines have well-established power law distributions (Mandelbrot 1977) as do features of forest communities (Levin and Buttrel 1997; Sole and Manrubia 1995), forest fires (Malamud, Morein, and Turcotte 1996), and even wars (Roberts and Turcotte 1998).

We first investigated the structure of shrines along the pilgrimage circuit of Mt. Kailash in Tibet, the most sacred mountain of south Asia by measuring the positions of the 54 major shines of its Kora with GPS. We found evidence for self-organization in the presence of a power law in the spacing of adjacent shrines. The frequently distribution of separation varies with a power of -1.5. We extended our measurements to the 108 shrines of the Panchakroshi yatra and found a similar distribution with a power of -1.4. Further measurements of all of the shrines along the four inner yatras of Varanasi, a total of 324 shrines, gave a distribution with a power of-1.5.

The recurrent power law in these two major pilgrimage circuits of Asia is a remarkable result. Although a power law is a necessary but not a sufficient condition for self-organization, these results do suggest pilgrimage landscapes can mimic the natural world. It provides a fascinating new perspective on an issue that has challenged philosophers for millennia (Prigogine 1997). The old dualistic concept of a fundamental difference between nature with its laws and humans with their creativity finds no support in these pilgrimage landscapes. When people become pilgrims and behave in a spontaneous manner as members of a self-interacting group, they become one with nature. In contrast, when a pilgrimage tradition is taken over by authority or rigid tradition, it loses its spontaneity and its characteristics of self-organization. There should be a full range of pilgrimage landscapes across the world, some self-organized and others with imposed structures, some remaining open to newness, spontaneity, and self-discovery, and others closed by rigid tradition.

Patterns in Time

When coherence and inter-connectedness prevail in an open system, small "disturbances" such as new ideas or new concentrations of people may not be locally contained or suppressed but may spread across the land. In such systems these of information, ideas, or people have no fundamental scale, which means that their sizes have a power law distribution. There is a new physics involved that is not taught in our introductory university courses: departures from equilibrium yield the most interesting forms of nature and fundamental particles no longer are the goal of all our searches. In a manner similar to the concept of emptiness in Buddhism, one searches but cannot find an absolute and fundamental scale that is the "building block" for all structures.

Forest fires are well-studied examples of pulses of energy in which, as we have already noted there is a power law distribution of sizes of fires (Malamud, Morein and Turcotte 1998). It is a small matter to extend the concept of pulses of forest fires to pilgrimage in which the "ignition" by an idea or motivation causes moving pulses of people, igniting multiple cascades of further pilgrims and even new types of pilgrimages.

The Gangetic basin and the whole of the sub-continent serve as the catchment basin for pilgrimage to Varanasi using the terminology of the Turners (Turner 1969; Turner and Turner 1978). If the catchment area functions as a self-organized landscape, pulses of people that move through the catchment basin on their way to Kashi should have distributions of sizes that also follow a power law. In order to test this proposal we recorded the hourly visitors to Asi Ghat over a period of 600 days between November 1999 and May 2001. All together, we have records of more than 1.3 million visitors.

Visitors to Asi Ghat arrive in great numbers at the time of festivals, and they also come every morning throughout the year. Festivals are established by the lunar-solar calendar, and we discovered a strong connectivity in time among the pilgrims. The following table gives the total numbers of visitors to Asi Ghat during major festivals of 1998, 1999, and 2000 and the specific festival of the lunar-calendar (Singh 1994). Note the small differences from one year to the next for specific festivals, which are most remarkable considering that people are coming from separate points of origin and from great distances. Consider, for example, the visitors during Shivaratri in the two years, 1999 and 2000, the numbers of which differed by only 1556 or 1.7 per cent.

Numbers of Visitors to Asi Ghat

				%diff
1.	Makara Samkranti			
		1999	2000	
	January 14-15	37802	45293	4.51%
2.	Maha Shivaratri	14-Feb-99	4-Mar-00	
	Shiva's night	21712	23262	1.73%
	Phalguna, K-13			
3.	Karttika Purnima	4-Nov-98	23-Nov-99	
	Kartikka, S-15	33536	37382	2.71%
4.	Margasira Purnima	3-Dec-98	22-Dec-99	
	Margashira, S-15	21658	22090	0.49%
5.	Surya Shasthi		15-Nov-99	
	Chhatha		38265	
	Karttika, S-7			
6.	Magha Amavasya	17-Jan-99	5-Feb-00	
	Mauni Amavasya	10344	10569	0.54%
	Magha, K -15			
7.	Magha Purnima	31-Jan-99	19-Feb-00	
	Magha, S-15	5809	5246	2.55%
8.	Prabodhini Ekad-ashi Karttika, S-11	31-Oct-98	19-Nov-99	
		9292	8649	-1.79%
9.	Basant Panchami	22-Jan-99	10-Feb-00	
	Magha, S-5	7163	2196	-26.54%

Table 1

Festival	*Dates*	*Numbers*	*Average Atter-nance*	*Annual Differ-ence*	*Percent Differ-ence*
Makara Samkranti	14-15 Jan1999	37802			
January 14/15	14-15 Jan 2000	45293	41547.5	7491	18%
Maha	14 Feb 1999	21712			
Shivaratri	4 March 2000	23268	22490	1556	7%
Karttika	4 Nov 1998	33536			
Purnima	23 Nov 1999	37382	35459	3846	11%
Margasira	3 Dec 1998	21658			
Purnima	22 Dec 1999	22090	21874	432	2%
Magha	17 Jan 1999	10344			
Amavasya	5 Feb 2000	10569	10456.5	225	2%
Magha	31 Jan 1999	5809			
Purnima	19 Feb 2000	5246	5527.5	563	10%
Prabodhini	31 Oct 1998	9292			
Ekadashi	19 Nov 1999	8649	8970.5	643	7%

When we look at the numbers of hourly visitors to Asi Ghat we find that they fall into three major categories : (1) On those days, especially in the cool mornings of winter, when there are fewer than approximately 300 people arriving per hour, the system has not achieved self-organization and the pulses of visitors do not have a power law distribution. (2) When there are between approximately 300 and 2500 people per hour arriving at Asi Ghat, the system has achieved sufficient connectivity and mutual interactions that the system becomes self-organized. The sizes of pulses of people follow a power law with a power of -2.9. (3) At the time of major festivals when there are more than 2500 people arriving per hour, the system continues to be self-organized, but with a slightly different form. In this case the frequency of arrival of different sizes of groups has a power of-2.3. If people arrived entirely at random their numbers should follow a Poisson or an exponential function, which would be quite different from the power law distribution we have measured.

Consulting Remarks

These examples of power law distributions are consistent with pilgrimage as a coherent self-organized process. When pilgrims always walk across the land as members of a moving community they create enduring patterns, sometimes in parallel to the patterns of the sun and moon. The Turners speak of the *communitas* of pilgrimage (Turner and Turner 1978), and in many pilgrimage landscapes that community extends from earth to the heavens.

In the great trajectory of time that has swept through the universe since the onset of expansion some 15 billion years ago new patterns have emerged from the nearly infinite possibilities of Primordial Chaos. The future is a perpetual new construction, not a guaranteed product of deterministic laws.

In this study we have compared pilgrimage with biological and geological phenomena that similarly display self-organization. We believe, however, that the human processes that resulted in the placement of shrines and pulses of pilgrims are vastly more complex than the geophysical processed that generate fractal patterns in physical landscapes or even the intricate biological processes operating in complex ecosystems.

In self-organized pilgrimages, it is necessary that the system be open, that energy and ideas come and go, that individuals be spontaneous and free. In India, the scale of coherence and interaction is mind boggling in its vastness, extending across thousands of km of the subcontinent, involving the coherent behaviour of millions of people who individually and collectively are seeking an experience of the holy and sacred. By the movement of their feet pilgrims provide maps and new meaning for an entire land.

Appendix

Fractals and Power Laws

Self organization is characterized by a power law distribution of the sizes of its elements such the number of elements of a size r is given by

$N = Ar^{-D}$

where the power, D, may be defined as the fractal dimension.

Scale invariance of self-similarity is demonstrated by changing the scale of measurement from r to kr, where k is a scaling factor, as if one were to magnify or demagnify an image. The image in its essence remains. The power law behavior remains unchanged and retains the same dimension:

$N = Ar^{-D}$ becomes $Ak^{-D}r^{-D}$

or simply

$N = Br^{-D}$

We may test for scale invariance by means of log-log plots of geographic features and of time series.

Pattern	*Dimension (Cambel 1993)*
Koch snowflake	1.262
Sierpinsky triangle	1.585
Atmospheric clouds	2.35
Woods Plants	1.28-1.79
Sea anemone	1.6
Coast lines	1.05-1.25
Turbulant flames 2.33	
Pilgrimage circuits 1.5	
Time Series:	1.3-1.5 (Malamud,
Forest Fires	Morein,Turcotte 1998)
Pilgrims to Asi Ghat2.3-2.9	

Square or rectangular geometries with a dimension precisely equal to 2 are found in planned pre-conceived ritual landscapes such a royal city designed as the geometrically perfect "cosmic" cities of China or a Hindu temple built according to precise mathematical rules. With only a single dimension, these structures do not show power law distributions.

Scale invariance and self-similarity are fundamental characteristics of fractals. First introduced by Mandelbrot, fractals were so named because of their fractional dimensions, such as 1.6 for the sea-anemone or 2.35 for clouds. Freedom from imposed dimensions of 1, 2 or 3 make fractals common features of the natural world. The real fractals found in nature are not geometrically precise or mathematically deterministic like the Mandelbrot set or other well-known fractals such as the Sierpinski triangle, or the von Koch snowflake. Like the actual snowflake with its damaged edges and broken symmetries, fractals of nature posses a statistical self-similarity in that patterns at different levels of scale are similar but never exactly duplicated.

Acknowledgments

We are most grateful for the field assistance we have received from Dasarath, Ryan Gaylord, Ryan Keenan, Ryan Wallace, and Colin Flahive.

References

Bak, Per 1996. *How Nature Works: The Science of Self-Organized Criticality*. Copernicus, New York.

Cambel, A.B.1993. *Applied Chaos Theory, A Paradigm for Complexity*. Academic Press, Boston.

Eck, Diana. 1983. *Banaras, City of Light*. London: Routledge and Kegan Paul.

Eidt, R.S. 1977. Detection and Examination of Anthroposols by Phosphate Analysis. *Science* 197: 1327-1333.

Kaufmann, Stuart. 1995. *At Home in the Universe*. New York: Oxford University Press.

Levin, Simon. 1999. *Fragile Domain: Complesity and the Commons*. Reading: Prscus Books.

Levin, Simon and Linda Buttel. 1997. *Measurements of Patchiness in Ecological Systems.* Ithaca: Cornal University.

Malamud, Bruce D., Gleb Morein, and Donald L. Turcotte. 1998. Forest Fires: An Example of Self-Organized Critical Behaviour. *Science* 281: 1840-1841.

Malville, John McKim. 2001. "The Paradigm of Self-Organization: From Village to Pilgrimage" in *The Nature of Man and Culture: Alternative Paradigms in Anthropology,* edited by B.N. Saraswati. Delhi: Indira Gandhi National Centre for the Arts.

Mandelbrot, B.B. 1977. *Fractals: Form, Chance, and Dimension.* San Francisco: Freeman.

Prigogine, Illya. 1980. *From Being to Becoming. Time and Complexity in the Physical Sciences.* New York: W.II. Freeman and Co.

..... 1997. *The End of Certainty: Time, Chaos, and the New Laws of Nature.* New York: The Free Press.

Roberts, D.C. and Donald L. Turcotte, 1998. Fractality and Self-Organized Criticality of Wars. *Fractals* 6: 351-357.

Saraswati, B.N. 1985. "Kashi pilgrimage: the End of an Endlesss Journey," in *Dimensions of pilgrimage.* Edited by M.Jha. New Delhi: Inter-India Publications.

Singh, Rana P.B. 1987. The Pilgrimage Mandala of Varanasi (Kashi). *National Geographical Journal of India* 33: 493-524.

— 1991. *Pancakroshi Yatra, Varanasi: Sacred Journey, Ecology of Place and Faithscape.* Varanasi: Tara Book Agency.

— 1993. "Varanasi: the Pilgrimage Mandala, Geomantic Map, and Cosmic Numbers," in *Banaras (Varanasi): Cosmic Order, Sacred City, Hindu Traditions.* Edited by Rana P.B. Singh, pp. 37-64. Varanasi: Tara Book Agency.

— 1994. "Time and Hindu Rituals in Varansi: a Study of Sacrality and Cyclcs," in *Pilgrimage Studies: Text and Context.* Edited by L. Gopal and D.P. Dubey, pp.67-72. Allahabad: The Society of Pilgrimage Studies.

Solc, Ricardo V. and Susanna C. Manrubia. 1995. Are Rainforests Self-organized in a Critical State? *Journal of Theoretical Biology* 173: 31-40.

Turner, V.1969. *The Ritual Process. Structure and Anti-Structure,* Chicago: Aldine Publishing Company.

Turner, V. and E. Turner. 1978. *Image and Pilgrimage in Christian culture. Anthropological Perspectives.* New York: Columbia University Press.

8

Ayodhya in Ancient Sanskrit Texts

Shashi Tiwari

Ayodhya the most sacred city, is a prominent centre of religious pilgrimage for the Hindus, Buddhists and Jains from the ancient times. The earliest reference to the Ayodhya is in the Atharvaveda, where the word is used as a epithet of the city (pur) of the gods. We find its first detailed description by Maharisi Valmiki Ayodhya derives its historical as well as religious importance due to its association with solar dynasty. Risi Vasistha and particularly the Rama legend. Mahabhasya of Patanjali had referred to it as Saketa in several contexts. There are several references of Ayodhya in ancient Sanskrit texts and inscriptions, relating to the period between Lord Buddha and Guptas. The Puranas, specially Visnudharmottara and Skanda Puranas, Present detailed information on Ayodhya.

India is a land of deep spiritualism. Most of the Indians believe in the doctrines of *Karma* and transmigration of the soul. It is their firm belief that this life is the result of deeds done in previous births and the kind of future life beyond death will be determined by the acts of the present life. The holy scriptures, therefore, prescribe various religious rites and moral duties for becoming enlightened and liberated. Among the diverse modes or pious deeds one is 'pilgrimage' (*tirtha-sevana),* which can be performed in various ways, i.e., bathing in sacred rivers, visit to and residence in holy places, having darsana of the deities there and offering worship to them. The word *'tirtha'* literally means, 'one which purifies'. It can also mean, 'one which is helpful in crossing the world or this birth', it derived from the root *tr* (to cross). Accordingly pilgrimages are regarded of special importance for washing off the sins and attaining salvation. They, the highest mode of worship, comprise various geographical entities. Any river, lake, well, pool, mountain, forest, land or city can be an object of pilgrimage. Not only the Hindus, but the Buddhists and the Jainas also have their places of pilgrimage. In the *Mahabharata* and the Puranas we found their specific and detailed treatment.

Ayodhya, the most sacred city, is a prominent centre of religious pilgrimage for the Hindus, Buddhists and Jainas from the ancient times. It is found that 'Ayodhya' had a great imprint on the Hindu mind and whereever the Hindus settled, they named their towns 'Ayodhya'. The old capital of Thailand, called by this name, testifies to this fact.[1] Today it is a symbol of a varied and rich cultural heritage of the Indian people. At present the holy city of Ayodhya pre-eminently a temple town, is situated on the right bank of the river Sarayu (Ghagara) on latitude 26^0 48 foot sign north and longitude 82^0 13' east in north India, just 8 kms. north-east of Faizabad. Numerous religious edifices and temples of importance to pilgrims are located within the small town of the old city and also on the bank of the holy Sarayu. Ayodhya is associated with countless fairs and festivities related specifically to Rama's saga. While it attracts pilgrims all the year round, the gathering assumes mammoth dimensions on certain occasions such as the Ramanavami, Dasahara and Kartika Purnima. Apart from the religious edifices of various faiths, the Jaina shrine is particularly noteworthy. The *Brahmakunda* is a place of reverence for the Buddhists as well as the Sikhs. Due to the presence of some important mosques and tombs, Ayodhya has become the sacred land of the Muslims also.

Ayodhya is a city of immense antiquity, full of historical significance and sacred monuments. All these make it a well-known centre of pilgrimage. Ancient Indian texts shed light on its origin, development and historical authenticity. While the name 'Ayodhya' is found in the Vedas, the oldest extant literature, its mention or description is available in the *Ramayana,* the *Mahabharata,* the *Astadhyayi,* the Puranas, Buddhist and Jaina literature and also in Sanskrit poetic compositions. Though a systematic description of the rise of Ayodhya as a sacred centre is difficult due to the uncertainty of chronological order of the literary sources its significance and continuous popularity as a pilgrimage centre can be very well examined on the basis of the textural evidence. Information from the literary sources may be supplemented or checked by the archaeological and epigraphic evidence. In this paper an effort will be made to study the main references to Ayodhya available in the ancient *texts* to find out its origin and also the factors that led to the development of this ancient centre of pilgrimage.

The word 'Ayodhya' is traced from the root √*yudh* (to fight)— A + √*yudh* + *nyat.*[2] It literally means a place which cannot be attacked or conquered. It is unassailable and therefore a place of peace. The etymology of the word A-yodhya is clearly given in the *Taittiriyaranyaka*[3] and the Puranas.[4] The *Ramayana* has justified the significance and reality of its name.[5] The *Skanda Purana* has explained the term mythologically, stating that it represents the combined form of Brahma, Visnu and Siva—'A' for Brahma, 'Ya' for Visnu and 'Dha' for Ṛudra.[6]

The earliest reference to Ayodhya is in the *Atharvaveda* where the word is used as an epithet of the city (*pur)* of the gods, as prosperous as the paradise itself. It is described that this city of the gods consists of eight circles and nine entrances, surrounded by light on all sides.[7] Definitely here it is a mythical or spiritual city, not the geographical one. Gradually in pre-historic India a place must have borne this name. The region around Ayodhya is generally identified with the term *'Janapada'* i.e., the country of the Kos'alas, in the *Satapatha Brahamana* and The Astadhyayi.[8] But in the Brahmana literature it is described as a village (*grama).*[9]

During the *Ramayana* period Ayodhya rose to the prominence of a capital city of the kingdom of Kos'ala along the banks of the river Sarayu. We find its first detailed description by Maharisi Valmiki. "The famous city of Ayodhya was founded by Manu himself — that foremost of man. The city was twelve *yojanas* long with a breadth of three *yojanas*. It was a magnificent city, full of wealth and paddy. It had wide streets and fine roads regularly sprinkled with water. It had an abundance of full bloomed flowers. It had lofty gates furnished with doors and bolts, and well-arranged rows of shops. It was fully protected with mechanical contrivances and arms. It was the home of skilful artisans, dramatic parties and theatres for women. It contained palatial buildings, gardens and mango-groves. The city was rendered impregnable being encircled by the deep moat filled with water. It abounded in horses and elephants, cattle, camels and asses".[10] It was decorated with mountain like palaces glittering with gems.[11] And was like an aerial car obtained in the heaven by the *siddhas* through penance.[12]

According to *Ramayana* the succession to the throne of Ayodhya was generally determined by the law of primogeniture in the Iksvaku family.[13] Ayodhya had many well-known kings who are described in the various Puranas.[14] Iksvaku, son of Manu, was the founder[15] of the illustrious solar dynasty, which ruled the country from the capital city Ayodhya. It is interesting to note that the *Rigveda* refers to a rich and powerful prince called Iksvaku.[16] Generally all the kings of the solar race were connected with the Vas'istha family. The Vas'lsthas were their hereditary family priests.[17] The kingdom of Ayodhya rose to great eminence under Yuvanas'va and especially his son Mandhatr.[18] The supremacy of Ayodhya waned and the Kanyakubja kingdom rose into prominence under its king Jahnu. The Haihayas overcame Ayodhya and the foreign tribes settled there after its conquest.[19] Ayodhya again became famous under Bhagiratha and Ambarisa Nabhagi.[20] Dasaratha, the fifty-sixth monarch of the solar line in descent from Raja Manu, sought the help of the sage Rsyasrnga from Anga Desa.[21] The eastern and the southern kings and the kings of he distant Punjab were invited to

Dasaratha's horse sacrifice at Ayodhya.[22] Dasaratha had improved the city to a great extent and therefore during his reign the glory of the dynasty reached its highest point. Till the time of Rama, the eldest son of Dasaratha, the city of Ayodhya maintained its pomp and show. This town played an important part in the story of the *Ramayana,* as all the major events of his youthful days took place there. Later kng Rama was regarded as the incarnation of Visnu in the Hindu scriptures and religious traditions. After the reign of Rama Ayodhya was destroyed by the flood of the Sarayu river, but his son Kusa, ruling from Kusasthali at that time, restored its lost glory, according to some Hindu traditions and the 16th canto of the *Raghuvamsa* of Kalidasa. After the fall of the last of he solar dynasty, Raja Sumitra, the one hundred and thirteenth monarch, Ayodhya is said to have been rendered a desert. Several historians have raised question about the historicity of Ayodhya, of the *Ramayana,* as according to the epic Lord Rama, the king of Ayodhya, was born in the ' Treta Yuga', which spanned thousands of years before the arrival of the 'Kaliyuga', to them it seems a creation of the poet's imagination. But there are other scholars, who are convinced about the correctness of the popular belief of the Indians that the Ayodhya of today, geographically situated on the bank of the river Sarayu, is the same as the Ayodhya of the epic literature.[23] No doubt, Ayodhya derives its historical as well as religious importance due to its association with the solar dynasty, Risi Vasistha and particularly the Rama legend.

The *Mahabharata* refers to Ayodhya as the capital of king Kalmasapada, the thirty-fifth monarch of the solar dynasty, in whose time Vasistha came to Ayodhya.[24] In the age of the composition of the *Mahabharata* probably the city lost its importance as a metropolis and the cities of Indraprastha and Hastinapura occupied its position. However, in the course of Bhima's conquest of the eastern territories, there is a mention of his conquest of Ayodhya,[25] which was no more a capital of the kingdom of Kosala. It has the status of a city state, as is evident from the fact that Bhima after his conquest of Vrhadvala, the Kosala king, attacked Dirghayajna, the king of Ayodhya. This epic has mentioned a route that connected Kosala with Avanti.[26] The road must have passed through the Kosala city of Ayodhya.[27] It is quite noteworthy that the place from where Rama departed to the heaven, mentioned by the name Gopratara in the *Ramayana,* has also figured in the list of holy places given in the *Mahabharata.*[28]

While Panini (500 B.C.) has mentioned the term 'Kosala', which seems to refer to the region nearby Ayodhya, the *Mahabhasya* of Patanjali (150 B.C.) has referred to it as Saketa in several contexts.[29] Alexander Cunningham states that both the names are identical.[30] Hans Bakker opines that Ayodhya is the name of the town in its earliest phase, and Saketa refers to it during the period of Buddha (6th century B.C.) and thereafter.[31] Hence both the names represent the same city. It is a fact that the Buddhist texts routinely call the site of Ayodhya 'Saketa' and the Jains texts refer to the town by the same name or call it by other names, 'Vinita' and 'lksvakubhumi'.[32]

Ayodhya's recognition as an important town may be seen in the history of Jainism and Buddhism.[33] It was twelve *yojanas* long and nine *yojanas* broad, according to the Jaina account.[34] It was the birthplace of the first and the fourth pathfinders or fordmakers (*tirthankaras*) of Jainism.[35] According to the Jaina tradition, out of the twenty four, five *Tirthankaras* of the present era hailed from Ayodhya—Rsabhadeva, Ajitanatha, Abhinanda, Sumatinatha and Anantanatha.[36] Lord Adiguru attained enlightenment here. Kumarapala, the king of the Calukyas, installed a Jaina image in the city. The temple of Nabhiraja also still exists.[37] A Jaina terracotta found in the excavations belongs to the third-fourth centuries A.D. It proves the presence of Jainism during that period in the region.[38]

Like Jainiam, Ayodhya is held in great reverence by the followers of Buddhism. Lord Buddha is said to have visited the sacred soil of Ayodhya several times. A number of monasteries and Buddhist *stupas* existed in the area. In the Buddhist literature both the names Saketa and Ayodhya are found. Some think that Saketa and Ayodhya were identical, but T.W. Rhys Davids holds the view that both the cities existed separately in Buddha's time.[39] According to the Buddhist sources, Saketa and Ayodhya were different cities, because Saketa was located on the river Ganga, not on the river Saryu, where the present day Ayodhya is situated.[40] But others do not agree with this view.[41] Perhaps they were adjoining cities.[42] In any case the importance of Ayodhya is continuous in the contemporary literature. In the days of Buddha and Mahavira the Kingdom of Kosala was divided into north and south. The capital of northern Kosala was Ayodhya and of southern Kosala was Sravasti.[43] The Pali texts refer to a few kings of Ayodhya.[44]

There are several references of Ayodhya in ancient Sanskrit texts and inscriptions relating to the period between Lord Buddha and Guptas, which prove its existence at that time, though it is quite difficult to arrange them chronologically. The *Kathasaritsagara* refers to the camp of Nanda in Ayodhya[45] which testifies to the historicity of Ayodhya during fourth century B.C. Saketa figures prominently in the important text of the *Yugapurana* which relates to the period of the downfall of the Maurya empire.[46] The *Yoginitantra* mentions this city.[47] During the Sunga period Ayodhya seems to have been included in the kingdom of Pusyamitra Sunga (2nd century B.C.). An inscription found here mentions the fact that Pusyamitra performed two horse sacrifices (*asvamedha*) during his reign.[48] This has enhanced the archaeological importance of Ayodhya. Kalidasa, the famous Sanskrit poet of the first century B.C. (or according to some scholars of the fifth century A.D.), has used the names Ayodhya and Saketa interchangeably in his *Mahakavya Rahhuvamsa* several times,[49] which point to one and the same city.

Ptolemy, the famous Greek scholar of the first century A.D. has mentioned Saketa as Sogeda.[50] B.B. Lal's exacavations in Ayodhya have not found anything from the period between the 3rd century and the 11th century A.D.[51], yet those who conclude therefrom that there was no habitation then in Ayodhya are contradicted by a number of literary sources and also by the accounts of the Chinese travellers and the inscriptions found during that period. The Gaya copper plate inscription of Samudragupta mentions the city, situated on the river Sarayu.[52] But during his reign

Saketa was placed under the direct rule of Pataliputra. The Chinese pilgrim Fa-Hien, who visited Saketa probably during the time of Chandragupta II in the beginning of the 5th century A.D., called it Sha-Chi. He did not find the Buddhists and Brahmanas on friendly terms. He also saw a tape there, where four Buddhists walked and sat. He found the city almost in ruins.[53] The fifth century A.D. may therefore, be a crucial phase in the history of Ayodhya.

Soon after Fa-Hien left India, Kumaragupta I (415-455 A.D.) ascended the Gupta throne. The Karamdanda inscription near Ayodhya during his reign informs that in 436 A.D. some offerings were made to the Brahmanas hailing from Ayodhya. From the Chinese sources we know that Skandagupta (455-467 A.D.) had the royal court installed in Ayodhya. Possibly the royal court had moved from Pataliputra to Saketa/Ayodhya during the reign of Kumaragupta, as the first inscription featuring the name Ayodhya dated from the reign of this king.[54] Thus Saketa was clearly identified as Ayodhya in the late fifth century A.D., when the royal court of the late Guptas was installed there.

Another Chinese traveller Hsuan Tsang, who visited India in the beginning of the 7th century A.D., after travelling more than 600 li and crossing the Ganga to the south, reached the Ayodhya region. According to him, it was the temporary residence of Asanga and Vasubandhu. He has mentioned in detail that the country yielded good crops, was clothed in luxuriant vegetation and had rich fruit orchards and a genial climate. The people had good manners and devoted themselves to practical learning. He has called Ayodhya by the name O-yu-t'o having a circuit of 5000 *li*. The city measured 20 *li* in circumference, which corresponds to the present old centre of Ayodhya. The *Kasikavrtti* on Panini's *Astadhyayi* (650 A.D.) furnishes the additional information that the moat around the town was like that of Pataliputra.[55] The account of Hsuan Tsang states that in this period Ayodhya retained its former glory and status. The identification of Ayodhya with Sha-Chi and O-yu-t'o visited by the Chinese pilgrims is quite important. Most of the historians are in favour of their identity. As Cunningham states, Fa-hian's Sha-Chi is the same as Hsuan Tsang's Visakha and both are identical with Saketa and Ayodhya.[56] Watters has identified Hsuan Tsang's O-yu-t'o with Ayodhya.[57]

The Puranas, the most exhaustive source of our knowledge for the geography of ancient and medieval India, vividly describe various religious and sacred places, popularly known as *'tirtha'*. Almost all the major Puranas refer to Ayodhya,[58] Saketa or the kings of Ayodhya related to the lksvaku or some other dynasty. The *Vishnudharmottara Purana* and the *Skanda Purana* present detailed information on Ayodhya.[59] The compilation of the Puranas is spread over centuries. It is for this reason that the dates of the different Puranas are also controversial. Most scholars put them in two groups - Early and Late. The Mahapuranas or at least the important ones among them were finalised in the Gupta period, as they provide an account of the Guptas. R.C. Hazra maintains that the composition of the *Vishnudharmottara Purana* took place between 400 and 500 A.D.[60] A.B.L. Awasthi thinks that the *Skanda Purana's* Ayodhya Mahatmya represents the relic of the so-called dark period of the ancient Indian history, i.e., the period beginning from the fall of the Maurya dynasty to the dawn of the Gupta empire, because of certain references to the Guptas there.[61] Therefore it may be concluded that the town which withnessed many political upheavals was never out of the minds of the Indian rulers and people.

In the Puranas Ayodhya is stated to be a city (puri, nagari),[62] which gives liberation (*moksa*)[63] and is auspicious (*punyatama*).[64] It is one of the seven sacred places which are regarded the most important for washing off the sins and leading to salvation. It should be noted that the seven names of the group are not uniform in the different Puranas. However, Ayodhya's name occurs in most of the references.[65] It is 'Aryatirtha' according to the *Garuda Purana,* 'Ramanagri' according to the *Brhaddharma Purana* and Saketa' and 'Dasarathipuri' according to the *Skanda Purana.*[66] The *Agni Purana* narrates the story of the *Ramayana* in detail. The *Narada* and the *Padma*

Puranas also deal with the events related to the reign of Rama.[67] The thirteenth chapter of the *Vishnudharmottara Purana* mentions the glorious state of Ayodhya in the kingdom of Kosala situated on the bank of the river Sarayu and built by Manu. It also describes the kings the solar dynasty from Iksvaku downwards. According to the *Skanda Purana* this great city was situated on the wheel of Vishnu named *Sudarsana.* It looked like a fish. It was in extent one *yojana* from the Sahasradhara in the east, one *yojana* from the Sarayu in the south, one *yojana* from the Sama in the west and one *yojana* from Tamasa in the north.[68] Situated on the bank of the river Sarayu, it was the capital of the Iksvaku kings. It contained ramparts, gateways, streets and beautiful places.[69] The Ayodhya Mahatmya upholds the divinity of Ayodhya and its sacredness, being the birth place of Rama.[70] It describes a number of *tirthas,* such as the *Brahmakunda, Cakrahari, Guptahari, Chandrahari, Papamocana, Svargadvara, Sitakunda, Gopratara, Ksirodaka, Siddhapeetha,* etc. Even Prayaga personified used to come to Ayodhya for its purification.[71] Thus this ancient city is glorified in the Ayodhya Mahatmya of the *Skanda Purana.*

Ayodhya's sanctity is also enhanced by the myths, associated with it. One such myth speaks of a king named Vikramaditya, probably of Ujjaina, who miraculously rediscovered it. This story may be taken to highlight the continuity of Ayodhya as one and the same city. It does not relate any other historical event.

Ayodhya's glory lies in its cultural-religious heritage. From the very beginning it remained under the halo of spiritualism and holiness. Undeniably it has derived its importance from its association with Rama legend in the epics. It is well known that the famous poet Tulasidasa went to Ayodhya to compose the *Ramacharitamanasa,* the immortal classic on Sri Rama. Ayodhya occupies a significant position as a sacred place of religious pilgrimage in the Puranas. It has also been regarded as a sacred land for the Jainas and the Buddhists. Its greatness, popularity and attraction as a centre of pilgrimage through the ages is borne out by widely dispersed literary sources.

References

1. Singh, Sukhdev, *Uttar Pradesh,* New Delhi, 1978, p. 146.
2. Yoddhum asakya ayodhya l
3. Karmagatimantarena kenapi praharttumasakya I *Tai Aras* 1/27/3.
4. Nayodya sakyate yasmattamayodhyam tato viduh l *Skanda P,* Vaisnava, Ayo.61.
   Ayodhya namatah puri l *Vishnudharmottara P.*,1/13/1.
   Ayodhyan amayodhhyayam rajandasarathau sthite I
   Harivamsa P., 1/54/26; *Vishnudharmottara P.,* 1/202, 1—240/2.
5. Sa satyanama prakasyate l *Ramayana,* Bala K., 6/26.
6. Akaro brahma ca proktam yokaro visnurucyate I
   Dhakaro rudrarupasca ayodhya nama rajate II *Skanda P.,* Vaisnava, Ayo.60.
7. Astacakra navadvara devanam purayodhya I *Atharvaveda,* 10/2/31.
8. *Satapatha Brahmana* 1/4/1/14; *Astadhyayi,* 4/1/171.
9. *Sankhayana Srautasutra,* 15/17. *Aitareya Brahmana,* 7/3/1.
10. Kosalo nama muditah sphito Janapado mahan !
    Nivistah sarayutire prabhutadhanadhanyavan !!
    Ayodhyanama nagari tatrasillokavisruta !
    Manuna manavandrena ya puri nirmita svayam !!
    Ayata dasa ca dve ca yojanani mahapuri !
    Srimati trini vistirna suvibhaktamahapatha !!
    Rajamargena mahata suvibhaktena Sobhita !
    Muktapuspavakirnena jalasiktena nityasah !!
    Kapatatoranavatim suvistrtantarapanam !
    Sarvayantrayudhavatimusita sarvasilpibhih !!
    Vadhunatakasamghaisca samyukta sarvatah purim !
    Udyanamravanopetam mahatim salamekhalam !!
    Durgagambhiraparikham durgamanyairdurasadam !
    Vajivaranasampurnam gobhirustraih Kharaistatha !!
    Ramayana Bala K., 5/5-8,10,12, 13.
11. Prasadaratnavikrtaih parvatairiva sobhitam ! *Ramayana,* Bala. K. 5/15.
12. Vimanamiva siddhanam tapasadhigatam divi *I Ramayana,* Bala, K 5/19.
13. Iksvakunamidam tesam rajyam vemse mahatmanam I *Ramayana,* Bala K, 5/3.

14. *Vayu P.*, 99/270; *Matsya P.*, 50/77; *Agni P.*, 272/5-7; *Kurma P.*, 1/20/4-6; *Harivamsa P.*, 11/660; *Padma P.*, 5/8/130-62, etc.
15. *Bhagavata P.*, 9/8/17-19.
16. *Rigveda*, 10/60/4; Macdonell, A.A., *A History of Sanskrit Literature*, Varanasi, 1965, p. 133.
17. *Vishnu P.*, 4/3/18; *Padma P.*, 6/219/44.
18. *Mahabharata*, III/126.
19. Law, B.C., *Historical Geography of Ancient India*, Delhi, 1976, p.69.
20. *Vayu P.*, 88/171-2; *Padma P.*, 6/22/7-18; *Linga P.*, 1/66/21-22, etc.
21. *Ramayana*, Bala K.9 and 10.
22. *Ramayana*, Bala K. 13/21-29.
23. Bakker, Hans, *Ayodhya*, Groningen, 1986, p.10;
Nayak, Pradeep, *The Politics of the Ayodhya Dispute*, Delhi, 1993, p. 69.
24. Mani, V., *Puranic Encyclopaedia*, Varanasi, 1975, p. 85.
Mahabharata, Adi, *P.*, 175-176.
25. Ayodhyayam tu dhrmajyam dirghayajyam mahabalam I
Ayajat pandavasrestho natitivrena karmanu II
Asa pantha Vidarbhanamasau gacchati kosalan II *Mahabharata*, Sabha P., 30/2.
26. *Mahabharata*, Vana P., 61/23.
27. Banerjee, S.K., *Economic life in the Great Epic*, Calcutta, 1990, p. 127.
28. *Ramayana* 7/110/22; *Mahabharata*, 3/82/63-65.
29. *Mahabhasya*, 1/3/25, 3/2/111.
30. Alexander Cunningham, *Ancient Geography of India*, 1924, p. 464 (*Archaeological Survey Reports*, 1,2,6,20); H.H.Wilson, *Sanskrit Dictionary;* B.N. Puri *Patanjalikalina Bharata* (Hindi), p. 123.
31. Bakker, Hans, *Ayodhya*, p. 4.
32. *Avassaka* commentary, p. 244 a; *Avassaka Nirjjuti*, 382.
33. Stevenson, S., *Heart of Jainism*, pp. 50-51.
34. *Vividhatirthakalpa*, ch. 34.
35. *Avassaka Nirjjuti*, 382.
36. Sinha, R.K., *Glimpses of Faizabad*, Delhi, 1975, p. 38.
37. Law, B.C., *Some Jaina Canonical Sutras*, p. 173.
38. Nayak, Pradeep, *The Politics of the Ayodhya Dispute*, p. 71.
39. Davids, T.W. Rhys, *Buddhist India*, Calcutta, 1950, p. 39;
Law, B.C., *Geography of Early Buddhism*, p.5.
40. *Samyukta Nikaya;* Nayak, Pradeep, *The Politics of the Ayodhya Disputs*, p. 70.

41. Elst, Kaenraad, *Ram Janmabhoomi vs Babri Masjid,* Delhi, 1990, pp. 24-25.
42. J.R.A.S., 1917, p. 52.
43. *Aitihasika Sthanavali* (Hindi); Bakker, Hans, *Ayodhya,* p. 2.
44. Fausboll, V., *Jataka,* III, p. 270; IV, 82-83.
45. *Kathasaritsagara,* Tawney's ed., p. 37.
46. Bakker, Hans, *Ayodhya,* p. 18-19; *Yuga Purana,* 2/89—95.
47. *Yoginitantra,* 2/4, pp. 128-9.
48. *Epigraphia Indica.,* XX,p. 57.
49. Kalidasa, *Raghuvamsa,* 5/31, 13/59, 13/61, 13/62, 14/13, 14/29.
50. *Ptolemy's Geography,* ed, S.N. Majumdar, 2.25.
51. Elst, Koenraad, *Ram Janmabhoomi vs Babri Masjid,* p. 23.
52. J.F. Fleet, *Corpus Inscriptionum Indicarum,* III, London, 1888.
53. James Legge, Tr., *A Record of Buddhistic Kingdoms* (An Account of Fa-hien's Travels), Oxford, 1886, pp. 54-55;
    Law, B.C., *Historical Geography of Ancient India,* p. 68.
54. Bakker, Hans, *Ayodhya,* pp. 27-30;
    Panikkar, K.M. *A Historical Overview,* pp. 24-25.
55. *Kasikavrtti* on Panini, 5/1/116.
56. Cunningham, *Ancient Geography of India,* Calcutta 1924, pp. 339, 401-407.
57. Watters, T., *On Yuan Chwang's Travels in India,* London, 1905, I,pp. 354-9.
58. *Vishnu P.,* 4/2, 4/4/97; *Brahma P.,* 5/46, 67/58, 123/5; *Linga P.,* 2/5/45, 75, 78; *Brahmanda P.,* 2/48/1, 2/49/10, 24, 2/53/5, 2/54/5, 2/63/21, 93; *Narada P.,* 1/27/35, 1/73/68, 153, 2/14/61, 2/75/21; *Padma P.,* Sristi, 8/82, 30/140, 143, 33/170, 37/148, 38/73, Svarga, 18/92, Bhumi, 42/2, Patala, 3/25, 7/23, 23/8, 28/63, 37/29, Uttara, 71/235, 114/28, 201/11, 242/44; *Bhavisya P.,* Prati, 1/2/10, 3/42, III/14/15, IV/8/1, 17/29, 21/55, 23/29, 26/9; *Siva P.,* Vidyesvara, 25/9, Kotirudra, 21/52, Uma, 44/45-46; *Agni P.* 5/14, 6/7, 30, 47, 49, 10/31, 109/24, 130/11, 176/18, 184/18, 242/73, 273/6; *Varaha P.,* 97/37, 163/49, 51; *Vamana P.,* 64/62; *Brhaddharma P.,* I 14/11, 19/16, 29, 2/50/69, 54/6, 7.
59. *Visnufharmottara, P.,* I ch. 13, 202/2, 221/14, 240/2. chs. 240-245;
    Skanda P. Vaisnava, Ayodhya Mahatmyam, chs. 1-10.

60. Hazra, R.C., *Studies in the Upapuranas,* Vol. I, Calcutta, 1958, p. 138.
61. Awasthi, A.B.L., *Purana Index,* New Delhi, 1992, pp. 179-183.
62. *Visnudharmottara P.,* 1/13/1; *Narada P.,* 1/73/68; *Brhaddharma P.,* 1/14/11.
63. *Narada P.,* 1/27/3; *Agni P.,* 109/24.
64. *Brahmanda P.,* 3/40/91.
65. Ayodhya mathura maya kasi kanci avantika I
Puri dvaravati caiva saptaita moksadayikah II
Brhaddharma P., 2/54/16; *Narada P.,* 1/27/35.
Ayodhya mathura maya kasi kanci hyavantika I
Eta punyatamah proktah purinamuttamottamah II *Brahmanda P.,* 3/40/91.
66. *Garuda P.,* 1/44/7; *Brhaddharma P.,* 2/54/7; *Skanda P.* Vaisnava, Ayo. 3/31, 6/117.
67. *Narada, P.* 1/73/68; *Padma, P.,* Patala, 37/29.
68. *Skanda, P.,* Vaisnnava, Ayo. 4/6, 1/64-65.
69. *Ibid.,* 1/32-34.
70. Tasmatsthanata aisane ramajanma pravarttate I
Janmasthanamidam proktam moksadi phalasadh- anam II *Ibid.,* 10/18.
71. Yatra prayagarajo' pi snatumayati kartike I
Suddhayartham sadhukamo' sau prayage munisattamah II *Ibid,* 6/181-82.

9

Pilgrimage in Shakti Tradition : A Textual and Contextual Study*

Professor (Dr.) K.G. Gurumurthy

Anthropologists have used Redfield's conception of a Civilization as a compound structure of Little and Great Traditions (1956). This approach popularly known as Western approach, classifies civilizations into classical and folk and tell in terms of Great and Little traditions (cf., Cohn 1971, Singer 1972) Orientalists have their own approach to study the phenomenon though it sometimes appears like a modified version of the former. Srinivas (1952, 1956), ventured to write on this, by using the concept of Sanskritization to explain the process. He divided the Hinduism into four levels—Universal, Peninsular, Regional and Local, on the basis of level of Sanskritic contents in them.

Ishwaran, a North America based Indian scholar, who studied the Lingayats of South India (1974, 1977, 1983,1989 1993), says that the 'Sanskritization process which is told after the Western model of Great and Little (*Marga* and *Desi*) traditions answers that situation to some level and certainly

* The author gratefully acknowledges the help extended to him by Prof. C. G. Hussain Khan and Dr. K. C. Tarachand. Deptt. of Anthropology, Karnatak University, Dharwad, in writing this paper.

not beyond Sanskritization'. So he proposes a five fold typology, which according to him is more consistent with historical and contemporary facts' (1983 : 111). He further says that like the western anthropologists, Srinivas, advocates not only a two fold level typology but also supports them with his Coorg data. Srinivas, Ishwaran say further, is of the view that there will be no scope for change in (classical) religious traditions and certainly not in the form of religious movements since the classical tradition adhere to a text. But, Ishwaran with his data on the Lingayats, argues that a movement for change is possible. He also shows how a 'Little tradition can refuse to fuse with either Classical (Great) or Local (Little) traditions and become a protest religious tradition' (1983 : 112). We agree with Ishwaran and also support his stand on the basis of our data on Pilgrimage collected about a Mother Goddess' ritual tradition from South India (cf Gurumurthy 1989, 1991, 1992, 1995, 1996).

Secondly, according to Singer, textual studies tell 'much about what is transmitted but very little about how, and to or for whom. The result tends to be a collection of disembodied 'ideas' logically manipulatable into a systematic 'Philosophy' (1972:39). Text in the form of religious dogma, is the result of writings by a group of learned men who sat in an isolated place and formulated certain ideas which they later, strived to propagate. They reduced their ideas to writing and often sealed them with divine approval that 'god gave it' or 'His messenger brought it from heaven for the good of mankind'. These scholars were few in number and also were aware that what they have produced is deviant and different from that which is already practiced by the masses and it will be opposed by the propagators of the already existing ritual tradition. They also had the fear of retaliation and so often did not publish it or left it in hiding, for posterity to discover at an appropriate time. They also presented these ideas in symbols, lest they are easily known to masses and also without instructions, as to whom they are directed and how they are to be given and by whom. These 'ideal' forms called classicals, are different and often opposed to what it is actually practiced or lived by the masses.

Pilgrimage is one of the areas discussed by those learned men since it is concerned with all the three components of the sacred complex.

In classical Hinduism pilgrimage to a sacred centre is a spiritual obligation (cf Saraswati, 1975). The places of pilgrimage are seats of deities, saints, birth or confluence spots of rivers, mountain tops, valleys, banks of lakes; with mythological significances. The devotees are obligated to spend certain number of days in a year here and this in turn helped the sacred specialists to transmit definite religious ideas to them.

Here in our study we will deal with pilgrimage at contextual level, as viewed by the folk level devotees and sacred specialists. Singer says that the contextual informations refers to 'incidence of religious beliefs and practices in the context of daily life' (1972:39). For the Folk religion is a way of life and they also have a pantheon of Local environmental beings, taken as personal, favourite, family, caste and community level deities. It is possible that a single deity is taken in all these forms by different groups and on this ground the categories of devotees are formed. People treat gods and goddesses as some one who live with them responding to their prayers and day-to-day needs. Their religious lore constitutes the beliefs, wraths, worships, vows and booms bestowed on them by the deities. It is believed by them that it would be more beneficial if the pilgrimage is made during the annual fair of the sacred centre; since that period would be convenient for them and the deity would also be active and available, to receive their vows and offerings personally.[1]

In order to understand a pilgrimage it becomes necessary to study the entire sacred tradition, in which it is made. According to Vidyarthi (cf. 1961) a Sacred Complex comprises of three components—sacred centre, sacred specialists and sacred specialists and sacred performances. In our study we have included Devotees as the fourth component. Further, we have also added *Jogati* and *Jogappa*. Mendicant functionaries and *Tanika*-hereditary owner of the sacred centre, as sub-categories of sacred specialists, along with the temple priests since they perform a number of folk level ritual roles which are contextual in nature (cf. Gurumurthy 1996 : 117-147 and 233-270).[3]

Sacred Centre

For our discussion we have chosen a sacred centre of an active and powerful goddess-Renuka - Yallamma, who has lakhs of devotees in the drought prone, poverty stricken, backward districts of several southern and western Indian states. It is well known in the religious history of India as one of the ancient *Shakti* centres. The goddess was claimed by several ritual traditions during different levels of civilization. Originally She was the goddess of food hunters and gatherers and had no definite idol form and abode. She symbolised in the form of green neem leaves placed in a bamboo pan and carried on head by women folk. When these devotees who went about collecting wild leafy and vegetable food became agriculturists and had a shift from collection to production, She became their goddess and controlled a host of local environmental deities. With the sedantarization of group, started Sanskritization of Her sacred complex. In this process, as we can see later, several attempts were made to absorb the local tradition into Sanskritic tradition, whenever favourable political situation arose for the propagation of the new tradition.

Myths Connected with the Sacred Centre

According to our survey there are sixty-one sacred units at the sacred centre (Tarachand 1987:111-114, 1991:77-78, Gurumurthy 1996:180). Each unit has a myth connecting it with the goddess either at folk or Sanskritic levels. A detailed study of these units will help in understanding the textual and contextual background of pilgrimage in this ritual tradition.

According to the folk level myth "The goddess, younger sister of the headman of a village located by the side of the sacred centre, had contracted a 'disease' and became inactive and so was isolated on a hillock. She was allowed to come to the border of the village only to collect her daily necessities. As days passed, one day she met two holymen who, after hearing Her plight cured the 'disease' using their divine powers and took Her into their fold. As Her duty towards them, She visited the villages around the sacred centre daily to propagate their glory and to collect alms. By the time the two holymen became old and died, the goddess had become 'active' by acquiring the power needed from them to cure the 'diseases' of men and animals. That it how the devotees started coming on pilgrimage to Her with vows and votive offers. In due course of time her own sacred centre, devotees and ritual tradition were formed. Her brothers also came and settled at the sacred centre as Her priests. This set-up continues even today in the sacred centre".

The Sanskritised myth has several versions as it takes a twist back and forth, according to the change in the rulers of the land; who propagated their own ritual tradition. It says:

"Son of God came down from the Himalayas in the guise of a sage, and chose the spot on which the sacred centre under study stands today, to do penance. After few years his ancestors asked him to become a householder. So he went to the nearby kingdom and asked the king to give his daughter, in marriage to him. After their marriage the couple lived there itself and over the years they begot four sons."[2]

From that time onwards the religious history shows, under one pretext or other, the goddess and her children were eliminated from the myth to propagate the tradition as a classical one, where only vedic gods were worshipped. Similarly, attempts were also made to include them back in the myths by the folk level believers because they were linked to the tradition through them. They also used it as a survival mechanism to fight the hostile environmental conditions. The first change in the folk level tradition came during the 14th century, when the territory was under the Saivite Vijayanagara rulers. According to this:

"Securing water from the nearby river, for Her husband's ritual needs, was one of the daily duties of the wife goddess. To bring the water She made a pot daily, using the sand grains from the river bank and, carried it on Her head, resting it on the coil of a live snake (cf. Gurumurthy, 1991). She could do all these miraculous acts owing to the divine powers She had acquired as a devout wife (*Mahasati*).

One day, the wife goddess saw an angel and his wives wading in the river water and lost Her mental composure. Later remembering Her duty, She started making the pot, but could not accomplish. On seeing Her empty handed, using His hindsight, the husband god could visualise as to what had happened at the river. Becoming angry on Her for losing Her loyalty (*Nisthe*) and dedication to Him, he cursed Her to lose the ritual influence (*Prabhava*) and form (*Rupa*), which She had earned by marrying Him and, also ordered Her out of the hermitage. Later He sat in penance.

When the wife goddess was roaming without devotees and a place to stay, one day She was spotted by the doctors of gods, who also cured Her of the curse. Regaining youth and charm, She returned to Her husband, who welcomed Her back and together they lived happily thereafter."

By 15th Century when the propagators of Vaishnava tradition took over the sacred centre, they once again attempted to eliminate the goddess from the ritual tradition and so altered the myth to narrate that the revived wife goddess was not accepted by the husband god, as under:

"When husband god saw the wife goddess having regained Her form and ritual influence with the help of some one other than him (*Saivas*), he became very angry and ordered his sons to chop-off Her head for the insult and disgrace that She has brought on Him. The first three sons[3] refused to obey Him and were cursed to become eunuchs[4]. After punishing them He called the last son, who dutifully carried out the orders. After eliminating Her, the husband god established himself there itself as the principal deity an the son returned for penance".

By the early 17th century, the *Shaktas* took over the territory and revived *Shakti* ritual tradition in the sacred centre. To make the goddess all powerful there was a need to eliminate the husband god. There developed a myth with a twist as follows:

"Soon after carrying out the orders, the father god became very happy and granted him a boon. The dutyful son asked for the revival of his mother. Father god sensing an unity pact between the Mother and Son, went away for penance, to Himalayas. The revived goddess pities for Her three cursed sons and decides to stay with them. However, the fourth son too goes away for penance. With the hostile husband god and son going away, the goddess becomes the principal deity in the ritual tradition.

During the latter part of the 17th century the territory came under the Vaishnava rulers, who once again revived the classical tradition. During their periods a myth developed as under :

"After the revival of the wife goddess the divine couple lived together. One day the king of the land, a Saiva by tradition and brother of the slained (Saiva version) wife goddess, visited them with his courtiers and soldiers. They were treated to their satisfaction, with the help of the *Kamadhemu*[5], the celestial cow which was with them. The king gets amazed by its capacity and claims it for himself by force and, in the struggle the husband god was killed.

Seeing Her husband god killed, the wife goddess calls Her (Vaishnava) son, for help. To avenge his father's death he goes round the earth twenty-one times, one for each wound that was inflicted on the body of his slained father, to kill the entire ruling class. He also brings their women and children for the service of his mother. When these helpless prisoners prayed for mercy the goddess pardons and takes them as Her devotees. To 'Protect' his widowed mother, the son go stays there itself. Over the years She becomes the presiding deity of the sacred centre".

There comes a twist in the myth during the last part of the 17th century, when a last attempt was made to revive the husband god, under the Vaishnavite Peshwa rule. It says:

"On hearing the news of husband god's death, His father came down from the Himalayas and revives Him and establishes the Vaishnava tradition. Both the days on which the husband god was killed and revived were fullmoon days with a three months difference. On seeing Her husband god revived, the wife goddess and children gods become happy. The devotees celebrate this day as a festival and also came on pilgrimage".

This ritual tradition however survived for a short while, till the Peshwa lost their territory to the Moghals and they in turn, to the Bijapur Sultans. The new rulers gave the sacred centre to a feudal lord for certain amount of revenue to the state. Later, when the territory came under the British East India Company, they too continued the same system. During this period the representatives of the feudal lord revived the Mother Goddess tradition and a number of folk level rituals, which facilitated them to collect the required amount, from the folk. Even today this version of ritual tradition continues in the sacred centre and the descendants of the traditional temple administrators have also become the sacred specialists claiming the status and accompanying roles as their hereditary right.

Sacred Socialists

Since there is a close relation between the sacred specialists and the pilgrimage performed, there arises a need to know their ritual status and roles and the mythical connections they have with the goddess and Her devotees. It has already been noted there is lot of confusion and contradiction in the statuses and roles of the sacred specialists-the temple priests, *Tanika* and the ritual mendicants who now belong to different level ritual traditions (cf. Gurumurthy, 1991, 1992, 1996).

(a) **Temple Priests :** The goddess has had both priestesses and priests, depending upon the level of civilizations She belonged. As Mother Goddess She was without a temple and the women who took and worshipped Her wherever they went, by keeping in a basket. Later, While under the *Shakta tradition*, She got Her own sacred centre and the *Jogappa* - a set of dedicated men, as Her priests. They propagated myths narrating that the goddess is their elder sister.

During the 16th century, when the sacred complex came under the rulers who belong to Sanskritic tradition, they sent Brahmin prists who had introduced a male deity here and reduced the goddess to the status of a wife. However, during the later part of the 17th century, under the feudal lords, when the *Shakta* tradition was revived; the Brahmin priests vacated their position and the *Tanika,* non-Brahmin householders came as temple priests. So they occupy two positions - the priests and *Tanika* of the sacred centre. By propagating a myth they became Her elder brothers. Today this type of ritual tradition and priests continue in the sacred centre and they propagate a contextual level ritual tradition.

(b) ***Tanika*** : Whenever the classical ritual tradition was introduced in the sacred centre, along with Brahmin priests the king of the land also appointed an administrator - *Tanika,* to the sacred centre so that the ritual activities are conducted properly. He was given some land grant for this purpose. Whenever the territory was taken over by another conqueror normally this person continued in the position as long as the ruler was a Hindu and of the same sect and changed otherwise. Later the post became hereditary and powerful. When the non-Hindu rulers conquered the territory they demanded a fixed amount of revenue from the sacred centre against demolition or takeover. The extra state concession to the temple were also withdrawn. The *Tanika* stood guarantee for this payment and collected the same from the devotees as entry and ritual fee (*Kappa* and *Kanike*), the former going to the state and the latter to the temple maintenance fund.

In case of this sacred centre, to facilitate the *Tanika* in collecting the required amount he propagated a myth that the devotees are his subjects (*Praja*) and he the custodian and guardian of the ritual fertility of the goddess. He had also proclaimed that he is responsible for the retention of the goddess at the sacred centre lest She went and settled with more devout devotees or captured by more powerful rival beings and rendered 'inactive'. To keep Her 'active' and 'safe', he propagated that he needs more and more ritual offerings. Since the devotees are the beneficiaries; he demanded the same from them. Thus, through the mendicants he prompts the devotees to come on pilgrimage throughout the year and the defaulters are also threatened with the wrath of the goddess.[6]

In this capacity he even barred the devotees who failed to pay the entry fee and also those who came without votive objects, from performing pilgrimage. He also kept track of defaulters and summoned them using the mendicants, under his control. Often threatened that he would report their imprudence to the goddess and bring Her wrath on them. The folk level, illiterate, superstitious, leaderless and poor devotees accepted all his demands and performed their pilgrimage.

To save the devotees from the autocratic *Tanika,* successive governments have brought checks on him by taking away ritual and other roles from him. Being influential and rich they went to the king or court of law and have retained the same with them. Now with the abolition of hereditary posts and appointment of Charity Commissioner as the administrator of the temple, they have officially lost all their roles and privileges. But traditionally they still continue in their customary position and exploit the devotees who come for pilgrimage.

The first *Tanika* had four sons and through them developed four lineages. As of 1991 there were 127 families of these people. They have customarily divided their devotees into four groups and claim ritual tax from them. Each of them owns an establishment at the sacred centre and his linked devotees on pilgrimage, report to him here as a must. Only after paying his dues and agreeing to offer votive objects to the goddess to his satisfaction, that he allows them to perform the pilgrimage. As an indication of this satisfaction, he also accompanys them to the temple to recommend their vows to his younger sister, the goddess.[7]

The folk level devotees considered as the children of the goddess, are obligated to come on pilgrimage regularly and offer ritual objects such as food, clothing, bangles, vermilion and turmeric powder to make Her active. Owing to cronic droughts and poverty, they fail to do so. But they believe that without these votive objects the goddess becomes 'weak' and 'inactive' towards them. She may even leave the sacred centre to settle with more devout devotees. Without devotees and the active deity, the *Tanika* also loses his livelihood. So he, as the guardian of the ritual fertility of the goddess and controller of devotees, intervenes by using the mendicants to convey the threat of the wrath of goddess and motivates them to come on pilgrimage.[8] Wrath of the goddess results in the form of loss of life, virility, fertility, property, mental peace and other mundane and vital things of life. The illiterate and superstitious devotees fail to connect these problems with drought conditions, lack of development, exploitation, venerial diseases, malnutrition, unhygenic conditions, lack of health and medical facilities and get mortally scared. So they borrow or even sell come property and some on pilgrimage.

(c) **Religious mendicants** : In this *Shakti* tradition, the mendicant functionaries act as a link between the devotees and sacred centre. There are seven categories of them with certain ambiguities in their ritual, social, sexual statuses and roles. They belong to all castes and age groups and trace their origin to and links with the goddess (cf. Gurumurthy 1992:56-64). According to their background they carry a sacred object with them which has its myth of origin indicating the mendicant's connection with the goddess. They are well versed with the religious lore of the goddess and convey it among the devotees when they go about collecting alms and pilgrims. In this tradition since only the devotees accompanied by a mendicant are allowed to come on pilgrimage, we can see them always with a group of devotees. They are not recognised as sacred specialists by the classical tradition. So they motivate and bring only the folk level devotees linked to them, on pilgrimage and hand them over to the *Tanika*.

Unlike the ascetics of Kashi (cf. Saraswati and Sinha 1974, Vidyarthi *et.al.* 1979), the mendicants here have a few folk level ritual statuses and roles. Each one is assigned with certain number of villages, where the linked devotees of their mentor *Tanika* reside and whom they visit regularly on week days, to bless on behalf of the goddess, to collect alms to the priest and ritual tax for the *Tanika*. The devotees show them due respect and offer them with ritually clean seat, food and also alms. Since the mendicants are chosen from among the local devotees whom they visit regularly, they know all good and bad that happens to them. When something bad occurs, they advise the devotees to have full faith in the all powerful goddess and also take vows in Her name. When the devotees are hackled by the *Tanika,* for costlier votive objects and delays permission to visit the goddess or to leave the sacred centre after the pilgrimage, for non-payment of his dues, the mendicant mediates on their behalf and help them.

Each *Tanika* initiates his required number of mendicants to control and collect ritual tax from his linked devotees. There are thousands of them moving in the villages of devotees and on the way to and also at, the sacred centre. To signify their category they carry with them the sacred object which they get at the time of initiation. Some of the positions are hereditary and others are transferred to a disciple. All temple girls (*dēvadāsi*) according to their category, automatically become mendicants to become again divine and to earn their maintenance. A few devout housewives on becoming old and destitute women, can also become mendicants, by undergoing the initiation rite. Eunuchs and transvestites from another category.[9] All of them are well-versed in the folk level religious lore of the tradition and propagate it among the devotees. They are more popular with folk level devotees who practice contextual level rituals.

Sacred Performances

Rituals offered at the sacred centre today, are neither *Vedic* nor *Agamic* but belong to a local tradition, which is a mixture of both classical and folk traditions. The devotees come with mundane contextual problems. The sacred specialists who belong to folk level and claim their right on hereditary ground and as her brothers, also allow them to do that. No purity and pollution rules are observed and instead propagated that the entire day and all days in a year are 'favourable' to come on pilgrimage. So the pilgrims trickle throughout the year, whenever it suits them. Now, because of the selective Sanskritization of the sacred complex, the *Tanika* cum folk level priests have 'copied' a few sanskritic customs and practices to continue in that position. They have also started imposing purity and pollution rules on the pilgrims. At the entrance of the sanctum sanctorium, the priest takes the votive objects and symbolically offers them to the goddess and returns the same as sacred material.

The mendicants and the devotees coming from ritually lower castes, sacrificial animals and cooked food are tabooed from the sanctum sanctorum. However, the devotees offer these customary rituals to the goddess, first in the folk level sacred units which are located at the sacred centre, through the *Tanika* and mendicants, and then come to the sacred unit of the goddess with ritually cleaner objects.

Depending upon their category, the devotees are allowed to take vows for a number of worldly desires such as landed property, good health, mercy, love and affection of the beloved, a male child and for protection. These are all contextual in nature. Each vow is accompanied by votive objects or services. Often the very objects or benefits got from the goddess are vowed back to the goddess. Because the urge is not only to get the objects but also to become free from the stigma on them as defaulter or as cursed person. In this ritual tradition prayers and performances are offered not keeping in view the matters which the sanskritic tradition holds high such as salvation, heaven and so on.

Devotees

As a powerful and active deity, with long and rich ritual tradition, the goddess has a large number of devotees and also at folk and classical levels. They form into three categories : Those who have the goddess as their family deity, favourite or as merciful deity (cf. Gurumurthy 1996: 190-191). The first group are Her children and are free to come on pilgrimage whenever they want and only they have the right over the material potentials of the goddess. So while taking vows, they pray to the goddess saying 'give me' such and such a thing, in the manner a child demands from its mother. There are vows to pressurise and pester the goddess for benefits and only these devotees are allowed to take them. Immediately on arrival at the sacred centre, these devotees on pilgrimage meet the *Tanika* for help. He, stands in the position of their maternal uncle and the mendicant, in the position of their sorrorate aunt, are totally trusted by them. It is also customarily believed that the goddess will be always angry on Her children for not coming on pilgrimage frequently and offer Her with the ritual objects. So they are forced to accept the mediation of these two local level sacred specialists to pacify Her. Knowing the helpless condition of the devotees, these two exploit them in the name of pilgrimage, vows and votive objects.

The second category of devotees are those who need only the support and expect no material benefits from the goddess. They become the devotees of the goddess because their original family deity is angry on them or some evil force is coming in their way of getting these benefits. Since there is provision to take help from any powerful deity to ward-off such obstacles, these persons have taken shelter under the goddess by taking Her as their favourite deity. While taking vow, they pray saying 'help us to get benefits from our deity' or 'protect us from evil beings'.

The last category of devotees too have a family deity of their own, by tradition. But they have become the devotees of this goddess because of Her wrath on them for insulting Her. As a punishment She goes on giving them a claim of troubles - loss of materials, health, virility, mental peace, and beloved ones. When mendicants come across such victims, advice them to come under the shelter of their merciful goddess and repent for their imprudence. When such devotees take a vow for help, they pray saying 'show mercy on us'. During the pilgrimage they offer not only the vowed ritual objects but also their pride to the goddess. As a mark of total surrender to Her, they parade in nude, go rolling on their body around Her temple, travel the entire distance from their home to Her sacred centre by foot or by postrating to the goddess at every step they take or offer their services by becoming a *Devadasi* or mendicant. It is in this manner that the devotees align with the deity and the priests on kin ground and not on spiritual. Their vows are mundane and not for spiritual gains. Thus their links and pilgrimages are contextual in nature.

In this ritual tradition, when the devotees are in trouble or bestowed with material and other benefit, believe that it is certainly due to the wrath or grace of the goddess. So they are motivated to take a vow to Her and come on pilgrimage to offer votive objects and services for their worldly benefits. They also take the mediation of their ritual kin - the mendicant and the *Tanika,* the way the kin ties are used in their society to survive the difficult conditions. There is no provision to take vows for spiritual gains and so these are no spiritual leaders in this ritual tradition. Though of late, many changes have come due to Sanskritization of the sacred complex the pilgrimage made in this ritual tradition is still at the folk level. Due to historical-political reasons the process of change was not continuous and complete. Therefore, today, we have a mixed version of ritual tradition which Ishwaran (1983) has termed it as Populistic. The tradition has also successfully resisted fusion with either Classical or Folk traditions. This was made possible by adopting the populistic version of Mother Goddess ritual tradition and through the *Shakta* movement, as a survival mechanism. The masses too adopted this tradition to fight the chronic drought and famine conditions, poverty, exploitation, illiteracy etc., which prevail in the region.

Foot Notes

1. At contextual level, the pilgrimage made during the fair of the sacred centre has a few secular functions (cf. Bose 1961, Sinha 1958, Saraswati, 1972) since they served as meeting places of many cultures. In the past during the absence of commercialised and specialized markets and agencies, the annual fairs, where thousands of pilgrims, craftsmen and entertainers, converged, served as places of buying, selling and exchanging of household and agricultural articles and information. Of late, both government and private agencies set exhibitions to educate masses on several governmental plans and programmes.

2. According to the Saiva ritual tradition, Renuka and Jamadagni had four sons by name - Sulochana, Vilochana, Brahmalochana and Parashurama. The couple had no daughters. In the Vaishnava ritual tradition the divine couple had five sons and a daughter. The sons are-Srivasu (Agni Vamsha), Viswavasu (Vayu Vamsha), Bhruhad Bhanu (Surya Vamsha) and Parashurama (Vishnu Vamsha). The name of the daughter is Trikaladēvi.

3. The sons mentioned here are not actually persons but represent groups of devotees. Earlier, they belonged to Mother Goddess tradition and later got affiliated to the Jamadagni and

Renuka ritual tradition (cf. Gurumurthy 1991, 1996).

4. It is told that symbolically Jamadagni the father god, curses his sons, to become eunuchs. The potency or virility that is supposed to have been removed from his sons (minor gods of the ritual tradition) was not of biological but ritual. As his followers, these groups, had received some ritual powers from their father (principal deity) who was the founder of the Vaishnave ritual tradition. When they disobeyed him, i.e., refused to disassociate themselves with the Mother Goddess, he withdrew this ritual powers from them. As a result of which they could either belong to the ritual tradition of their mother, i.e., Mother Goddess, which they had left earlier, or to their father's, i.e., classical tradition, which they had joined now and became neither (powerless) persons. This is told in the folk level myths that they became eunuchs.

5. *Kamadhenu* though literally means the celestial cow in Sanskritic literature, symbolically represents the sacred centre in this context (cf. Gurumurthy, 1991). The sacred centre, like the mythical wish fulfilling cow, gives the priest or the one who controls it, with all that he wants since these things and services are demanded of the devotees in the name of the presiding deity.

6. It is propagated by the *Tanika* that the goddess will go away or desert them and settle elsewhere if She is not visited or worshipped by using the ritual offerings brought by a fresh batch of devotees, every day This is told in the form of a myth and pressurise the devotees to come on pilgrimage in all the seasons to the year. So there is no question of auspiciousness or inauspiciousness of time element involved to perform the pilgrimage. It has been also told at populistic level that the goddess becomes inactive if She is not regularly offered with these ritual objects by the devotees since these are needed by Her to look 'attractive' to draw the attention of the male deity.

7. The myth says that only on the recommendation of the *Tanika,* Her brother, the goddess accepts the vows and votive objects from the devotees. So the devotees beg, cry and persue him to oblige them. Since all the votive objects offered to the goddess finally go to the *Tanika,* he makes use

of his position and exploits the devotees.

8. As of today the *Tanika* also works as the temple priest at the sacred centre. The position and benefits are equally distributed among the male members belonging to the four lineages by dividing the year into four equal parts and working on rotation. When not attending to his duties at the temple, the *Tanika* sits in his establishment at the sacred centre awaiting for the arrival of pilgrims. In addition, they own agricultural land in their village and also business establishments at the sacred centre. They visit their linked devotees in their villages during every harvest season and collect ritual tax. They also occupy a number of offices at local level civic bodies and temple committees. All these aspects have made them influential persons in the region.

9. Though it is a fact and this still has to be confirmed by a medico-social survey, a few categories of mendicants are eunuchs. But the question here is why the eunuchs end-up as mendicants. According to our findings in a patriarchal-virilocal, close rural society it becomes difficult for eunuchs to make a normal living. So the religious tradition has provided them with an opportunity to become mendicant functionaries, which exempts them from marrying and having a family. These mendicants claim their origin to a myth where they are the first three sons of the goddess who were cursed by their father god to lose their virility, when they had refused to chopp-off the head of their mother (goddess). So they do not feel ashamed or guilty of their status and freely move about in the society, propagating the glory of their mother.

There is another category of eunuch mendicants who get this status because of the wrath of the goddess. According to a version of the myth earlier they propagated a different ritual tradition and came to subdue the goddess. But the powerful goddess reduced them to this status by removing their ritual power, which is symbolised here by their virility, and enslaved them.

References

Bose, N.K. 1961, *Peasant life in India: A Study in Indian Unity and Diversity*, Calcutta.

Cohn, Bernord S.1971, India: Social Anthropology of a Civilization,

Englewood Cliffe, N.J., Prentice-Hall.

Ishwaran, K.1974, Shivapura - A South Indian Village. Routledge and Kegan Paul, London.

—, 1977. *A Populistic Community and Modernization in India.* Vikas, New Delhi.

—, 1983. *Religion and Society among the Lingayats of South India.* Vikas, New Delhi.

—,1989, Basavanna and Lingayat Dharma. Prasaranga, Karnatak University, Dharwad (Kannada).

—, 1993, Speaking of Basava: Lingayat Religion and Culture in South Asia. Westview Press, Oxford.

Gurumurthy, K.G.1989, Sacred Complex of Saudhatti. UGC Special Lectures delivered at the School of Archaeology, History and Anthropology, Telugu University, Sresailam.

—, 1991, "Symbolism in Rçnuka- Yallamma Ritual Tradition." In, *Samshodhana. Falicitation volume in honour of* Dr. M. Chidanandamurthy. Ed. Laxman Telagavi, Bangalore (pp.273-300) (Kannada).

—,1992, "Ritual Mendicants of a Shakti Shrine." In, *Science, Culture and Development. Facilitation volume in honour of Dr.L.K.Mahapatra.* Eds. N.K. Behura and C.K. Tripati, Paragan, Bhubaneshwar (pp.43-69).

—, 1995, "Pilgrimage to the Goddess at the Seven Valleys." In, *Pilgriamage: Concepts, Themes, Issues amnd Methoology.* Ed. Makhan Jha. Inter-India, New Delhi (pp.170-202).

—, 1996, *Religion and Politics: A Cultural Study of Ritual Tradition of Renuka-Yallamma.* Vimochana, Athani (Kannada).

Redfield, Robert 1956, *Peasant Society and Culture: An Anthropological Appoach to the Human Whole.* Chicago University Press, Chicago.

Saraswati, B.N.1975 Kashi: Myth and Reality of a Classical Cultural Tradition. Institute of Advanced Study, Simla.

—,1983 Traditions of Tirthas in Insia - the anthropology of Hindu Pilgrimage, N.K. Bose Memorial Foundation, Varanasi.

Saraswati, B.N. and Sinha, Surajit 1978, Ascetics of Kashi: *Myth and Reality of a Classical Cultural Tradition.* Institute of Advanced Study, Simla.

Singer, Milton 1972, *When a Great Tradition Modernises.* Prager Publications, New York.

Sinha, Surajit 1958, "Tribal Cultures of Peninsular India as a

Dimension of the Little Tradition: A Preliminary Statement. In, *Traditional India: Structure and Change*. Ed. Milton Singer (pp.298-312).

Srinivas, M.N. 1952, *Religion and Society among the Coorgs of South India*. Oxford, London.

Tarachand, K.C. 1987, Women in Sacred Prostitution: A study of Devadasi custom in Karnataka. Ph.D. thesis accepted by Karnatak University, Dharwad, for a degree in Anthropology.

—, 1991, *Devadasi Custom: Rural Social Structure and Flesh Markets*. Reliance, New Delhi.

Vidyarthi, L.P., Saraswati B.N. & Makhan Jha 1961, *The Sacred Complex of Hindu Gaya*. Asia

Publishing House, Bombay. 1979, *The Sacred Complex of Kashi*. Concept, New Delhi.

10

Pushkar Tirtha of Rajasthan, India An Anthropological Appraisal

Yadu Nath Pandey

Introduction

In Indian Anthropology, the study of Hindu place of pilgrimage was initiated after India's independence when a team of American Anthropologists took up researches in India. Under that trend of research Robert Redfield and Milton Singer influenced their counterparts in India and a number of researches on the Hindu traditional cities were taken up for studying them as a dimension of Indian Civilization. Milton Singer (1972) had earlier studied the city of Madras and had developed a set of concept like "cultural centres", "cultural performances", "cultural specialises", "cultural media" etc. However, when L.P. Vidyarthi studied The Sacred Complex of Hindu Gaya, (1961)", he modified some of the concepts developed earlier by Milton Singer and suggested that a Hindu place of pilgrimage should be studied in terms of trictometic elements viz. the sacred centres, the sacred performances, the sacred specialists and according to Vidyarthi (*ibid*) these are the universal specialities of the Hindu places of pilgrimages.

Under the influence of these researches Makhan Jha studied " the Sacred Complex of Janakpur in Nepal (1971)", the first work of this kind after Vidyarthi, when

Jha attempted to test the hypothesis that "Boundary of a nation is not the boundary of a civilization". Earlier, Saraswati also studied "the temple organization in Goa (1962)", and " the Holy circuit of Nimshar" (1965), which accelerated the researches on Hindu places of pilgrimage in Indian Anthropology. In this connection Jha further accelerated his interests in the study of Hindu places of pilgrimage and among which special mention may be made of his works viz, the "Sacred Complex of Ratanpur" (1972), the "Sacred Complex of Puri" (1979), the "Sacred Complex of the Himalayas" (1981, 1986), the "sacred complex Kathmandu" (1995), etc. In addition to these major works a number of young anthropologists in India have undertaken researches on the different little known sacred centres situated in both the tribal and non-tribal dominated regions of India. A few anthropologists, however, have recently studied, the Buddhist sacred centres as well as the Islamic sacred centres in both India and Nepal (Jha, 1995).

Influenced by these trends of researches in Indian Anthropology, I have attempted to throw light on the Pushkar tirtha in Rajasthan, which is called the king of all the tirthas of the Hindu Universe. I, therefore, discuss below the different aspects of this famous place of Hindu pilgrimage of western India, in the present paper.

Location of Pushkar

Pushkar Tirtha, named after a big Sarover (lake) created by Lord Brahma, the creater of the Hindu universe, is situated at a distance of nearly thirteen kilometres from Ajmer in the state of Rajasthan. One can reach Pushkar Tirtha from Ajmer only by road. However, the last railway station for reaching Pushkar is only at Ajmer.

From Ajmer pilgrims and other devotees usually engage auto rickshaw or go by buses which usually poly regularly on Ajmer-Pushkar road.

The Myth associated with Pushkar Tirtha

It is believed, as also mentioned in the various *Purans*

that a drop of nector fell at Pushkar which turned into a big lake. Later on, Lord Brahma along with his wife Savitri came to reside at Pushkar followed by several gods and goddesses. It is further mentioned in the Puran, that a holy bath in the Pushkar lake would earn a religious merit equal to several hundred *Ashwamedh Yaga.* It is narrated that the pilgrim would get *Moksha* (salvation) after getting a sacred bath in the holy lake of Pushkar. In course of time, the Purans say that various *rishis* (ascetics) including Brihaspati and Gods like Lord Vishnu, Lord Shiva, etc., all came to Pushkar to worship Lord Brahma.

The Pushkar tirtha is also famous for offering *pindas* (rice balls) to the past ancestors for their salvation. The Puranas, further mention that the Gaya Tirtha, famous for *pind-dan* which is located in the state of Bihar, is believed to come here in the Hindu month of Kartik Purnima (full Moon day) to receive oblations from the descendants of the deceased ancestors. Various other sacred rivers like Saraswati, Yamuna, etc. also reside there around the Pushkar lake. In this way various myths and legends have been associated with the Pushkar Tirtha which influence the Hindu pilgrims to visit the Pushkar tirtha at least once in their life time.

Although, there are various Puranas wherein we get a detail references and descriptions of Pushkar tirtha, but most elaborately Pushkar tirtha has been described in the Padmapuran where several chapters have been devoted on the description of Pushkar tirtha. However, I describe mostly the contextual aspect of the sacred centres of Pushkar tirtha with a view to examine as to how in course of time, the sacred centres grow at a Hindu place of pilgrimage and here it binds together people belonging to various castes and sects.

Sacred Centres of Pushkar

Broadly speaking Pushkar Tirtha is famous for its lake known as *Pushkar Sarovar.* The *Pushkar Sarovar* is divided into three parts, viz. the eldest Pushkar is represented by Suprava river, Middle Pushkar by the

Sindha river and the little Pushkar finds representation through the rivers like Kanka, Hand, Prachi rivers, etc.

The Pushkar lake is surrounded by various hills over which a large number of sacred centres are situated and the pilgrims are expected to make at least a circumambulation of all these shrines to earn religious merit.

As mentioned earlier, the main holy place of Pushkar is Pushkar Sarover where there are fifty two bathing ghats, among them special mention may be made of *Gau Ghat,* the *Barah Ghat,* Brahma Ghat, etc. These bathing Ghats were built by the Hindu Kings and queens of Rajasthan as well as by the Marahta rulers from time to time. For example, one of the Marahta rulers built one beautiful umbrella in memory of Santu Ram Bawalia at the cost of Rs. 1 lakh and several thousands at *Gau Ghat.* Again, in Sambat 1762 (corresponding to 1705 A.D.) Guru Govind Singh Ji visited Pushkar and preached the lessons of tolerance and universal brotherhood at Pushkar.

Thus, since the dawn of civilization Pushkar has attracted the attentions of great personalities from all over India irrespective of any religious or political affiliations. In this connection it may be further noted that when big national leaders like Mahatma Gandhi, Jawarharlal Nehru, Lal Bahadur Shastri etc. were cremated, their ashes were immersed in the Pushkar Sarovar for salvation of their souls.

Besides this Pushkar lake, the other main attraction is the temple of Lord Brahma, the only Brahma temple found in the Hindu world. Nowhere in India nor Nepal, the only Hindu Kingdom in the world, there is any temple of Lord Brahma. However, at Pushkar the famous temple of Lord Brahma is one of the main attraction when pilgrims from different parts of India come for darshan of Brahma. The priest at the Brahma temple at Pushkar reported that no householder is allowed to perform Puja in the temple of Brama, because only the ascetics have right to performs *puja* in the temple of Brahma. However, the general Hindu pilgrims offer flowers and other sacred ingredients from a distance through the priests of Brahma temple.

Performance at Pushkar

One of the important sacred performances of Pushkar is to take bath in the *Pushkar Sarovar* and, thereafter, to offer the *Pindas* to their past ancestors. Thus, after Gaya tirtha, Pushkar is a second important tirtha for *pinda dan.* As mentioned earlier, Gaya tirtha comes personally to Pushkar on full moon day in the month of Kartik to receive the *Pindas* offered in the names of past ancestors, when pilgrims assemble here in large number.

On the occasion of Kartik Purnima the biggest animal fair is arranged here when animal traders reach *Pushkar* a week ahead for selling varieties of animals, like camels, horses, cows, etc. On this occasion there is a heavy rush of tourist also who come not only from different parts of India, but also from various foreign countries. On such occasion the races of camels, horses etc. are also arranged and thereby tourists arc attracted to visit Pushkar mela.

The Pilgrims have been found to visit only a few important sacred centres, after taking the sacred bath in the Pushkar *Sarovar* and among those famous temples, special mountain may be made of Brahmaji temple, *BarahVishnu* temple, Savitri temple, or Raghunathji, the Atmeshwar Mahadeo, Baikunthaji temple etc. It may be mentioned have that there are three hundred fifty sacred centres at Pushkar but pilgrims do not visit almost all the sacred centres mainly due to lack of time at their disposal. However, it has been found during my field work at Pushkar that almost all the pilgrims visit the temple of Lord Brahma followed by the worship of Gayatriji and then they go to other sacred centres as mentioned above. The pilgrims get all sorts of facilities during the period of their stay at Pushkar. The priests of Pushkar, who are Brahmins belonging to Parasar gotra, have residential houses where provisions are made for the accommodation of pilgrims who have jajmanika (pilgrims priests) relationship. Besides the priests houses, there are many *dharamshalas* like the Surja *dharamshala,* Krishna *dharamshala,* Gujarati *dharamshala,* Maheshwari *dharamshala,* Sindhis *dharamshala,* Govt. rest houses and a few private lodgs for the stay of the pilgrims at Pushkar. However, it has been further observed that a few pilgrims and devotees who visit Pushkar by their own vehicles prefer to return to Ajmer in the evening to pass night at Ajmer city. The pilgrims at Pushkar are also provided with many restaurants where they take snacks, lunch etc., without much difficulties. In this way, although Pushkar is comparatively a small town of temples but almost all facilities are available for pilgrims who are the main sources of income and livelihood for the priests, the traders, and other local inhabitants who entirely depend on this is called "pilgrims industry" (Saraswati 1975; Jha 1971, 1995, Vidyarthi, Jha and Saraswati 1978).

Sacred specialists

Among the sacred specialists (Vidyarti 1961), the Brahmanas belonging to the Parasar Gotra are in overwhelming number. From an estimate, there are seven hundred Brahmin priests who entirely depend on income received from the pilgrims. Various donations. remunerations etc. given by the pilgrims from time to time are the main sources of their livelihood. They have not much cultivable lands and whatever lands they have, those are neither fertile nor provide sufficient yields for their annual consumption. In this way, the Brahmin priests mainly depend on income received from the pilgrims. However, some Brahmin priests have recently established few shops and restaurants to earn some extra money for their better survival. In this way, some changes have taken place in the economic structure of the sacred specialists of Pushkar.

Besides the Brahmin priests there are other functionariess like the flowermen, the barbers, the *Prasad* sellers etc, who also earn money by selling flowers and other sacred ingredients. According to Vidyarthi (*Ibid*) these people also fall under the category of "Sacred specialists", and these "Sacred specialists", no doubt, maintain their livelihood by conducting religious services.

The sacred centres of Pushkar have been patronised by kings and queens of Rajasthan princely states and Marathas, in particular, and by the rich pilgrims of India, in general. The constructions of various bathing ghats at the Pushkar lake, the various umrellas at the different bathing ghats, the different *dharamshalas* and several other inns for the use of visiting pilgrims, have been made from time to time by the Rajput rulers which shows that Pushkar tirthas have been patronised by the rulers of different dynasties of Rajasthan and other neighbouring states. As a matter of fact, tirthas survive only by extending patronage and continue to be centres of "great traditions" (Redfield :1955) in Indian Civilization.

Observations

Hindu Tirthas, since time immemorial, have been the centres of civilization where pilgrims belonging to various castes and tribes come together and interact with each other and thereby it promotes the national integration and social cohesion in India. Pushkar tirtha is the only Hindu tirtha in India where Lord Brahma is the presiding deity and it is the only temple in the whole Hindu universe. The Hindu pilgrims, irrespective of castes and sectarian affiliations aspire to visit at least once in their life time. It is a binding force and reflects a universal sense of socio-religious solidarity when the pilgrims from far north-eastern India visit Pushkar situated at the western India and thereby exchange views for the mutual benefit of cultural integration. This is the highest benefit a tirtha provides for promoting national integration and socio-religious solidarity irrespective of its locations, geological and ecological variations.

References

Jha, Makhan : 1971, *The Sacred Complex of Janakpur in Nepal* The United Publishers. Allahabad.

—, :1978, *Aspects of a Great Traditional City in Nepal* : Krishore Vidya Niketan Varanasi. : The Sacred Complex of Kathmandu, Nepal. Gyan Prakashan, New Delhi.

—,1995, *Pilgrimage : Issues, Themes, Concepts and Methodology*, Inter India Publication, New Delhi.

Panday Yadunath : 1995, The Bhadrakali of Itkhori, India. Paper presented at thirteenth I.C.A.E.S., Mexico

Published in M. Jha's edited volume on *Pilgrimage: Issues*, Themes, Concepts and Methods: Inter India Publication, New Delhi.

Redfield, Robert Milton Singer : 1955, Social Organisation of Traditions: Far Eastern quarterly, Vol. 15.

Saraswati, Baidyanath : 1975, *Kashi : Myth and Reality of a Classical, Cultural Traditions*; Published by Indian Institute of Advanced Study, Simla.

Singer, Milton : 1972, *When a Great Tradition Nodernizes*: Prentice Hall, New York.

Vidyarthi, L.P :1961, *The Sacred Complex of* Hindu Gaya, Asia Publication House, Bombay.

Vidyarthi, L.P, M.Jha and,B.N. Saraswati : 1978, *The sacred complex of Kashi* : Concept Publishing Company, New Delhi.

11

Pilgrims and Pilgrimage : A Case Study of Sakti Pitha-Kalighat, India

Purabi Nandi

Thc Shakti Pitha of Kalighat is situated in the predominantly urban area of Calcutta. It is a Shakta religious Centre. A myth link most of the Sakti Pitha within a scheme of unity.

The legend concerns the goddess Sati, daughter of Daksha and wife of Siva. Daksha decided to hold a great sacrifice (Yajna) to which he invited neither his daughter nor son-in-law. Sati was offended by this slight and attended the sacrifice uninvited. There she was insulted by Daksha and humiliated, she took her life. On hearing this news, Siva hastened to the house of Daksha, destroyed the Yajna, killed Daksha and claimed the body of his wife. In consolable at his loss, he placed Sati's body on his shoulder and began a mad dance through the three universe. His dance threatened to destroy all creation. The gods became distraught at this prospect. One version of the story of Dakshayajna has it that the gods approached Visnu to restrain Siva. Visnu sent arrows or his *Sudarsan Chakra* (discus) to dismember the body of Sati limb by limb. An alternative vision states that the deities Brahma, Visnu, and Sani entered Sati's body and caused it to disintegrate when Siva was thereby deprived of Sati's body, he ceased his mad dance.

The parts of Sati's body fell from Siva's shoulder to the earth and the places where they landed became the sacred Sakti Pitha. Fifty-one Pitha established one of them is Kalighat. As conceived by Dr. Sailendra Ghosal Shastri (1957) after the death of king Asoke, a maximum number of people of Nalanda were engaged in austere worship of God Buddha. Among them some mendicant friar and mendicant nun began to study the scripture. Generally, *Tantra* is the system of the religious worship. But some mendicant friar and mendicant nun were explained, "*Tantra* means to study the different parts of body". There are fifty-one important parts of body which are awaken by the yoga. These sixty four mendicant friar and mendicant nun were given away from the Nalanda by the other mendicant friar and mendicant nun. Then they were incorporated within a group. They were present different comprehend places of India and established the one part of the body of one place. Thus there are established the fifty-one holy places in India. Kalighat is the one of the holy place among these places. This religious centre contains the daksinapadanguli (figure of the right leg) of the goddess. The Sakti is related to that of Siva as will be discussed in a pitha by the presence of a Bairava, a named manifestation of Siva, as the associate of the particular aspect of the goddess found in that place. The union of Siva and Sakti, often conceived symbolically as a wedded couple, is represented in every Sakti Pitha by having Siva installed as a lingo in a small shrine near that of goddess. There he receives oblation from the priests and pilgrims, but is always accorded secondary status to the goddess.

Since early times the pitha of Kalighat has received the attention of sovereign power of Northern India, it is evident from Mansinghs' (the General under the Mughal Akbar and later on of Jahangir) connection with Lakshminkanta, an inmate of the Ashrama. It is stated that under his initiative Lakshmikanta, secured royal patronage and the jagir from the Mughal King. In course of time his family became the powerful landlords of Kalighat and contributed towards the construction of the temple of the mother and helped in popularising the Sakti-cult in the area. Later on after the Britishers purchased dihi-Kalikata (Calcutta) from the family and a deed was signed on the 9th of November in 1698, the urbanisation of the area started and the pithas came to be visited more, and more by sophisticated people which naturally had its effect upon the total life of the place. Thus the cremation ground here is at a distance from the main centre of the mother and on enquiry it could be gathered from on Oriya ritualist, in the *Smasana* (cremation ground) that, people here consider the cremation ground as a deity place and a possible breading ground of various germs and viruses, while as he reported, the case is otherwise in other pithas where it is expected that the maha *Smasama* should be at a close proximity to the centre of worship. The impact of the Britishers and the growing sophistication had its effect upon some of the important rituals also.

The life giving, protective, creative capacites of the goddess provide the motives for most pilgrims visit to Sakti pitha, where they seek out the powerful Mother to aid them in this life or for help in procuring a better future life. The goddess is sought out for all the spiritual, material and physical needs of her children. In this role the goddess is creator and provide and it is this aspect of the goddess that most pilgrims seek to propagate or benefit from in their worship.

People take their bath in the river Adiganga before visiting this temple. The very name 'Adiganga' is significant and indicates that this was at one time the old and original bed of the river. It is said that the cardinal factor in the latter history of the delta of Bengal has been the east ward shift of the Ganges water from a main out let along the western margins the Bhagirathi-Hooghly to the present main cause the Padma-Meghna, with such streams as Ichamati, Jalangi, Mathabhaga, Gorai representing intermediate positions of the most important channel. This Bhagirathi or one of its several branches (Hooghly, Saraswati, Adiganga or 'Tolly's Nullah) was an important distributary in the seventeenth century, but has been sitting since 1770 when the Damodar, which helped it to keep it clear, shifted its mouth eight miles to the south. The present situation of the river in respect of volume of water has undoubtedly affected the life of the centre.

History of the Temple Patronage

There are different traditions which suggest that the temple of Devi Kalika accommodating here petrified figures kept in a box inside her image was constructed by more than one man leaving in different periods of history. It is believed that Vasanta Roy (brother of Vikramaditya, the ruler of Jessore in the sixteenth century A.D.) built this temple when he came there on a routine visit and found the existing one in a very wretched condition. It is said that, he did it out of his devotion for his Guru Bhuvaneswar Chakraborty, the then Sevait of the temple. This seems to be quite possible when it is noted that Kalighat was at the time part of the State Jessore. Another tradition affirms that Mansingh built it when he came to Bengal.

As both Vasanta Roy and Mansingh lived almost in the same period. The issue as to who constructed the improved edition of the temple gets all the more complicated. But it is to be noted that Mansingh's visit to Bengal and clash with Pratapaditya (the nephew of Vasanta Roy) took place when Vasanta Roy was already dead.

This is evident from the fact that Kachu Roy, the son of Vasanta Roy helped Mansingh against Pratapaditya in order to avenge his father death at the hand of the former.

After scrutinising the above facts it may be concluded that Vasanta Roy and Mansingh helped in piece-meal construction of the temple at two different times. The story connected with temple construction by Santosh Roy of the Sabarna Chowdhury is equally interesting when Churamoni Dutta of Shova Bazar, Calcutta died, Kaliprasad Dutta faced much difficulty in inviting the Brahmanas of the locality at the Shradha ceremony of his relative owing to mischief done by his rival party. At this he sought the help of Santosh Roy. He favourably responded and the brahmins who attended the ceremony were given enough *daksina* (gift in the form of money) besides food. In accordance with the wish of their leader. Santosh Roy, the brahmins dedicated the money received towards the expansion of the Devi's temple. Though the progamme was undertaken by Santosh Roy, it could not finished during his life time ; it was completed by his son in 1809 A.D. No major construction of temple has taken place after this date.

The pitha can be divided into five number of Centres.

(1) The temple of the goddess Kalika.

(2) The Nakulesvara Siva temple.

(3) The Kalikunda.

(4) The deities of Syamarai and Govindarai.

(5) The cremation ground by the side of Adiganga.

The temple of the goddess Kalika with four Siva Lingas surrounding it, the Saubhagua Kunda in east, the Syamarai in the west from one secred cluster, because the rituals concerning these centres are done entirely in accordance with requirement of goddess. In that sense the temple of Nakulesvara is also a part of this cluster as Nakulesvara is her consort and the life in both the centres are turned together as well be evident from the discussion of the ritual pattern.

It is interesting that Govindaraj who is at present nearer in space to the Devi than Nakulesvara (situated at a distance on the Haldarpara Road) is treated as an outside which has interesting history at the back. It is said that, the original shrine of Govindaji was established by the trading communities like the Seths and Basus in the village of Govindapura (now a part of Calcutta). The village is evidently named after the deity situated at a little distance from Kalighat.

It is to be noted that the place of cremation or burning ghat which forms an integral part of a pithas in general, is at a distance from the temple unlike is other pithas where Tantric rules are more strictly observed. Another thing that attracts one's notice is the increasing number of studios and tea stalls centering round the burning ghat. Very recently in addition to the old burning ghat a modern electrified oven has been constructed to meet the increasing demand of the over populated area. Lighting arrangements have improved so that there is not the slightest difficulty in going to the cremation ground in the dark hours. There is proper resting place as well. All these are due to impact of city life.

The temple of the goddess Kali was constructed on the eight katha land. The height of this temple is sixty hand and the wide within the temple is thirty hand. At that time, the expenditure to construct this temple was Rupees sixty thousand (approx.)

The Image of Goddess Kali

Any pilgrim visiting the image of the goddess Kalika at the temple of Kalighat will be surprised to see that though she is supported to represent Dakshina Kalika, she according to the dhyana of the goddess, does not stand upon the chest of her consort Siva there by making a great departure from the usual scense in other centres. Here we find a bust, with four hands and an uncouth face with a long potruding tongue of gold. We may naturally enquire what might be the reason of this deviation from the general practice. It may be noted that though a Sakti Centre, Kalighat has a Yoga tradition of Lakulisa Pasupata order centering round the temple of Nakulesavara. Here therefore the mother goddess serves the object of high concentration tune with the Yoga Sutra of Patanjali.

Thus, in the truer spirit of Yoga tradition emphasis has been put on the symbol (taking in it a part of Sati's body) instead of on the fuller image.

A true follower of Kali pays only secondary homage to Siva and the fanaties go so far as to assert that Siva is nothing but a darwan (door keeper) or the Great Mother Kingdom where the goddess is the supreme queen. According to them the interior status of Siva is reflected by the image where he lies under the feet of the goddess. The Saivas of Kalighat did not like it and so under their influence a new type of image was constructed at the centre.

One tilak was printed on the nose of goddess Kali, it represent the Baisnav cult. The most influential sevait Bhavanidas Chakraborty was originally Baisnav cult. At last he accepted the sakta cult.

Rituals : The Sakti pitha ritual-performances can broadly be divided into two categories, daily performance and occasional performance.

There is the usual daily routing a Sakti pitha which provides for *Nitya Puja* for the period November to February (around 7.30 a.m.) *Balidan* at 11.00 a.m., and *anna-bhoga* at 2.30 p.m. to 3.00 p.m. *Arati* (between 6.30 p.m. to 7.00 p.m.) *Sitala-Bhoga* (after 7.00 p.m.) and after a light meal of the Devi, *Sayana* (sleeping) at night. One loudly utters here the words "Visvambhara Jago" in order to awaken Visvambhara (equated with Siva), followed by mangala arati (morning Prayer). It is the first ritual act done in the name of visvambhara in a place where the Devi Kalika is supreme. The period of March to October the time of Nitya Puja is maintained before one hour, i.e., 6.30 a.m.

Ramnavami celebration in Kalighat is another performance of considerable importance. It is to be noted that on this occasion Krishna and his consort Radha are worshipped with pomp and grandeur and inmates of the pitha there are given new clothings (The usual practice in other areas is that people were new cloths during Durga Puja). It is held each year on a day of *Chaitra* (April-May). The ceremony is divided into two parts. One is *'Nandatsava'* when takes place on the birth day of Krishna. In the evening hours the image of Radha and Mahadeva are given a sacred bath with *'Dahi'* (curd) and *'Haludi'* (turmeric). Then another ritual takes place on the following day and is known as *'Dalotsava'*.

On this occasion the deities are places on a swing. Then they taken out in a procession through the different streets of locality. After this they are placed at the feet of Devi Kalika. The ritual signify the different stages of the growth of Krishna. During *Nandatsava* he remains a mere child. He gradually matures and when he is an adult, he marries and lies a happy conjugal life. This is symbolised by the scene of the owing. But even in adulthood he remains devoutly attached to his mother here who is Devi Kalika. The entire ritual programme suggests a familiar tone of a Bengali family. Here Radha, Krishna and Devi Kalika have been cast in a distinctly human mould. The presence of

Radha and Mahadava and the rituals connected with them bring in it a Vaishavic tone, but as Devi Kalika is their mother, the predominance of the Sakti cults becomes well apparent.

It was learnt that a religious gathering in front of the temple is organised each year in order to facilitate to *Sadhakas* and inmates of the religious centre in matter of receiving higher spiritual and religious knowledge. It is believed *jnana* (knowledge) is one of the *Yoga* ways by which *Kundalini* is roused in the body of *Sadhaka*. This gathering is known as Siva-*bhakti pradayini-sabha*. It is interesting to note that this assembly has replaced the formen one called *Sarvarth-asadhini Sadha*. It used to be held within the precinct of Kalika Devi's temple on the *Chaitra Samkranti* day (Last day of Bangali month Chaitra which coincides with a day in mid April of the English Calendar), and *Paila Vaisakh* (the first day of Bengali year).

The Ritualists : Persons connected with temple and helping in its ritual can broadly be grouped into the following categories :- (i) *Purohits* (ii) The *sevaits* (iii) The *Daladharas* (iv) A group of man belong to casts other than Brahmin.

Ritualist of three categories are Brahmins of the *Halder* groups, origin from the Bhabanidas Chakraborty, while the non-Brahmins belong mainly to the *Bagdi* class, a proto Austroloid original inhabitant of the place. The *halder* families even to this day remain responsible for every thing related to the temple of Mother while position and prestige of all other groups are virtually determined in terms of their relation with these *Halder* Sevaits.

The fact of Bhavanidas Chakraborty coming to this pithasthan from East Bengal has been referred to earlier. He is considered to be earliest *Halders Sevaits* of Kalighat from whom the different Halders families trace their origin. Though he was already married Bhavanidas took another daughter of Bhubaneswara Brahmachari in wed lock. It has been noted already that Bhuvaneswara was the first recognised *Mahanta* or chief Sevait of the *pitha*. By this marriage he got four sons. His first son Jadavendra was by her first wife whom he got married before coming to Kalighat.

Later on Jadavendra came to Kalighat and these five members constituted the original Halder family, the title of Halder being conferred upon them during the regime of Allivardi Khan.

They ultimately became the properties of the property of Kalika Devi. This family of Halders has expanded so much today that it is hardly possible now for any individual of this family to scene more than one *pala* in a year. The *pala* here means the daily change of worship of the goddess but on occasions like Snanyatra, Syamapuja, Durgapuja etc. all the sevaits unite and share their duties. During these occasions they act in joint responsibility. The Halders have practice of selling their *palas* or terms within their own community. No outsider is entitled to purchase it. It is to be noted that the sale transference of *pala* in no way takes away the responsibility of looking after the ritual performance from the sevait concerned. The responsibility was first handed over by Sri Bhabanidas upon his five sons and that is being continued through generations.

With the advancement of time the number of pilgrims increased. This brought a pressure upon the sevaits who in order to cope with load of work began appointing additional hands for temple service and thus special purohits were appointed for performing the actual *puja* ceremony. Ultimately many of them became their *gurus* (spiritual guides) or *Purohhit.*

The function of the Daladhara group of ritualists is to mediate between the *purohitas* and the pilgrims mainly. They also help the priests directly according to the later direction by holding the *Dala* a sacred pot where articles of worship are placed and at the same time guide the pilgrims in having *darsan* of the different sacred centres of the pithasthan.

A new phase developed in the life centering the pithasthan after partition of India in 1947, when a large number of refugees who lived on priesthood in the East Bengal, came here and tried to act as such in the temple. They were accepted, but not given the status of *Purohita.* Naturally they then accepted the job of *Daladharas* and became *Sathis* of pilgrims. It has been noted that of the non-brahmin caste engaged in the service of the *Bagdis* figures prominently. The Bagdis have been assists the landlords Halders and they are slaying animals for sacrifice. These *Bagdis* are still at a very low level of culture and so do not hesitate to continue their old practice.

The *Sadgopas* (another section of the low caste Hindus) sell articles for worship. Their shops are called 'Dalardokan'.

Patras are another class who help in the propagation of knowledge about Mother and her temple. They earn their bread by selling pictures relating to deities and religious themes. As the pilgrims generally are of modest means, these artists take care that the finished product in saleable at a small figure. In this way men of different caste orders and tastes have been rendering indirect service to the temple of the Mother since ages.

As a place of Hindu pilgrimage, Kalighat has attracted many people from diverse areas for a long time. On an average three to four thousand pilgrims, come daily to this place. This number increases manifold of such occasions as Snanjatra, Durgapuja, Kalipuja, Ramnavami, Chaitra Sankranti, Payla Baishak, Aksoythithiya, when one lack of people congregate here. The attendance of pilgrims is found to exceed the average on every Tuesday, Saturday, Sunday and usual holidays throughout the year. I have contracted with ritual specialists and people of various socio-economic strata the elites, the common men and women of various caste groups and professions. In course of conversation with them, I realise that it concern not only with the sacred complex pilgrim centre but also with the socio-economic aspects of its presence in area and especially importance of the cult for the town.

The main objective of the study is :

1. Nature and Type of Pilgrims.
2. Different type of rituals usually performed by the pilgrims and it causes.
3. To find out the reason by which the people are attracted to the sacred place.

Two hundred data have been collected by interview with males 110 and female 90 over the age 10+ to 70 above.

Available documents are being consulted whereever available to examine the authenticity of statements are responses.

Thus, my main method have been schedule, interview, observations, case studies, sampling etc. through which the scientific data have been collected. Photographs have been also taken of the type of ritual performed. Thus, my approach are largely synchronic and are based on empirical field work.

Standard Techniques of analysis of both quantitative and qualitative type have been applied for the analysis of data.

Table 1
Per centage Distribution of Sample Pilgrims by Age and Sex

	Male		*Female*	
Age	*No*	*Per centage*	*No*	*Per centage*
10 -20	02	1.80	02	2.20
20 -30	04	3.60	08	8.90
30 -40	15	13.60	16	17.80
40 -50	37	33.70	22	24.40
50 -60	40	36.40	27	30.00
60 -70	07	6.40	07	7.80
70+above	05	4.50	08	8.90
Total	110	100.00	90	100.00

Table-1 shows that within 10 + to 30 years of male pilgrims are very poor but within 20 - 30 years of female pilgrims are 8.90 per cent Within 50 - 80 years of male pilgrims are 36.40 per cent contrast to the 30 per cent female pilgrims. Within 40 - 50 years of male pilgrims are 33.40 per cent contrast to the 24.40 per cent of female pilgrims. Within 30 to 40 years of male pilgrims are 13.60 per cent contrast to the 17.80 per cent of female pilgrims. Within 60 - 70 and above years of male pilgrims respectively

6.40 per cent and 4.50 per cent contrast to the 7.80 per cent and 8.90 per cent of female pilgrims.

Table-2 shows that Male and Female Pilgrims of Hindi language are greater than Bengali language. Female pilgrims of Bengali, language are greater than male pilgrims of Bengali language Male pilgrims of Oriya, Malayam and Assamese languages respectively 9.10 per cent, 6.40 per cent and 4.50 per cent contrast to the female pilgrims 5.6 per cent, 3.30 per cent and 2.20 per cent.

Table 2

Per centage Distribution of Respondents on the basis of Language

	Male		*Female*	
Language	*No.*	*Per centage*	*No.*	*Per centage*
Bengali	35	31.80	35	38.00
Hindi	53	48.20	45	50.90
Oriya	10	9.10	05	5.60
Malayam	07	6.40	03	3.30
Assamese	05	4.50	02	2.20
Total	110	100.00	90	100.00

Table 3

Per centage Distribution of Respondents on the Basis of Literacy

	Male		*Female*	
Educational level	*No.*	*Per centage*	*No.*	*Per centage*
Illiterate	15	13.64	13	14.44
Literate with nonformal	27	24.55	16	17.78
Primary to below High School	43	39.09	36	40.00

Contd.

Educational level	*Male* No.	*Male* Per centage	*Female* No.	*Female* Per centage
High School to intermediate	14	12.73	11	12.22
Graduate and Post graduate	08	7.27	14	15.56
Technical	03	2.72	-	-
Total	110	100.00	90	100.00

Table-3 exhibits the level of literacy of the sample pilgrims it is evident that the proportion of Primary to below High School male pilgrims 39.09 per cent and female 40 per cent are higher than other educational level. The peculiar feature is 2.72 per cent of the male pilgrims has received technical education but no female pilgrim has received technical education. The proportion of male and female illiterate pilgrim is slight difference. At the same picture shows High School in Intermediate education of male and female pilgrim 24.55 per cent literate with non-formal education of male pilgrim contrast to the 17.78 per cent female pilgrim. 7.27 per cent male graduate and post graduate pilgrim contrast to the 15.66 per cent female pilgrim.

Table 4
Per centage Distribution of Respondents On The Basis of Occupation

Occupation	*Male* No.	*Male* Per centage	*Female* No.	*Female* Per centage
Medical Doctor	02	1.81	03	3.33
Lawyer	04	3.64	04	4.44
Nurse	-	-	02	2.22
Politician	17	15.45	04	4.44
Lecturer	02	1.81	02	2.22
Teacher	09	8.18	10	11.11
Policeman	15	13.64	-	-

Contd.

Occupation	*Male*		*Female*	
	No.	*Per centage*	*No.*	*Per centage*
Fireman	08	7.27	-	-
Traditional Shop	21	19.09	-	-
Priest	03	2.73	-	-
Beggar	04	3.64	06	6.67
Servant	03	2.73	08	8.89
Military	03	2.73	-	-
Navy	02	1.81	-	-
Sadhu	04	3.64	-	-
Unemployed	05	4.55	33	36.67 (Housewife)
Retired	03	2.73	06	6.67
Student	05	4.55	12	13.34
Total	110	100.00	90	100.00

Table - 4 exhibits the proportion of traditional shop male pilgrim is higher 19.09 per cent than other occupation. The proportion of unemployed female (housewife) pilgrim is higher 36.67 per cent other occupation. 15.45 per cent of male politician pilgrim contrast to the 4.44 per cent female politician pilgrim. 4.55 per cent of male student pilgrim contrast to the 13.34 per cent of female student pilgrim. The proportion of other occupational male and female pilgrim is slight difference.

There are two type of pilgrims come to this pilgrimage centre-one regularly another occasionally.

Table 5

Per centage Distribution of Pilgrims Area And Type

No. of Sample Pilgrim - 200

Type of Pilgrim

Area District	*Regularly*		*Occasional*	
	No.	*Per centage*	*No.*	*Per centage*
Calcutta	65	52.00	20	26.68
24 Parganas	45	36.00	15	20.00
Howrah	10	8.00	10	13.33

Contd.

Area District	*No.*	*Regularly Per centage*	*No.*	*Occasional Per centage*
Hooghly	05	4.00	18	24.00
Burdwan	-	-	04	5.33
Nadia	-	-	01	1.33
Midnapur	-	-	02	2.68
Bankura	-	-	01	1.33
Birbhum	-	-	01	1.33
Murshidabad	-	-	01	1.33
West Dinajpur	-	-	01	1.33
Maldha	-	-	01	1.33
Total	125	100.00	75	100.00

Table-5 shows that 52 per cent and 36 per cent pilgrim comes regularly and 26.68 per cent and 20 per cent pilgrim comes occasionally from the Calcutta and 24-Parganas District. The next two districts, Howarah and Hooghly pilgrims comes regularly 8 per cent and 4 per cent respectively. 13.33 per cent and 24 per cent pilgrim comes occasionally from the Howrah and Hooghly Districts. Pilgrim of other eight districts comes occasionally and this proportion is very poor. They are making different types of vow such as for personal health, husband and children welfare, for other welfare, for job, to regain memory, for setting child, for business, for examination, for daughters marriage, for safe delivery of child, for resolution of family problem, to find lost child, to cure child's dumbness.

Fullfilling the above vow they come to this pilgrimage centre. The different type of rituals usually performed by the pilgrims.

Darshan

This is the simplest of all sacred performances denoting an act of seeing or visiting the deity in order to pay homage. No elaborate rite is needed in it. In formal worship, one has to take a look at the deity first, but that is different from a casual visit in that the former is done as a part of worship while the latter exclusively without performing the worship. For instance some resident of Kalighat possess the habit of visiting the temple regularly just to have a look at the deity. Similarly, many people come from outside once or twice a week only to have an auspicious view of God.

Puja

The worship takes place everybody in the temple of Kalighat. Different kinds of worshippers do it different manners and personal worships with prayer and incantations and the resident of the town and pilgrims from outside perform it by offering some articles like *Nakuldana,* coconut, kinds of sweets (*para*), flowers, *Dhup,* garlands in earthen source known as *dala.*

Snan

The water of Adiganga and Kalikunda is considered holy and meritorious by the pilgrims. In the month of *Aswin* (September-October) people comes from local and neighbouring areas, particularly the poor Hindu perform the *tarpan* (water offering to the names).

Dandi

When a desire is fulfilled and believed to be so through the deity's grace some devotees undergo an austerity called dandi. It consists of traversing a part of whole of the way to pilgrimage through successive prostrations, each equal to measure of one's body length and is common sight at many other centres of pilgrimage in India.

Dhil-bandha

Although restricted to the women devotees of local and regional areas, some 10-12 persons come here every day to perform a ritual known as *dhil-bandha.* As the name suggests, it is an act of tying a lump of hard clay or a potsherd with one's own hair or with a rope and suspending it to a tree or any object in front of the deity. This is a folk rite suggesting a sort of contractual relation between the devout and the deity. The nodule is the token of contact kept at the deity's custody. The act of tying, i.e. the bandhan seems to symbolic the contact. The deity may or may not fulfil the vow but if it does, the devout must honour the unilateral contact and offer the worship.

After fulfilling the sacred vow, other rituals are performed—Goat sacrifice to the Goddess, money offering, silver and Gold offering, etc.

There is widespread belief among worshippers of Kali in the powerful efficag of sacrificial offerings to the goddess, and *bali* continues to be performed in vast numbers today even in urban Bengal Calcutta male goats are the most commonly used live animals offered in sacrifice. At Kalighat Temple a daily sacrifice of a single goat in commissioned by the Brahmins in charge of ritual (paladors). The meat of this animal is later cooked and offered to the deity as part of her daily food offering (Bhog). Portions of *bhog* are subsequently purchased and consumed by worshippers as *prasad* (divine grace). At the temple goat sacrifices are individually made to Kali as vow related offering (*manater bali*). Here the worshipper makes a vow to offer an animal in sacrifice should the goddess alleviate a crisis such as illness of penury. In this type of offering made after the individual's problem has been resolved by Kali, the meat of the animals taken home, cooked and consumed as *prasad* by members of the sacrifice's family. At Kalighat Temple 70 or more goats may be offered in sacrifice (usually vow-related) on any of several auspicious festive days, including Kalipuja, Tuesday, Saturday, are especially auspicious for Kali's worship and have an average of 30 or more goat sacrifices in one day.

Bali sacrifice is the experiential high point of the goddess rituals a successful *bali,* namely a clean immolation with one stroke of the sacrificial sword, is perceived at being critical to the 'well being' (*mangal*) of the sacrifier and his family. Conversely, a failed *bali*, i.e., where more than one stroke is required, is seen as a condition of being struck being hundred (bansha para) Its consequences are perceived as being catastrophic, the sacrifier or his family going in danger dead and general calamity, such as insanity, poverty and disease. The evident power of *bali* is obviously integral to its 'meaning' and continuing popularity, suggesting that a great deal lies a stake for the scarifier.

The structure of *pathabali* may be divided into five board phases :

(i) *Baliprakara.* A prolongue in which a male goat of 'auspicious signs' namely one that is entirely black and in good health, is prepared for sacrifice through rites of purification and sacrilization.

(ii) *Kharagapuja.* The consecration and worship of the sacrificial sword.

(iii) *Stambhapuja.* The and worship of the iron post where the immolation takes place.

(iv) *Chedan.* The immolation of the animal.

(v) *Sankalpa/ Utsarga* : The declaration of intent by the sacrifier as he surrenders the offering of blood with flesh to Kali and her consort Siva, here as *Mahakalabhairaba* the 'fearsome Great Time'.

The amount of money is offered by the pilgrims Rs. 22,000 to Rs. 28,000 approx each Tuesday, Saturday, Sunday in a weak, other's day. Amount of money is Rs. 18,000 to 20,000. The day of occasion this amount increase three times of each Saturday. Daily sevait of that day receive this amount.

Silver and Gold are offered by the pilgrims, these materials are deposited under the custody of Temple Committee. The value of ornaments of Devi Kalika image is Rs. 6 lakh (approx).

The dresses of Devi Kalika is changed by the pilgrims twice or three times within a year. The amount of expenditure is Rs. 22,000 to Rs. 25,000 to this purpose. Because there is very short time to change the dress. (Sayana to Mangal Arati). All ornaments of Devi Kalika maintains this time.

I find a peculiar feature that there are competition between the pilgrims to offer this money.

To examine the nature of relationships between the various purpose of visit and the selected few societal characteristics of the pilgrims, there are many reasons. These reasons are classified into three broad categories —spiritual, material and recreation.

Spiritual

This category includes such desires to which no

materialistic motive can be imputed when a pilgrim comes for *darshan* (auspicious view of deity) or making a tirtha, he goes to desire spiritual satisfaction e.g. *Santi* (peace), *tripti* (satisfaction), *ananda* (joy) or simply feeling better. The purpose is primarily directed to individual emotional experience and not to earthly gains, welfare of society, or avoidance of evil. This type of purpose has been labelled as spiritual and includes certain desires, like *punya* (religious merit), *papa-skhalan* (redemption of sin) and *mukti* (salvation), also which admittedly have different meanings and implications. By philosophic interpretation while the *Santi-tripti ananda* motive involves individual satisfaction in a detached manner, the *punya-pap skhalan-mukti* motive reflects the pilgrims concept about the other world. Again accumulation of religious merit (*Punya*) and removal of sin (*Pap-Skhalan*), though not synonymous are more or less complementary, however, since only a few of our sample pilgrims had such desires they were lumped in the spiritual category. In my pilgrim sample, I found 20 persons, i.e., 10 per cent who came with spiritual motive.

Material

Included in this category are such desires which involves the therapeutic, socio-cultural, economic and allied aspects of life. The therapeutic purpose concerns the problems of health, e.g., curing illness, improving health, and so on. In other words, when a person visits a place of pilgrimage to seek divine remedies for any ailments his purpose may be termed as such. The socio-cultural purpose refers to the needs connected with the social and psychological life of a devotee. It involves certain rites, rituals, obligations and duties, e.g., *Upanayan* (investitute with sacred thread), *annaprasanna* (sacred rice taking) and so on. Besides these, purposes involving successful examination, marriage, and Parenthood, safe delivery, restoration of peace of family, and knowing whereabouts of absconding persons have all been included in the category. The economic motive includes purposes like success in business, getting an employment, service promotion, settlement of disputes concerning property, and so on. There are some people who come to the religious centre for any particular purpose. It may appear that these four sub-categories of motives do not have spiritual content. Their success depends on the close interaction of devotees with the supernatural power. The per centage of pilgrim coming for the purpose of therapeutic, socio-cultural, economic and general needs are 19.50, 13.50, 28.50 and 14.00 respectively.

Recreational

When pilgrimage is not motivated by either spiritual or material needs but mainly by curiosity fun and frolic, recreation leisure for change in the monotonus daily life, or similar other motives it can be labelled as recreation. Some other purposes like providing company to others, acting as guides or agents, and visit on account of business or service have also been included in this category. This category thus includes pilgrims whose main purpose does not concern with the sacred nature of the place. To them the deity or the pilgrim centres represents nothing more than a tourist spot. In my pilgrim sample, I found 29 person, i.e., 14.50 per cent who came with recreational motive.

There are peculiar feature at Kalighat, people perform her two important social ceremonies—one intermarriage or marriage between otherwise unequal partners and thread ceremony which is usually completed within a period of three days is done here in a day. The floor adjacent to the temple of Mother is also utilised for purpose of marriage and thread ceremony. This can be done at minimum cost. The two important ceremonies, i.e., marriage and thread require only an expenditure ranging from few *annas* to a rupee. For Kalkhata the usual rate is thirty one up only.

Nowadays the pilgrims has developed an agnostic attitude. As the secretary of the temple committee told me, in spite of the increasing number of people visiting the centre, the position in respect of the volume of sacred performance is not proportionately improving.

Pilgrimage in West Bengal is a voluntary act. The persistence of the institute depends on the choice of individuals to undertake journeys, to sacred shrines, and so from one point of view the explicit motives and beliefs of participants are important foundations of the institution.

Pilgrims go to pilgrimage for every imaginable reason. The motives of devotion, supplication, to gain earthly comforts, the alleviation of suffering or a desirable result, or to gain spiritual rewards, are certainly not unique to pilgrimage. The relationship is to be seen not only in the motives of pilgrims, but in the rituals, deities, architecture, symbols, myth and beliefs associated with pilgrimage.

The dust or water of the sacred place is said to possess holiness of an almost tangible variety-if cures, restores, bestows welfare etc. - because it has had direct contact with divine. Many sacred places house relies believed to retain some of the spiritual essence (and often miraculous power) of the saint or deity; who has left them.

It is also generally believed that various activities performed on a pilgrimage, such as austerities, offerings, self sacrifice, charity, sincere devotion and personal faith, increase the meritoriousness of pilgrimage. The merit (*Punya*) this accumulated can be applied to bring about changes in the existential conditions of the life of the pilgrim in the immediate or distant futures, and so in this life or the next, and can be brought to bear on immediate personal problems or general metaphysical conditions. Belief in Karma reincarnation merit-accumulation and the automatic efficiency of ritual, and concern for purity, status and divine favour are examples of such commonalities. In reflecting both the diversity and unity of Bengali Hinduism, Pilgrimage gives back a true image of the religious culture of the region at the historical moment. These elements of pilgrimage are significant not only for the reasons expressed by participants, but also because some important notions of Hindu theology, philosophy and eschatology are enacted through pilgrimage practice.

Kalighat witnesses the assemblage of pilgrims evenly distributed throughout the year.

References

Bhaltacharya, Nidjulal : 1958 : *Kalighater Aitihasik Katha*; Pub : Printers Sindicate, Cal-26.

Baghi, Sibendugbpal; 1988, *Eminent India Sakta Centres in Eastern India*;

(An Indisciplinary study in the Background of the Pithas of Kalighat, Vakresware and Kamakhya, Pub : Puthi Pustak, Calcutta.

Chakraborty, Radharaman :1993 : *Religious and interstate relations in Asia today,* Asian Studies, II (I) Jan June'93, (23-38) ISN = 14557.

Chakraborty, Prafulla; 1984 : *Social Profile of Tarakeswar study of a Pilgrim town inWest Bengal,* Calcutta Firma.

Das, Amarendra ; 1962 : *Kalighater Ghar Samsar,* Pub : Nirmal Mudran, Calcutta -6.

Eddy, Sherwood ; *1919 : How to find God,* Pub : Calcutta Association Press.

Ghosal, Dr.Sailendra Shastri Hanumantha Rao, M ; 1957 : Aloke Tirtha, Pub : Naba Jiban Press, Calcutta -6. ; 1993 : Is religiosity related to age *Man In India,* 73 (3) ; September' 93 (259-265) ISN = 14799.

Morinis, E. Alan ; 1984 : *Pilgrimage In The Hindu Tradition, A case study of West Bengal,* Pub : Oxford University Press.

Oommen, T.K. ; 1992 : Religious and development Hindu Society, *Social Compass,* 39 (I), March 92 ; 67-76 (ISN 1160).

Samanta, Suchitra ; 1994 : Self-animal and divine digestion : Goat sacrifice to the Goddess Kali in Bengal ; *A Journal of Asian Studies* 53(3) August - 94 ; 779- 803 (ISN-7144).

Index